21世纪应用型本科土木建筑系列实用规划教材

工程管理专业英语

主　编　王竹芳

北京大学出版社
PEKING UNIVERSITY PRESS

内 容 简 介

本书主要内容包括：项目管理组织；雇主；成本估算；项目预算；承包商；工程承包合同的类型；招标程序；项目融资；关键路径法；进度控制；创新和技术与经济的可行性；索赔、争端和仲裁；各类保证范例格式等。本书选材广泛、内容新颖、针对性强、难度适中，有助于提高读者阅读相关专业的英语书刊和文献的能力。

本书为高等院校工程管理专业本科学生学习专业英语而编写，亦可作为土木工程专业英语教材，同时也可供广大从事工程管理、土木工程，且具备一定英语基础的工程技术人员及自学者学习参考。

图书在版编目（CIP）数据

工程管理专业英语/王竹芳主编. —北京：北京大学出版社，2009.3
（21 世纪应用型本科土木建筑系列实用规划教材）
ISBN 978-7-301-14957-7

Ⅰ. 工… Ⅱ. 王… Ⅲ. 建筑工程—施工管理—英语—高等学校—教材 Ⅳ. H31

中国版本图书馆 CIP 数据核字(2009)第 020642 号

书　　　名：	工程管理专业英语
著作责任者：	王竹芳　主编
策划编辑：	张　玮　吴　迪
责任编辑：	张　玮
标准书号：	ISBN 978-7-301-14957-7/H · 2205
出 版 者：	北京大学出版社
地　　　址：	北京市海淀区成府路 205 号　100871
网　　　址：	http://www.pup.cn　http://www.pup6.com
电　　　话：	邮购部 010-62752015　发行部 010-62750672　编辑部 010-62750667
电子邮箱：	编辑部 pup6@pup.cn　总编室 zpup@pup.cn
印 刷 者：	北京虎彩文化传播有限公司
发 行 者：	北京大学出版社
经 销 者：	新华书店
	787 毫米×1092 毫米　16 开本　11.25 印张　245 千字
	2009 年 3 月第 1 版　2025 年 1 月第 13 次印刷
定　　　价：	32.00 元

未经许可，不得以任何方式复制或抄袭本书之部分或全部内容。
版权所有，侵权必究　　举报电话：010-62752024
　　　　　　　　　　　电子邮箱：fd@pup.cn

21世纪应用型本科土木建筑系列实用规划教材
专家编审委员会

主　任　　彭少民

副主任　　(按拼音顺序排名)

　　　　　陈伯望　　金康宁　　李　忱　　李　杰

　　　　　罗迎社　　彭　刚　　许成祥　　杨　勤

　　　　　俞　晓　　袁海庆　　周先雁　　张俊彦

委　员　　(按拼音顺序排名)

　　　　　邓寿昌　　付晓灵　　何放龙　　何培玲

　　　　　李晓目　　李学罡　　刘　杰　　刘建军

　　　　　刘文生　　罗　章　　石建军　　许　明

　　　　　严　兵　　张泽平　　张仲先

丛书总序

我国高等教育发展迅速，全日制高等学校每年招生人数至2004年已达到420万人，毛入学率19%，步入国际公认的高等教育"大众化"阶段。面临这种大规模的扩招，教育事业的发展与改革坚持以人为本的两个主体：一是学生，一是教师。教学质量的提高是在这两个主体上的反映，教材则是两个主体的媒介，属于教学的载体。

教育部曾在第三次新建本科院校教学工作研讨会上指出："一些高校办学定位不明，盲目追求上层次、上规格，导致人才培养规格盲目拔高，培养模式趋同。高校学生中'升本热'、'考硕热'、'考博热'持续升温，应试学习倾向仍然比较普遍，导致各层次人才培养目标难于全面实现，大学生知识结构不够合理，动手能力弱，实际工作能力不强。"而作为知识传承载体的教材，在高等教育的发展过程中起着至关重要的作用，但目前教材建设却远远滞后于应用型人才培养的步伐，许多应用型本科院校一直沿用偏重于研究型的教材，缺乏针对性强的实用教材。

近年来，我国房地产行业已经成为国民经济的支柱行业之一，随着本世纪我国城市化的大趋势，土木建筑行业对实用型人才的需求还将持续增加。为了满足相关应用型本科院校培养应用型人才的教学需求，从2004年10月北京大学出版社第六事业部就开始策划本套丛书，并派出十多位编辑分赴全国近三十个省份调研了两百多所院校的课程改革与教材建设的情况。在此基础上，规划出了涵盖"大土建"六个专业——土木工程、工程管理、建筑学、城市规划、给排水、建筑环境与设备工程的基础课程及专业主干课程的系列教材。通过2005年1月份在湖南大学的组稿会和2005年4月份在三峡大学的审纲会，在来自全国各地几十所高校的知名专家、教授的共同努力下，不但成立了本丛书的编审委员会，还规划出了首批包括土木工程、工程管理及建筑环境与设备工程等专业方向的四十多个选题，再经过各位主编老师和参编老师的艰苦努力，并在北京大学出版社各级领导的关心和第六事业部的各位编辑辛勤劳动下，首批教材终于2006年春季学期前夕陆续出版发行了。

在首批教材的编写出版过程中，得到了越来越多的来自全国各地相关兄弟院校的领导和专家的大力支持。于是，在顺利运作第一批土建教材的鼓舞下，北京大学出版社联合全国七十多家开设有土木建筑相关专业的高校，于2005年11月26日在长沙中南林业科技大学召开了《21世纪应用型本科土木建筑系列实用规划教材》(第二批)组稿会，规划了①建筑学专业；②城市规划专业；③建筑环境与设备工程专业；④给排水工程专业；⑤土木工程专业中的道路、桥梁、地下、岩土、矿山课群组近六十个选题。至此，北京大学出版社规划的"大土木建筑系列教材"已经涵盖了"大土建"的六个专业，是近年来全国高等教育出版界唯一一套完全覆盖"大土建"六个专业方向的系列教材，并将于2007年全部出版发行。

我国高等学校土木建筑专业的教育，在教育部和建设部的指导下，经土木建筑专业指导委员会六年来的研讨，已经形成了宽口径"大土建"的专业发展模式，明确了土木建筑专业教育的培养目标、培养方案和毕业生基本规格，从宽口径的视角，要求毕业生能从事土木工程的设计、施工与管理工作。业务范围涉及房屋建筑、隧道与地下建筑、公路与城市道路、铁道工程与桥梁、矿山建筑等，并且制定一整套课程教学大纲。本系列教材就是根据最新的培养方案和课程教学大纲，由一批长期在教学第一线从事教学并有过多年工程经验和丰富教学经验的教师担任主编，以定位"应用型人才培养"为目标而编撰，具有以下特点：

(1) 按照宽口径土木工程专业培养方案，注重提高学生综合素质和创新能力，注重加强学生专业基础知识和优化基本理论知识结构，不刻意追求理论研究型教材深度，内容取舍少而精，向培养土木工程师从事设计、施工与管理的应用方向拓展。

(2) 在理解土木工程相关学科的基础上，深入研究各课程之间的相互关系，各课程教材既要反映本学科发展水平，保证教材自身体系的完整性，又要尽量避免内容的重复。

(3) 培养学生，单靠专门的设计技巧训练和运用现成的方法，要取得专门实践的成功是不够的，因为这些方法随科学技术的发展经常改变。为了了解并和这些迅速发展的方法同步，教材的编撰侧重培养学生透析理解教材中的基本理论、基本特性和性能，又同时熟悉现行设计方法的理论依据和工程背景，以不变应万变，这是本系列教材力图涵盖的两个方面。

(4) 我国颁发的现行有关土木工程类的规范及规程，系 1999 年—2002 年完成的修订，内容有较大的取舍和更新，反映了我国土木工程设计与施工技术的发展。作为应用型教材，为培养学生毕业后获得注册执业资格，在内容上涉及不少相关规范条文和算例。但并不是规范条文的释义。

(5) 当代土木工程设计，越来越多地使用计算机程序或采用通用性的商业软件，有些结构特殊要求，则由工程师自行编写程序。本系列的相关工程结构课程的教材中，在阐述真实结构、简化计算模型、数学表达式之间的关系的基础上，给出了设计方法的详细步骤，这些步骤均可容易地转换成工程结构的流程图，有助于培养学生编写计算机程序。

(6) 按照科学发展观，从可持续发展的观念，根据课程特点，反映学科现代新理论、新技术、新材料、新工艺，以社会发展和科技进步的新近成果充实、更新教材内容，尽最大可能在教材中增加了这方面的信息量。同时考虑开发音像、电子、网络等多媒体教学形式，以提高教学效果和效率。

衷心感谢本套系列教材的各位编著者，没有他们在教学第一线的教改和工程第一线的辛勤实践，要出版如此规模的系列实用教材是不可能的。同时感谢北京大学出版社为我们广大编著者提供了广阔的平台，为我们进一步提高本专业领域的教学质量和教学水平提供了很好的条件。

我们真诚希望使用本系列教材的教师和学生，不吝指正，随时给我们提出宝贵的意见，以期进一步对本系列教材进行修订、完善。

本系列教材配套的 PPT 电子教案以及习题答案在出版社相关网站上提供下载。

《21 世纪应用型本科土木建筑系列实用规划教材》
专家编审委员会
2006 年 1 月

前 言

随着世界经济全球化的深入发展，工程项目管理也越来越国际化。我国加入WTO后工程项目管理面临的挑战和建筑业实施项目管理的实践表明我国的工程项目管理国际化是必然趋势，中国工程项目管理的深化和推进必须进一步加快管理方式的国际化，努力学习借鉴国际上先进的项目管理经验，在学习中借鉴，在借鉴中研究，在研究中提升，在提升中完善，不断提高项目管理水平。

不论项目主体如何多元，工程项目如何多样，实行工程项目管理的国际化是共性的，因此有必要向我国工程管理专业本科生以及工程管理从业人员提供并讲解国外相关资料，帮助他们掌握更多新的专业知识，提高他们的专业英语阅读能力。

本书主要取材于国际咨询工程师联合会(FIDIC)与世界银行编写的、通用于国际工程市场的正式出版物，国外近几年工程管理领域的经典教材、专著。本书旨在使读者掌握工程管理专业英语知识，培养和提高读者阅读专业英语文献资料的能力。读者在学习语言知识的同时，可以了解相关专业知识。本书特点是选材较新，实用性强，适合作为高校工程管理专业英语教材，也适用作为相关工程管理人员和工程技术人员的培训教材。

本书共分16个单元，主要内容包括：项目管理组织；雇主；成本估算；项目预算；承包商；工程承包合同的类型；招标程序；项目融资；关键路径法；进度控制；创新和技术与经济的可行性；索赔、争端和仲裁；各类保证范例格式等。内容覆盖面广，系统性较强。在每一单元内，均列出本单元相关的专业词汇，并根据本单元重点内容提出问题，读者在回答问题的同时，可以巩固对课文的理解，进而掌握相关专业知识。

本书的读者对象为普通高等院校工程管理专业及相关专业的学生，以及从事工程管理的管理人员和技术人员等。

为了方便使用本书的教师和学生，每单元都附有参考译文，并附有教学课件和问题答案。

由于作者水平有限，书中内容涉及面较广，也由于我国高校开设相关专业的历史较短，可供学习、参考、借鉴的资料不多见，所以书中难免出现不足之处，敬请专家和读者批评指正。

编 者

2009年1月

目　　录

Unit 1　Organizing for Project Management 1

Unit 2　The Employer 14

Unit 3　Cost Estimation 21

Unit 4　The Project Budget(1) 32

Unit 5　The Project Budget(2)——Forecasting for Activity Cost Control 42

Unit 6　The Contractor 52

Unit 7　Types of Construction Contracts 68

Unit 8　Tendering Procedure(1) 76

Unit 9　Tendering Procedure(2) 84

Unit 10　Project Finance 91

Unit 11　The Critical Path Method 106

Unit 12　Schedule Control(1) 121

Unit 13　Schedule Control(2) 130

Unit 14　Innovation and Technological & Economic Feasibility 139

Unit 15　Claims, Disputes and Arbitration 147

Unit 16　Sample Forms of Securities 157

参考文献 168

Unit 1   Organizing for Project Management

Organization of Project Participants

The top management of the owner sets the overall policy and selects the appropriate organization to take charge of a proposed project. Its policy will dictate how the project life cycle is divided among organizations and which professionals should be engaged. Decisions by the top management of the owner will also influence the organization to be adopted for project management. In general, there are many ways to decompose a project into stages. The most typical ways are:

- Sequential processing whereby the project is divided into separate stages and each stage is carried out successively in sequence.
- Parallel processing whereby the project is divided into independent parts such that all stages are carried out simultaneously.
- Staggered processing whereby the stages may be overlapping, such as the use of phased design-construct procedures for fast track operation.

It should be pointed out that some decompositions may work out better than others, depending on the circumstances. In any case, the prevalence of decomposition makes the subsequent integration particularly important. The critical issues involved in organization for project management are:

- How many organizations are involved?
- What are the relationships among the organizations?
- When are the various organizations brought into the project?

There are two basic approaches to organize for project implementation, even though many variations may exist as a result of different contractual relationships adopted by the owner and builder. These basic approaches are divided along the following lines:

- **Separation of organizations.** Numerous organizations serve as consultants or contractors to the owner, with different organizations handling design and construction functions. Typical examples which involve different degrees of separation are: traditional sequence of design and construction; professional construction management.
- **Integration of organizations.** A single or joint venture consisting of a number of organizations with a single command undertakes both design and construction functions. Two extremes may be cited as examples: owner-builder operation in which all work will be handled in house by force account; turnkey operation in which all work is contracted to a vendor which is responsible for delivering the completed project.

The organization for the management of construction projects may vary from case to case. On one extreme, each project may be staffed by existing personnel in the functional divisions of the organization on an ad-hoc basis as shown in Figure 1.1 until the project is completed. This arrangement is referred to as the matrix organization as each project manager must negotiate all resources for the project from the existing organizational framework. On the other hand, the organization may consist of a small central functional staff for the exclusive purpose of supporting various projects, each of which has its functional divisions as shown in Figure 1.2 This decentralized set-up is referred to as the project-oriented organization as each project manager has autonomy in managing the project. There are many variations of management style between these two extremes, depending on the objectives of the organization and the nature of the construction project. For example, a large chemical company with in-house staff for planning, design and construction of facilities for new product lines will naturally adopt the matrix organization. On the other hand, a construction company whose existence depends entirely on the management of certain types of construction projects may find the project-oriented organization particularly attractive. While organizations may differ, the same basic principles of management structure are applicable to most situations.

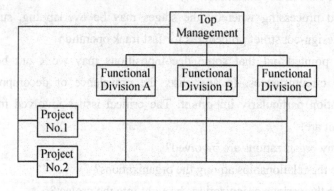

Figure 1.1　A Matrix Organization

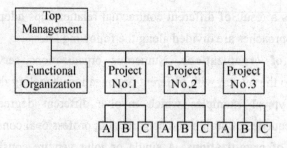

Figure 1.2　A Project-Oriented Organization

To illustrate various types of organizations for project management, we shall consider two examples, the first one representing an owner organization while the second one representing the organization of a construction management consultant under the direct supervision of the owner.

Traditional Designer-Constructor Sequence

For ordinary projects of moderate size and complexity, the owner often employs a designer (an architectural/engineering firm) which prepares the detailed plans and specifications for the constructor (a general contractor). The designer also acts on behalf of the owner to oversee the project implementation during construction. The general contractor is responsible for the construction itself even though the work may actually be undertaken by a number of specialty subcontractors.

The owner usually negotiates the fee for service with the architectural/engineering (A/E) firm. In addition to the responsibilities of designing the facility, the A/E firm also exercises to some degree supervision of the construction as stipulated by the owner. Traditionally, the A/E firm regards itself as design professionals representing the owner who should not communicate with potential contractors to avoid collusion or conflict of interest. Field inspectors working for an A/E firm usually follow through the implementation of a project after the design is completed and seldom have extensive input in the design itself. Because of the litigation climate in the last two decades, most A/E firms only provide observers rather than inspectors in the field. Even the shop drawings of fabrication or construction schemes submitted by the contractors for approval are reviewed with a disclaimer of responsibility by the A/E firms.

The owner may select a general constructor either through competitive bidding or through negotiation. Public agencies are required to use the competitive bidding mode, while private organizations may choose either mode of operation. In using competitive bidding, the owner is forced to use the designer-constructor sequence since detailed plans and specifications must be ready before inviting bidders to submit their bids. If the owner chooses to use a negotiated contract, it is free to use phased construction if it so desires.

The general contractor may choose to perform all or part of the construction work, or act only as a manager by subcontracting all the construction to subcontractors. The general contractor may also select the subcontractors through competitive bidding or negotiated contracts. The general contractor may ask a number of subcontractors to quote prices for the subcontracts before submitting its bid to the owner. However, the subcontractors often cannot force the winning general contractor to use them on the project. This situation may lead to practices known as bid shopping and bid peddling. Bid shopping refers to the situation when the general contractor approaches subcontractors other than those whose quoted prices were used in the winning contract in order to seek lower priced subcontracts. Bid peddling refers to the actions of subcontractors who offer lower priced subcontracts to the winning general subcontractors in order to dislodge the subcontractors who originally quoted prices to the general contractor prior to its bid submittal. In both cases, the quality of construction may be sacrificed, and some state statutes forbid these practices for public projects.

Although the designer-constructor sequence is still widely used because of the public perception of fairness in competitive bidding, many private owners recognize the disadvantages of using this approach when the project is large and complex and when market pressures require a shorter project duration than that which can be accomplished by using this traditional method.

Professional Construction Management

Professional construction management refers to a project management team consisting of a professional construction manager and other participants who will carry out the tasks of project planning, design and construction in an integrated manner. Contractual relationships among members of the team are intended to minimize adversarial relationships and contribute to greater response within the management group. A professional construction manager is a firm specialized in the practice of professional construction management which includes:

- Work with owner and the A/E firms from the beginning and make recommendations on design improvements, construction technology, schedules and construction economy.
- Propose design and construction alternatives if appropriate, and analyze the effects of the alternatives on the project cost and schedule.
- Monitor subsequent development of the project in order that these targets are not exceeded without the knowledge of the owner.
- Coordinate procurement of material and equipment and the work of all construction contractors, and monthly payments to contractors, changes, claims and inspection for conforming design requirements.
- Perform other project related services as required by owners.

Professional construction management is usually used when a project is very large or complex. The organizational features that are characteristics of mega-projects can be summarized as follows:

- The overall organizational approach for the project will change as the project advances. The "functional" organization may change to a "matrix" which may change to a "project" organization (not necessarily in this order).
- Within the overall organization, there will probably be functional, project, and matrix suborganizations all at the same time. This feature greatly complicates the theory and the practice of management, yet is essential for overall cost effectiveness.
- Successful giant, complex organizations usually have a strong matrix-type suborganization at the level where basic cost and schedule control responsibility is assigned. This suborganization is referred to as a "cost center" or as a "project" and is headed by a project manager. The cost center matrix may have participants assigned from many different functional groups. In turn, these functional groups may have technical reporting responsibilities to several different and higher tiers in the organization. The key to a cost effective effort is the development of this project suborganization into a single team under the leadership of a strong project manager.
- The extent to which decision-making will be centralized or decentralized is crucial to

the organization of the mega-project.

Consequently, it is important to recognize the changing nature of the organizational structure as a project is carried out in various stages.

Owner-Builder Operation

In this approach an owner must have a steady flow of on-going projects in order to maintain a large work force for in-house operation. However, the owner may choose to subcontract a substantial portion of the project to outside consultants and contractors for both design and construction, even though it retains centralized decision making to integrate all efforts in project implementation.

Example 1.1   U.S. Army Corps of Engineers Organization.

The District Engineer's Office of the U.S. Army Corps of Engineers may be viewed as a typical example of an owner-builder approach as shown in Figure 1.3.

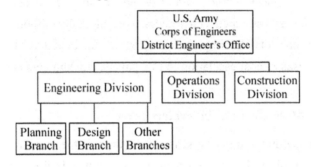

Figure 1.3   Organization of a District of Corps of Engineers

In the District Engineer's Office of the U.S. Corps of Engineers, there usually exist an Engineering Division and an Operations Division, and, in a large district, a Construction Division. Under each division, there are several branches. Since the authorization of a project is usually initiated by the U.S. Congress, the planning and design functions are separated in order to facilitate operations. Since the authorization of the feasibility study of a project may precede the authorization of the design by many years, each stage can best be handled by a different branch in the Engineering Division. If construction is ultimately authorized, the work may be handled by the Construction Division or by outside contractors. The Operations Division handles the operation of locks and other facilities which require routine attention and maintenance.

When a project is authorized, a project manager is selected from the most appropriate branch to head the project, together with a group of staff drawn from various branches to form the project team. When the project is completed, all members of the team including the project manager will return to their regular posts in various branches and divisions until the next project assignment. Thus, a matrix organization is used in managing each project.

Turnkey Operation

Some owners wish to delegate all responsibilities of design and construction to outside consultants in a turnkey project arrangement. A contractor agrees to provide the completed facility on the basis of performance specifications set forth by the owner. The contractor may even assume the responsibility of operating the project if the owner so desires. In order for a turnkey operation to succeed, the owner must be able to provide a set of unambiguous performance specifications to the contractor and must have complete confidence in the capability of the contractor to carry out the mission.

This approach is the direct opposite of the owner-builder approach in which the owner wishes to retain the maximum amount of control for the design-construction process.

Example 1.2 An Example of a Turnkey Organization.

A 150 MW power plant was proposed in 1985 by the Texas-New Mexico Power Company of Fort Worth, Texas, which would make use of the turnkey operation. Upon approval by the Texas Utility Commission, a consortium consisting of H.B. Zachry Co., Westinghouse Electric Co., and Combustion Engineering Inc., would design, build and finance the power plant for completion in 1990 for an estimated construction cost of $200 million in 1990 dollars. The consortium would assume total liability during construction, including debt service costs, and thereby eliminate the risks of cost escalation to rate payers, stockholders and the utility company management.

Leadership and Motivation for the Project Team

The project manager, in the broadest sense of the term, is the most important person for the success or failure of a project. The project manager is responsible for planning, organizing and controlling the project. In turn, the project manager receives authority from the management of the organization to mobilize the necessary resources to complete a project.

The project manager must be able to exert interpersonal influence in order to lead the project team. The project manager often gains the support of his/her team through a combination of the following:

- Formal authority resulting from an official capacity which is empowered to issue orders.
- Reward and/or penalty power resulting from his/her capacity to dispense directly or indirectly valued organization rewards or penalties.
- Expert power when the project manager is perceived as possessing special knowledge or expertise for the job.
- Attractive power because the project manager has a personality or other characteristics to convince others.

In a matrix organization, the members of the functional departments may be accustomed to a single reporting line in a hierarchical structure, but the project manager coordinates the activities of the team members drawn from functional departments. The functional structure within the matrix organization is responsible for priorities, coordination, administration and final decisions pertaining to project implementation. Thus, there are potential conflicts between functional divisions and project teams. The project manager must be given the responsibility and authority to resolve various conflicts such that the established project policy and quality standards will not be jeopardized. When contending issues of a more fundamental nature are developed, they must be brought to the attention of a high level in the management and be resolved expeditiously.

In general, the project manager's authority must be clearly documented as well as defined, particularly in a matrix organization where the functional division managers often retain certain authority over the personnel temporarily assigned to a project. The following principles should be observed:

- The interface between the project manager and the functional division managers should be kept as simple as possible.
- The project manager must gain control over those elements of the project which may overlap with functional division managers.
- The project manager should encourage problem solving rather than role playing of team members drawn from various functional divisions.

Questions

1. What are the most typical ways to decompose a project into stages?
2. How many issues are involved in organization for project management? What are they?
3. Say about the two basic approaches to organization for project management. How these basic approaches are divided?
4. What's the matrix organization for the management of construction projects?
5. What's the project-oriented organization for the management of construction projects?
6. Summarize the organizational features that are characteristics of mega-projects.
7. Why is it important to recognize the changing nature of the organizational structure as a project is carried out in various stages?
8. What organization is used in managing the owner-builder project?
9. The project manager is the most important person for the success or failure of a project, why?
10. How does the project manager gain the support of his/her team?

Vocabulary, Phrases and Expressions

project participants：项目参与方
sequential processing：串行处理；顺序加工
parallel processing：并行处理；多重处理
staggered processing：交叉处理；错列处理

separation of organizations：独立型组织
integration of organizations：集约型组织
owner-builder operation：业主自行建造项目
turnkey operation：交钥匙项目
matrix organization：矩阵式组织形式
project-oriented organization：以项目为导向的组织
an architectural/engineering firm：建筑/设计公司
a general contractor：总承包商
specialty subcontractors：专业分包商
supervise：监理
field inspectors：现场检查员
field observers：现场观察员
shop drawings of fabrication：车间安装图
construction schemes：施工计划；施工安排
designer-constructor sequence：设计施工顺序模式
subcontract：分包合同
quality of construction：建筑质量
construction management：施工管理
design and construction alternatives：设计或施工的替代方案
project cost and schedule：项目的成本和进度
procurement of material and equipment：材料和设备的采购
monthly payments：月度付款
cost center：成本中心
decision-making：决策
on-going projects：在建项目
engineering division：工程设计部门
operations division：运营部门
construction division：施工部门
outside contractors：外部承包商
authorization：授权
feasibility study of a project：项目可行性研究
project team：项目团队
performance specifications：设计任务说明书；规范(规格说明书)
liability during construction：建设期债务
debt service：还本付息；偿债
project manager：项目经理

参考译文

第1单元 项目管理组织

项目各参与方的组织

业主的高层管理负责设定总体方针,同时选择合适的组织来负责给定的项目。在业主的方针中会指出如何将项目生命周期中的任务划分给不同的组织,以及聘用什么样的专业人员。业主高层管理所做出的决策也将对被选出进行项目管理的组织产生影响。通常会有多种分解项目阶段的方法,其中最为典型的是:

- 顺序划分,项目被划分成独立的几个阶段,各阶段按连续顺序进行。
- 平行划分,项目被划分成独立的几个部分,各部分同时进行。
- 交叉划分,项目阶段可以进行搭接。例如,快速路径法的应用。

这里需要指出的是哪种分解方法更为有效,这完全取决于项目的具体情况。在多数情况下,按顺序划分的方法更为普遍一些。涉及项目管理的关键问题有:

- 项目涉及多少个组织?
- 各组织间的联系是什么?
- 各组织何时介入项目?

尽管由于业主和承包商之间所采用合同条件的不同会产生很多种完成项目的组织形式,但基本形式只有两种,并按照下面的思路来划分。

- **独立型组织**。相对于业主,会出现咨询方或承包商等多种分别处理设计和施工任务的组织,涉及这种类型组织的典型例子有:设计和施工的传统顺序模式;专业化的建设项目管理模式。
- **集约型组织**。由不同组织组成一个单一的联合体,以统一指令来承担设计和施工任务。这里介绍两种极端的例子:业主自行建造项目,在这里所有工作均由业主内部部门处理;交钥匙项目,即合同的所有工作内容都交给一个卖方,由他负责向业主提交完工项目。

建设项目的管理组织形式可视具体情况而定。一种情况是,项目所需人员由职能部门提供,由专职项目经理领导直至项目结束,如图1.1所示。在这种形式下,项目经理必须从现有的组织框架中协调并获取项目所需的各种资源,因而这种组织形式也被称为矩阵式组织。而另一种组织形式是如图1.2所示的直线式组织,在这种组织形式下,组织为每一个项目提供资源上的必要支持,因而也被称为以项目为导向的组织,每位项目经理都有管理项目的自治权。除此之外,还有其他类型的项目组织可供选择,这取决于组织目标和建设项目的特点。例如,一家由内部力量来计划、设计和建设新产品设备的大型公司很自然地会选择矩阵式组织。然而,完全依靠建设项目管理求生存的建筑公司,却倾向于选择以项目为导向的组织。尽管组织形式有所不同,但管理结构的基本原则却适用于大多数情况。

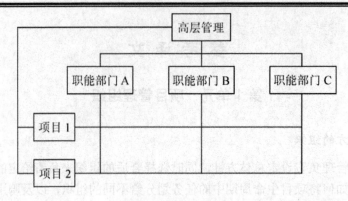

图 1.1 矩阵式组织

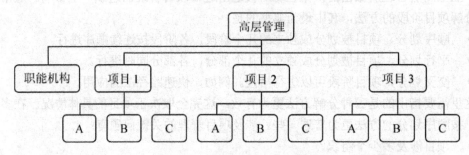

图 1.2 以项目为导向的组织

为了理解项目管理的不同组织形式，可以认为第一个例子所代表的是一个业主的管理组织，而第二个例子所代表的是一个业主直接监督下的建筑管理咨询方的管理组织。

传统的设计—承包模式

对于那些规模和复杂程度适中的普通项目，业主通常会选择一家设计单位(建筑设计公司)为承包商(总承包商)提供项目所需的详细规划和设计。设计单位同时代表业主在施工期间监督项目的执行。尽管具体工作由众多的专业分包商来承担，但却由总承包商对工程本身负责。

业主通常会跟建筑/设计(A/E)公司进行服务费用的谈判。除了承担设计责任外，A/E公司还行使一定程度的、由业主规定的、监督施工的职责。传统上，A/E 公司是把自己当作业主代表，并且不和潜在的承包商直接联系，以回避利益冲突的专业设计咨询人员。为A/E公司工作的现场监督人员通常在设计完成之后对项目实施跟踪检查，并且很少直接参与设计本身。由于在过去20年里诉讼之风渐盛，为避免诉讼纠纷，大多数A/E公司只向工地派观察员，而不再派现场监督。现在，由承包商提交获准的车间安装详图和项目计划，也被视作A/E公司推卸责任。

业主既可通过竞争性招标也可通过谈判来选择总承包商。一般公共机构被要求使用竞争性招标方式，而私人组织可采用两种方式中的任何一种。在竞争性招标中，业主将不得不采用设计—施工顺序模式，因为在邀请竞标者投标前，详细的规划和设计应已完成。如果采用谈判的合同方式，那么业主在选择建造模式方面有很大的余地。

总承包商可选择自己完成建设项目的全部工作或其中的一部分，也可以把建设项目全部分包给分包商，自己只作为管理者。总承包商同样既可用竞争性招标也可通过谈判来选择分包商。总承包商在向业主投标报价之前会先向分包商就分包合同进行询价。然而，分包商却不能强迫总承包商在中标后一定在项目上选择自己，这实际上就产生了所谓的"招标压价"和"投标兜售"。"招标压价"是指为了降低分包合同价格，总承包商在中标后并不与其报价已被采纳在中标合同中的分包商签分包合同，转而另寻求其他分包商。"投标兜售"则是指分包商的行为，即有些分包商为了挤掉其他报价比他早的分包商，愿意给总承包商提供更低价格的分包合同。在这两种情形下，建筑质量都会受到损害，因而有些州的法令禁止在公共项目中进行这些形式的操作。

尽管由于公众对于竞争性招标公正性的认同而使得设计－施工模式仍然得以广泛的使用，但许多私营业主也意识到了这种模式的缺点，即当项目规模巨大且较为复杂时，或者当项目迫于市场压力而需尽早完工时，该模式便显得力不从心。

专业化建设项目管理模式

专业化建设项目管理是指由专业建设项目经理(CM)和其他各方组成的项目管理队伍，这个项目管理队伍负责完成项目的规划、设计和施工等任务的集成与管理。这种模式试图将项目组织间的对立情绪降低到最低程度，同时有助于管理队伍内部的协调。专业化的 CM 是指从事下面工作的公司：

- 在项目前期，同业主和 A/E 公司一道工作，并就设计的改进、施工技术、进度安排和建筑经济提供参考建议。
- 如果合适，提议设计或施工的替代方案，并分析其对项目成本和进度的影响。
- 监督项目的进展，以防止目标的偏离。
- 处理与协调材料和设备的采购、承包商的施工活动、承包商月进度款的支付、设计变更、索赔和监督设计要求的落实。
- 执行业主和项目有关的其他服务要求。

当项目规模很大且较为复杂时，常常采用这种专业化的建筑管理模式。特大型项目的组织特征总结为以下几点：

- 随着项目的进展，项目总体的组织方式将发生变化，即由"职能式"组织变化成"矩阵式"组织，再变到"项目式"组织(不一定严格按照这个顺序)。
- 在整个组织内部，可能出现职能式、项目式和矩阵式等嵌套组织共生的情况。这虽然对总成本的控制有利，但却使管理的理论和实践趋于复杂化。
- 成功的巨型复杂组织通常都有一个强矩阵嵌套组织，使得基本的成本和进度控制责任得以落实，这个嵌套组织被称为"成本中心"或被当作一个"项目"为某个项目经理所领导。成本中心矩阵里的参与者往往从各个不同职能部门分派而来。而这些职能部门则负责向组织内更高的层级提交技术报告。有效成本管理的关键在于依靠一个很强的项目经理的领导，把这个嵌套组织发展成一个精干的团队。
- 决策的集权或分权程度对特大型项目组织而言至关重要。

总之，认识到组织机构在项目进行到不同阶段，其组织形式会发生改变是十分重要的。

业主—建造运营模式

在这种模式里，业主为了维持一个用于内部运营的、庞大的劳动力，必须有一个稳定的在建项目流。然而，即使业主为整合项目进展中的所有工作而保留集权式决策，他仍然可以将设计和建造的实质性部分外包给咨询师和承包商。

例 1.1　美国陆军工程公司组织。

美国陆军工程公司的地区工程师办公室可被认作是业主－建造运营模式的典型例子，如图 1.3 所示。

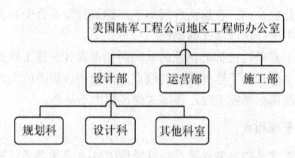

图 1.3　美国陆军工程公司的地区机构组织

在美国陆军工程公司的地区工程师办公室，通常有一个设计部和运营部，如果是一个大的地区，还会有一个施工部。每一个部门下设有若干个科室。由于项目通常经由美国国会发起和授权，所以为了便于操作，规划和设计通常分开进行。另外，由于项目可行性研究的授权通常比项目设计的授权要早几年，所以每一个阶段最好由设计部下面的不同科室来运作。如果项目的施工方案最终被批准，那么就由施工部门或外部的承包商来负责项目的施工。运营部则负责项目日常经营及各类设施的维修与养护。

当项目被批准后，应从最为合适的部门科室选择一位项目经理来领导项目，并连同从其他科室挑选出的人员一道组成项目团队。而当项目完成后，包括项目经理在内的所有项目团队成员都回归到其原来所在科室的岗位上，直到有新的项目任务。因此，该模式的项目管理采用矩阵式组织。

交钥匙运作模式

在交钥匙项目当中，由业主所选定的承包商来承担设计和施工的所有责任。承包商在业主提供执行标准的基础上，向业主提交完工建筑设施。如果业主愿意，承包商还可承担运营项目的责任。要想使交钥匙项目成功进行，业主需向承包商提供一套毫无歧义的执行标准，同时还应给予承包商完成项目的能力以足够的信任。

这种模式和前面所讲的业主—建造运营模式正好相反，在那里业主对设计—施工过程具有最大限度的控制权。

例 1.2　一个交钥匙组织范例。

1985 年，德克萨斯州的德克萨斯—新墨西哥电力公司推出一个采用交钥匙运作模式的 150MW 的电厂项目。征得德克萨斯州公用事业委员会的批准后，一个由 H.B.萨奇股份公司、威斯汀豪斯电力股份公司和克姆伯瑟工程有限公司组成的财团负责对该项目进行设计、施工和项目融资。该项目欲在 1990 年完工，其预计建设成本按 1990 年价格的可比价格为 2 亿美元。由于财团要承担包括贷款成本在内的建设期的所有债务，所以降低了对于贷款人、股东和公用事业管理公司的成本增加的风险。

项目团队领导和激励

项目经理,从这个术语的广义含义而言,是项目成败得失的关键。项目经理对项目的规划、组织和控制负有责任。反过来,项目经理拥有由管理组织授予的调动各项资源用以完成项目的权力。

为了领导项目团队,项目经理应施加其个人影响力。项目经理通过运用以下方法来获得团队成员的支持:

- 通过正式授权而得到发布指令的权力。
- 组织授予的根据个人表现对其实施直接或间接奖励或惩罚的权力。
- 当项目经理具备处理某项工作的专业知识和技能时的专家发言权。
- 项目经理本身具备的说服他人的能力。

在矩阵式组织当中,来自各职能部门的项目成员仍习惯于等级式结构里单线的汇报制度,这时项目经理应当协调这些选自不同职能部门的人员之间的活动。由于矩阵式组织中的职能部门仍会对影响项目进行的某些事情负责,所以在职能部门和项目团队之间就会有潜在冲突。为了使既定的项目方针和质量标准不受损害,则应当给予项目经理解决冲突的责任和权力。如果矛盾冲突有升级的趋势,则应立即引起高层管理的注意并予以及时化解。

一般而言,项目经理的权责不仅应当明确地予以定义,而且还应当予以确认,尤其是在矩阵式组织里。因为职能部门的经理们通常对其部门被暂时分派到项目上的人员仍保持着一定的影响力,所以应当遵守下面一些规则:

- 项目经理和职能部门经理之间的界面越简单越好。
- 当项目要素和职能部门发生重叠时,项目经理必须拥有对这些要素的控制权。
- 面对问题,项目经理必须采取积极解决的态度,而不是消极观望和无所适从。

Unit 2   The Employer

Right of Access to the Site

The Employer shall give the Contractor right of access to, and possession of, all parts of the Site within the time (or times) stated in the Particular Conditions. The right and possession may not be exclusive to the Contractor. If, under the Contract, the Employer is required to give (to the Contractor) possession of any foundation, structure, plant or means of access, the Employer shall do so in the time and manner stated in the Employer's Requirements. However, the Employer may withhold any such right or possession until the Performance Security has been received.

If no such time is stated in the Particular Conditions, the Employer shall give the Contractor right of access to, and possession of, the Site with effect from the Commencement Date.

If the Contractor suffers delay and/or incurs Cost as a result of a failure by the Employer to give any such right or possession within such time, the Contractor shall give notice to the Employer and shall be entitled subject to Sub-Clause 20.1 [Contractor's Claims] to:

(1) an extension of time for any such delay, if completion is or will be delayed, under Sub-Clause 8.4 [Extension of Time for Completion].

(2) payment of any such Cost plus reasonable profit, which shall be added to the Contract Price.

After receiving this notice, the Employer shall proceed in accordance with Sub-Clause 3.5 [Determinations] to agree or determine these matters.

However, if and to the extent that the Employer's failure was caused by any error or delay by the Contractor, including an error in, or delay in the submission of, any of the Contractor's Documents, the Contractor shall not be entitled to such extension of time, cost or profit.

Permits, Licences or Approves

The Employer shall (where he is in a position to do so) provide reasonable assistance to the Contractor at the request of the Contractor:

(1) by obtaining copies of the Laws of the Country which are relevant to the Contract but are not readily available.

(2) for the Contractor's applications for any permits, licences or approvals required by the Laws of the Country:

① which the Contractor is required to obtain under Sub-Clause 1.13 [Compliance with Laws].

② for the delivery of goods, including clearance through customs.

③ for the export of Contractor's Equipment when it is removed from the Site.

Employer's personnel

The Employer shall be responsible for ensuring that the Employer's Personnel and the Employer's other contractors on the Site:

(1) co-operate with the Contractor's efforts under Sub-Clause 4.6 [Co-operation].

(2) take actions similar to those which the Contractor is required to take under sub-paragraphs (a), (b) and (c) of Sub-Clause 4.8 [Safety Procedures] and under Sub-Clause 4.18 [protection of the Environment].

Employer's Financial Arrangements

The Employer shall submit, within 28 days after receiving any request from the Contractor, reasonable evidence that financial arrangements have been made and are being maintained which will enable the Employer to pay the Contract Price (as estimated at that time) in accordance with Clause 14 [Contract Price and Payment]. If the Employer intends to make any material change to his financial arrangements, the Employer shall give notice to the Contractor with detailed particulars.

Employer's Claims

If the Employer considers himself to be entitled to any payment under any Clause of these Conditions or otherwise in connection with the Contract, and/or to any extension of the Defects Notification Period, he shall give notice and particulars to the Contractor. However, notice is not required for payments due under Sub-Clause 4.19 [Electricity, Water and Gas], under Sub-Clause 4.20 [Employer's Equipment and Free-Issue Material], or for other services requested by the Contractor.

The notice shall be given as soon as practicable after the Employer became aware of the event or circumstances giving rise to the claim. A notice relating to any extension of the Defects Notification Period shall be given before the expiry of such period.

The particulars shall specify the Clause or other basis of the claim, and shall include substantiation of the amount and/or extension to which the Employer considers himself to be entitled in connection with the Contract. The employer shall then proceed in accordance with Sub-Clause 3.5 [Determinations] to agree or determine the amount (if any) which the Employer is entitled to be paid by the Contractor, and/or the extension (if any) of the Defects Notification Period in accordance with Sub-Clause 11.3 [Extension of the Defects Notification Period].

The Employer may deduct this amount from any moneys due, or to become due, to the Contractor. The Employer shall only be entitled to set off against or make any deduction from an amount due to the Contractor, or to otherwise claim against the Contractor, in accordance with this Sub-Clause or with sub-paragraph (a) and/or (b) of Sub-Clause 14.6 [Interim Payments].

The Employer's Representative

The Employer may appoint an Employer's Representative to act on his behalf under the Contract. In this event, he shall give notice to the Contractor of the name, address, duties and authority of the Employer's Representative.

The Employer's Representative shall carry out the duties assigned to him, and shall exercise the authority delegated to him, by the Employer. Unless and until the Employer notifies the Contractor, otherwise, the Employer's Representative shall be deemed to have the full authority of the Employer under the Contract, except in respect of Clause 15 [Determination by Employer].

If the Employer wishes to replace any person appointed as Employer's Representative, the Employer shall give the Contractor not less than 14 days' notice of the replacement's name, address, duties and authority, and of the date of appointment.

The Employer's personnel

The Employer or the Employer's Representative may from time to time assign duties and delegate authority to assistants, and may also revoke such assignment or delegation. These assistants may include a resident engineer, and/or independent inspectors appointed to inspect and/or test items of Plant and/or Materials. The assignment, delegation or revocation shall not take effect until a copy of it has been received by the Contractor.

Assistant shall be suitably qualified persons, who are competent to carry out these duties and exercise this authority, and who are fluent in the language for communications defined in Sub-Clause 1.4[Law and Language].

Delegated Persons

All these persons, including the Employer's Representative and assistants, to whom duties have been assigned or authority has been delegated, shall only be authorised to issue instructions to the Contractor to the extent defined by the delegation. Any approval, check, certificate, consent, examination, inspection, instruction, notice, proposal, request, test, or similar act by a delegated person, in accordance with the delegation, shall have the same effect as though the act had been an act of the Employer. However:

(1) unless otherwise stated in the delegated person's communication relating to such act, it shall not relieve the Contractor from any responsibility he has under the Contract, including responsibility for errors, omissions, discrepancies and non-compliances.

(2) any failure to disapprove any work, Plant or Materials shall not constitute approval and shall therefore not prejudice the right of the Employer to reject the work, Plant or Materials.

(3) if the Contractor questions any determination or instruction of a delegated person, the Contractor may refer the matter to the Employer, who shall promptly confirm, reverse or vary the determination or instruction.

Instructions

The Employer may issue to the Contractor instructions which may be necessary for the Contractor to perform his obligations under the Contract. Each instruction shall be given in writing and shall state the obligations to which it relates and the Sub-Clause (or other term of the Contract) in which the obligations are specified. If any such instruction constitutes a variation, Clause 13 [Variations and Adjustments] shall apply.

The Contractor shall take instructions from the Employer, or from the Employer's

Representative or an assistant to whom the appropriate authority has been delegated under this Clause.

Determinations

Whenever these Conditions provide that the Employer shall proceed in accordance with this Sub-Clause 3.5 to agree or determine any matter, the Employer shall consult with the Contractor in an endeavour to reach agreement. If agreement is not achieved, the Employer shall make a fair determination in accordance with the Contract, taking due regard of all relevant circumstances.

The Employer shall give notice to the Contractor of each agreement or determination, with supporting particulars. Each Party shall give effect to each agreement or determination, unless the Contractor gives notice, to the Employer, of his dissatisfaction with a determination within 14 days of receiving it. Either Party may then refer the dispute to the DAB in accordance with Sub-Clause 20.4 [Obtaining Dispute Adjudication Board's Decision].

Questions

1. When shall the employer give the contractor right of access to, and possession of, all parts of the site?
2. If the employer's failure was caused by any error or delay by the contractor, shall the contractor be entitled to extension of time, cost or profit?
3. What reasonable assistance should the employer provide to the contractor at the request of the contractor?
4. If the employer intends to make any material change to his financial arrangement, shall the employer notice to the contractor with detailed particulars?
5. When shall a notice relating to any extension of the defects notification period be given to the contractor?
6. What's authority of the employer's representative?
7. Who are included in the "delegated persons"?
8. Can delegated person issue instructions to the contractor?
9. The employer may issue to the contractor instructions, what shall the instructions state?
10. Once the contractor gives notices to the employer of his dissatisfaction with a determination, what will either party do?

Vocabulary, Phrases and Expressions

employer：雇主；业主
site：现场
right of access to the site：进入现场的权利
possession of the site：占用现场

the employer's requirements：雇主要求
performance security：履约担保
commencement date：开工日期
time for completion：竣工时间
an extension of time：延长期
contract price：合同价格
permits, licences or approvals：许可、执照或批准
protection of the environment：环境保护
financial arrangements：资金安排
material change to financial arrangements：重要的财务变更
defects notification period：缺陷通知期限
free-issue material：免费供应材料
employer's representative：雇主代表
resident engineer：驻地工程师
independent inspectors：独立检查员
delegated persons：受托人员
errors, omissions, or discrepancies：错误，遗漏或误差
dispute：争端

参 考 译 文

第 2 单元 雇 主

现场进入权

雇主应在专用条件中规定的时间(或几个时间)内，给承包商进入和占用现场各部分的权利。进入和占用权可不为承包商独享。如果根据合同，要求雇主(向承包商)提供任何基础、结构、生产设备或进入手段的占用权，雇主应按雇主要求中规定的时间和方式提供。但雇主在收到履约担保前，可保留上述任何进入或占用权，暂不给予。

如果在专用条件中没有规定上述时间，雇主应自开工日期起给承包商进入和占用现场的权利。

如果雇主未能及时给承包商上述进入和占用的权利，使承包商遭受延误和(或)成本增加，承包商应向雇主发出通知，根据第20.1款[承包商的索赔]的规定有权要求：

(1) 根据第8.4款[竣工时间的延长]的规定，如果竣工已经或将受到延误，对任何此类延误，给予延长期。

(2) 任何此类费用和合理利润应加入合同价格，给予支付。

在收到此通知后，雇主应按照第3.5款[确定]的规定，就此项要求做出商定或确定。

但是，如果出现雇主的违约是由于承包商的任何错误或延误，包括在任何承包商文件中的错误或提交延误造成的情况，承包商无权得到上述延长期、费用或利润。

许可、执照或批准

雇主应(按其所能)根据承包商的请求对其提供以下合理的协助。

(1) 取得与合同有关但不易得到的工程所在国的法律文本。

(2) 协助承包商申办工程所在国法律要求的任何许可、执照或批准：

① 根据第 1.13 款[遵守法律]的规定，承包商需要得到的。

② 为运送货物，包括结关需要的。

③ 当承包商设备运离现场出口时需要的。

雇主人员

雇主应负责保证在现场的雇主人员和其他承包商做到：

(1) 根据第 4.6 款[合作]的规定，与承包商进行合作。

(2) 采取与根据第 4.8 款[安全程序](a)、(b)、(c)项和第 4.18 款[环境保护]要求承包商应采取的类似的行动。

雇主的资金安排

雇主应在收到承包商的任何要求的 28 天内提出其已做并将维持的资金安排的合理证明，说明雇主能够按照第 14 条[合同价格和付款]的规定，支付合同价格(按当时估算)。如果雇主拟对其资金安排做任何重要变更，应将其变更的详细情节通知承包商。

雇主的索赔

如果雇主认为，根据本条件的任何条款或合同有关的其他事项，他有权得到任何付款，和(或)缺陷通知期限的任何延长，他应向承包商发出通知，说明细节。但对承包商根据第 4.19 款[电、水和燃气]和第 4.20 款[雇主的设备和免费供应的材料]规定的到期付款，或承包商要求的其他服务的应付款，不需发出通知。

通知应在雇主了解引起索赔的事件或情况后尽快发出。关于缺陷通知缺陷任何延长的通知，应在该期限到期前发出。

通知的细节应说明提出索赔根据的条款或其他依据，还应包括雇主认为根据合同他有权得到的索赔金额和(或)延长期的事实依据。然后，雇主应按照第 3.5 款[确定]的要求，商定或确定雇主有权得到承包商支付的金额(如果有)和(或)按照第 11.3 款[缺陷通知期限的延长]的规定，得到缺陷通知期限的延长期(如果有)。

雇主可将上述金额在给承包商的到期或将到期的任何应付款中扣减。雇主应仅有权根据本款或第 14.6 款[期中付款](a)和(或)(b)项的规定，从给承包商的应付款中冲销或扣减，或另外对承包商提出索赔。

雇主代表

雇主可以任命一名雇主代表，代表他按照合同内容工作。在此情况下，他应将雇主代表的姓名、地址、任务和权利通知承包商。

雇主代表应完成指派给他的任务，履行雇主托付给他的权利。除非和直到雇主另行通知承包商，雇主代表将被认为具有雇主根据合同规定的全部权力，涉及第 15 条[由雇主终止]规定的权利除外。

如果雇主希望替换任何已任命的雇主代表,应在不少于14天前将替换人的姓名、地址、任务和权利以及任命的日期通知给承包商。

其他雇主人员

雇主或雇主代表可随时对一些助手指派和托付一定的任务和权力,也可撤销这些指派和托付。这些助手可包括驻地工程师和(或)担任检验、和(或)试验各项生产设备和(或)材料的独立检查员。以上指派、托付或撤销在承包商收到抄件后生效。

这些助手应具有适当的资质、履行其任务和权利的能力,并能流利地使用第1.4款[法律和语言]规定的交流语言。

受托人员

所有这些人员包括已被指派任务、托付权力的雇主代表和助手,应只被授权在托付规定的范围内向承包商发布指示。由受托人员根据托付做出的任何批准、校核、证明、同意、检查、检验、指示、通知、建议、要求、试验或类似行动,应如同雇主采取的行动一样有效,但:

(1) 除非在受托人员关于上述行动的信函中另有说明,该行动都不免除承包商根据合同应承担的任何职责,包括对错误、遗漏、误差和未遵办的职责。

(2) 未对任何工作、生产设备或材料提出否定意见不应构成批准,不应影响雇主拒绝该工作、生产设备或材料的权利。

(3) 如果承包商对受托人员的决定或指示提出质疑,承包商可将此事项提交给雇主,雇主应迅速对该决定或指示进行确认、取消或更改。

指示

雇主可向承包商发出为承包商根据合同履行义务所需要的指示。每项指示都应是书面的,并说明其有关的义务,以及规定这些义务的条款(或合同的其他条款)。当任何此类指示构成一项变更时,应按照第13条[变更和调整]的规定办理。

承包商应接受雇主、雇主代表或根据本条受托相应权力的雇主代表或助手的指示。

确定

每当本条件规定雇主应按照第3.5款对任何事项进行商定或确定时,雇主应与承包商协商尽量达成协议。如果达不成协议,雇主应对有关情况给予应有的考虑,按照合同做出公正的决定。

雇主应将每一项商定或决定连同依据的细节通知承包商。各方都应履行每项商定或决定,除非承包商在收到通知14天内向雇主发出通知,对某项决定表示不满。这时,任一方可依照第20.4款[取得争端裁决委员会决定]的规定,将争端提交DAB。

Unit 3   Cost Estimation

Costs Associated with Constructed Facilities

The costs of a constructed facility to the owner include both the initial capital cost and the subsequent operation and maintenance costs. Each of these major cost categories consists of a number of cost components.

The capital cost for a construction project includes the expenses related to the initial establishment of the facility:
- Land acquisition, including holding and improvement.
- Planning and feasibility studies.
- Architectural and engineering design.
- Construction, including materials, equipment and labor.
- Field supervision of construction.
- Construction financing.
- Insurance and taxes during construction.
- Owner's general office overhead.
- Equipment and furnishings not included in construction.
- Inspection and testing.

The operation and maintenance cost in subsequent years over the project life cycle includes the following expenses:
- Land rent, if applicable.
- Operating staff.
- Labor and material for maintenance and repairs.
- Periodic renovations.
- Insurance and taxes.
- Financing costs.
- Utilities.
- Owner's other expenses.

The magnitude of each of these cost components depends on the nature, size and location of the project as well as the management organization, among many considerations. The owner is interested in achieving the lowest possible overall project cost that is consistent with its investment objectives.

It is important for design professionals and construction managers to realize that while the construction cost may be the single largest component of the capital cost, other cost components are not insignificant. For example, land acquisition costs are a major expenditure for building construction in high-density urban areas, and construction financing costs can reach the same order of magnitude as the construction cost in large projects such as the construction of nuclear power plants.

From the owner's perspective, it is equally important to estimate the corresponding operation and maintenance cost of each alternative for a proposed facility in order to analyze the life cycle costs. The large expenditures needed for facility maintenance, especially for publicly owned infrastructure, are reminders of the neglect in the past to consider fully the implications of operation and maintenance cost in the design stage.

In most construction budgets, there is an allowance for contingencies or unexpected costs occurring during construction. This contingency amount may be included within each cost item or be included in a single category of construction contingency. The amount of contingency is based on historical experience and the expected difficulty of a particular construction project. For example, one construction firm makes estimates of the expected cost in five different areas:

- Design development changes.
- Schedule adjustments.
- General administration changes (such as wage rates).
- Differing site conditions for those expected.
- Third party requirements imposed during construction, such as new permits.

Contingent amounts not spent for construction can be released near the end of construction to the owner or to add additional project elements.

Approaches to Cost Estimation

Cost estimating is one of the most important steps in project management. A cost estimate establishes the base line of the project cost at different stages of development of the project. A cost estimate at a given stage of project development represents a prediction provided by the cost engineer or estimator on the basis of available data. According to the American Association of Cost Engineers, cost engineering is defined as that area of engineering practice where engineering judgment and experience are utilized in the application of scientific principles and techniques to the problem of cost estimation, cost control and profitability.

Virtually all cost estimation is performed according to one or some combination of the following basic approaches.

(1) Production function. In microeconomics, the relationship between the output of a process and the necessary resources is referred to as the production function. In construction, the production function may be expressed by the relationship between the volume of construction and a factor of production such as labor or capital. A production function relates the amount or volume of output to the various inputs of labor, material and equipment. For example, the amount of output Q may be derived as a function of various input factors $x_1, x_2, \cdots, x_n$ by means of mathematical and/or statistical methods. Thus, for a specified level of output, we may attempt to find a set of values for the input factors so as to minimize the production cost. The relationship

between the sizes of a building project (expressed in square feet) to the input labor (expressed in labor hours per square foot) is an example of a production function for construction.

(2) Empirical cost inference. Empirical estimation of cost functions requires statistical techniques which relate the cost of constructing or operating a facility to a few important characteristics or attributes of the system. The role of statistical inference is to estimate the best parameter values or constants in an assumed cost function. Usually, this is accomplished by means of regression analysis techniques.

(3) Unit costs for bill of quantities. A unit cost is assigned to each of the facility components or tasks as represented by the bill of quantities. The total cost is the summation of the products of the quantities multiplied by the corresponding unit costs. The unit cost method is straightforward in principle but quite laborious in application. The initial step is to break down or disaggregate a process into a number of tasks. Collectively, these tasks must be completed for the construction of a facility. Once these tasks are defined and quantities representing these tasks are assessed, a unit cost is assigned to each and then the total cost is determined by summing the costs incurred in each task. The level of detail in decomposing into tasks will vary considerably from one estimate to another.

(4) Allocation of joint costs. Allocations of cost from existing accounts may be used to develop a cost function of an operation. The basic idea in this method is that each expenditure item can be assigned to particular characteristics of the operation. Ideally, the allocation of joint costs should be causally related to the category of basic costs in an allocation process. In many instances, however, a causal relationship between the allocation factor and the cost item cannot be identified or may not exist. For example, in construction projects, the accounts for basic costs may be classified according to:
- labor.
- material.
- construction equipment.
- construction supervision.
- general office overhead.

These basic costs may then be allocated proportionally to various tasks which are subdivisions of a project.

Types of Construction Cost Estimates

Construction cost constitutes only a fraction, though a substantial fraction, of the total project cost. However, it is the part of the cost under the control of the construction project manager. The required levels of accuracy of construction cost estimates vary at different stages of project development, ranging from ball park figures in the early stage to fairly reliable figures for budget control prior to construction. Since design decisions made at the beginning stage of a project life cycle are more tentative than those made at a later stage, the cost estimates made at the earlier stage are expected to be less accurate. Generally, the accuracy of a cost estimate will reflect the information available at the time of estimation.

Construction cost estimates may be viewed from different perspectives because of different institutional requirements. In spite of the many types of cost estimates used at different stages of a project, cost estimates can best be classified into three major categories according to their functions. A construction cost estimate serves one of the three basic functions: design, bid and control. For establishing the financing of a project, either a design estimate or a bid estimate is used.

- Design Estimates

For the owner or its designated design professionals, the types of cost estimates encountered run parallel with the planning and design as follows:

(1) Screening estimates (or order of magnitude estimates).

(2) Preliminary estimates (or conceptual estimates).

(3) Detailed estimates (or definitive estimates).

(4) Engineer's estimates based on plans and specifications.

For each of these different estimates, the amount of design information available typically increases.

In the planning and design stages of a project, various design estimates reflect the progress of the design. At the very early stage, the screening estimate or order of magnitude estimate is usually made before the facility is designed, and must therefore rely on the cost data of similar facilities built in the past. A preliminary estimate or conceptual estimate is based on the conceptual design of the facility at the state when the basic technologies for the design are known. The detailed estimate or definitive estimate is made when the scope of work is clearly defined and the detailed design is in progress so that the essential features of the facility are identifiable. The engineer's estimate is based on the completed plans and specifications when they are ready for the owner to solicit bids from construction contractors. In preparing these estimates, the design professional will include expected amounts for contractors' overhead and profits.

The costs associated with a facility may be decomposed into a hierarchy of levels that are appropriate for the purpose of cost estimation. The level of detail in decomposing the facility into tasks depends on the type of cost estimate to be prepared. For conceptual estimates, for example, the level of detail in defining tasks is quite coarse; for detailed estimates, the level of detail can be quite fine.

As an example, consider the cost estimates for a proposed bridge across a river. A screening estimate is made for each of the potential alternatives, such as a tied arch bridge or a cantilever truss bridge. As the bridge type is selected, e.g. the technology is chosen to be a tied arch bridge instead of some new bridge form; a preliminary estimate is made on the basis of the layout of the selected bridge form on the basis of the preliminary or conceptual design. When the detailed design has progressed to a point when the essential details are known, a detailed estimate is made on the basis of the well defined scope of the project. When the detailed plans and specifications are completed, an engineer's estimate can be made on the basis of items and quantities of work.

Unit 3 Cost Estimation

- Bid Estimates

For the contractor, a bid estimate submitted to the owner either for competitive bidding or negotiation consists of direct construction cost including field supervision, plus a markup to cover general overhead and profits. The direct cost of construction for bid estimates is usually derived from a combination of the following approaches.

(1) Subcontractor quotations.

(2) Quantity takeoffs.

(3) Construction procedures.

The contractor's bid estimates often reflect the desire of the contractor to secure the job as well as the estimating tools at its disposal. Some contractors have well established cost estimating procedures while others do not. Since only the lowest bidder will be the winner of the contract in most bidding contests, any effort devoted to cost estimating is a loss to the contractor who is not a successful bidder. Consequently, the contractor may put in the least amount of possible effort for making a cost estimate if it believes that its chance of success is not high.

If a general contractor intends to use subcontractors in the construction of a facility, it may solicit price quotations for various tasks to be subcontracted to specialty subcontractors. Thus, the general subcontractor will shift the burden of cost estimating to subcontractors. If all or part of the construction is to be undertaken by the general contractor, a bid estimate may be prepared on the basis of the quantity takeoffs from the plans provided by the owner or on the basis of the construction procedures devised by the contractor for implementing the project. For example, the cost of a footing of a certain type and size may be found in commercial publications on cost data which can be used to facilitate cost estimates from quantity takeoffs. However, the contractor may want to assess the actual cost of construction by considering the actual construction procedures to be used and the associated costs if the project is deemed to be different from typical designs. Hence, items such as labor, material and equipment needed to perform various tasks may be used as parameters for the cost estimates.

- Control Estimates

For monitoring the project during construction, a control estimate is derived from available information to establish:

(1) Budget estimate for financing.

(2) Budgeted cost after contracting but prior to construction.

(3) Estimated cost to completion during the progress of construction.

Both the owner and the contractor must adopt some base line for cost control during the construction. For the owner, a budget estimate must be adopted early enough for planning long term financing of the facility. Consequently, the detailed estimate is often used as the budget estimate since it is sufficient definitive to reflect the project scope and is available long before the engineer's estimate. As the work progresses, the budgeted cost must be revised periodically to reflect the estimated cost to completion. A revised estimated cost is necessary either because of change orders initiated by the owner or due to unexpected cost overruns or savings.

For the contractor, the bid estimate is usually regarded as the budget estimate, which will be used for control purposes as well as for planning construction financing. The budgeted cost should also be updated periodically to reflect the estimated cost to completion as well as to insure adequate cash flows for the completion of the project.

Questions

1. Which expenses are included in the capital cost for a construction project?
2. Which expenses are included in the operation and maintenance cost in subsequent years over the project life cycle?
3. Which cost may be the single largest component of the capital cost? Are the other cost components insignificant?
4. How does the construction firm estimate the amount of contingency?
5. Why is a cost estimate important at different stages of development of the project?
6. Say about the required levels of accuracy of construction cost estimates vary at different stages of project development.
7. How to classify cost estimates according to their functions?
8. For the owner or its designated design professionals, what types of cost estimates encountered run parallel with the planning and design?
9. How does a general contractor prepare a bid estimate?
10. How do the owner and the contractor control estimate?

Vocabulary, Phrases and Expressions

cost estimation：成本估算
initial capital：创办成本；初始投资
operation and maintenance costs：运行与养护费用
land acquisition：土地获得
field supervision of construction：现场施工监督
overhead：企业一般管理费用
project life cycle：项目生命周期
land rent：土地租金
periodic renovations：周期性更新
financial costs：财务成本
construction cost：施工建设费
unexpected costs：不可预见费用
cost engineers：造价工程师
cost engineering：工程估价
cost control：成本控制

production function：产出函数
the amount or volume of output：产出总量
production cost：生产成本
empirical cost inference：经验成本推论
bill of quantities：工程量清单
unit cost：单位成本
joint costs：联合成本
accuracy of cost estimates：估价精度
design estimate：设计估价
bid estimate：投标估价
screening estimates(or order of magnitude estimates)：筛选估计；匡算(或数量级估计)
preliminary estimates (or conceptual estimates)：初步估算(或概念性估算)
detailed estimates (or definitive estimates)：详细估计(或确定估计)
direct construction cost：直接施工成本
profits：利润
control estimate：控制估价
budget estimate：财务预算

参 考 译 文

第 3 单元　成 本 估 算

与建筑设施相关的成本

对业主来说，一项建筑设施的成本包括初始投资和随后的运行与养护费用。这两大项费用又是由许多分项费用组成的。

对于一个建设项目，其初始投资包括与建设该设施相关的各项资本投入：
- 取得土地，包括持有和再开发。
- 规划和可行性研究。
- 建筑和工程设计。
- 施工，包括材料、设备和劳动力。
- 现场施工监督。
- 建设融资成本。
- 建设过程中的各种保险和税费。
- 业主的一般行政管理开支。
- 不包括在施工中的设备和家具。
- 检查和试验。

在项目建成后全寿命周期中的运行与维护费用包括以下几个方面：
- 土地租金(如果有的话)。

- 运行人员费用。
- 维修和保养的劳动力和材料费用。
- 周期性翻新费用。
- 保险和税费。
- 财务成本。
- 公用事业费。
- 业主的其他开支。

以上这些费用的多少要由项目的性质、规模和地理位置，以及管理组织等多方面的因素来决定。业主总希望以尽可能少的投入来实现项目的目标。

设计者和施工管理者应当非常明确的重要一点是，施工建设费用是成本中最主要的一项费用，但是其他费用也不可忽视。例如，在高密度建筑的市区建设一个项目，取得土地的费用是一项主要的成本，而对核电站等这样的大型项目建设，融资成本可能与项目的建造成本基本持平。

站在业主方的角度看，为了分析项目全寿命周期的成本，对每个建设方案的运行和维护成本进行估计是同样重要的。有些项目，尤其是公共项目的物业保养成本巨大，这时刻都在提醒我们，不该像过去那样在项目的设计阶段忽视项目建成后的运行和保养。

在很多项目的预算中，总有一部分不可预见的费用准备用于施工中的意外情况，这些不可预见费用有可能包含在每一项费用中，也可能作为一项总的不可预见费用。不可预见费用的多少可根据历史经验和特定项目的建设难度来估计。例如，某一建筑公司对不可预见费用的估算包括5个不同方面。

- 设计变更。
- 进度调整。
- 总体管理方面的变化(例如，工资水平的变化)。
- 预测的现场条件的不同。
- 建设过程中第三方要求所产生的费用，如新的许可要求。

没有用掉的不可预见费用在工程末期可以退回业主方，或者用于项目新增部分的建设。

成本估算的方法

成本估算是项目管理中最重要的环节之一。它在项目建设的不同阶段为项目的成本建立了一条基准线。在项目开发过程中的某一特定阶段的成本估算就是造价工程师在现有数据基础上对未来成本的预测。根据美国造价工程师协会的定义，工程估价是运用科学理论和技术，根据工程师的判断和经验，解决成本估算、成本控制和盈利能力等问题的活动。

实际上，所有的估价活动都是基于以下这些基本方法中的一种或几种方法的组合。

(1) 产出函数。在微观经济学中把过程的产出和资源的消耗这两者之间的关系叫做产出函数。在建筑工程中，产出函数则可认为是建设项目的规模和生产参数(如人工或资金)之间的关系。产出函数建立了产出的总量或规模与各种投入(比如人力、材料、设备)之间的关系。例如，代表产出的 Q 可以用代表各种投入的不同参数 $x_1, x_2, \cdots, x_n$ 等通过数学和/或统计方法表达。因此，对某一特定的产出，可以通过对各个投入参数赋予不同的值，从而找到一个最低的生产成本。房屋建筑的大小(用平方英尺表示)和消耗的人力(用小时/平方英尺来表示)之间的关系就是产出函数的一个例子。

(2) 经验成本推论法。利用基于经验的成本函数估算成本需要一些统计技术，这些技术将建造或运营某设施与系统的一些重要特征或属性联系起来。数理统计推理的目的是为了找到最适合的参数值或者常数，用于在假定的成本函数中进行成本估算。在通常情况下，这需要利用回归分析法。

(3) 用于工程量清单的单位成本法。由工程量清单表达的各项任务或各个组成部分的单位成本能够明确，总成本就是各项产品的数量与其相应单位成本的乘积之和。单位成本法虽然在理论上非常直接，但是难以应用。第一步是将某工作分解成许多项任务，当然每项任务都是为项目建设服务的。一旦这些任务确定，并有了工作量的估算，用单价与每项任务的量相乘就可以得到每项任务的成本，从而得出每项工作的成本。当然，在不同的估算中对每项工作分解的详细程度可能会有很大差别。

(4) 混合成本分配法。有时候要从现有的会计账目上去分解，从而确定某项具体操作的成本函数。这种方法的基本思想是，每一项花费都能够对应地分配到操作过程中的某一特定步骤。理想情况是在成本分配过程中，混合成本能够有因果对应关系地被分解，并确定为某种基本成本。但是，在很多情况下，子项目和其分配成本之间难以确定或者根本不存在因果关系。例如，在建设项目中，基本成本可定义为以下5个方面：

- 人力。
- 材料。
- 建筑设备。
- 建设管理。
- 日常办公开销。

这几个基本成本有可能会按比例地分配到工程子项的不同任务中去。

建造成本估算的类型

建造成本是整个项目成本中的一部分，虽然很重要，但只是施工项目经理控制下的成本的一部分。在项目建设的不同阶段对估价精确度的要求也不一样，早期只是粗略估计，到施工前的预算就应当是相当可靠了。由于在项目生命周期早期设计方面的决策比后期更加具有不确定性，所以也就不能期望早期阶段的估价会准确。总的来说，估价的准确程度将反映估价时所获取的信息。

由于不同机构的要求不同，对建造成本估算也存在不同的观点。虽然在项目的不同阶段，建造成本的估算有许多不同的方法，但是根据其功用可分为3种主要方法。建造成本估算主要服务于以下3个方面：设计、投标和控制。要对项目进行融资，要么需要设计估价，要么需要投标估价。

- 设计估价

对于业主或他指定的设计者而言，在规划和设计过程中要平行进行的估价的种类如下：
(1) 匡算(宏观估价)。
(2) 初步估算(概念方案阶段估价)。
(3) 详细估算(明确估价)。
(4) 工程师基于施工计划和说明的估算。

对于以上每一个估价阶段，设计所提供的信息量是逐步增加的。

在项目的规划和设计阶段，不同的设计估算反映了设计进展的不同阶段。在最初阶段，投资匡算或者宏观估价通常是在项目设计之前做出的，因此必须依靠过去类似项目的数据。初步估算或者称为概念方案阶段估价主要基于概念设计方案进行估算，此时只明确了最基本的技术方案。详细估算或者称为明确估价是在工程范围基本明确、详细设计正在进行、项目的基本特征已经确定时做出的。工程师估算要以明确的施工计划和施工说明为基础，并且业主也可以据此发包选择施工承包商。在做这些估算时，设计人员应将承包商的日程管理费和利润考虑进去。

为了进行成本估算，可以把一项设施的有关成本分解成几个适当的层次。层次划分的详细程度取决于成本估算的种类，例如，对于概念设计方案阶段的估价，层次的划分就比较粗，而对于详细设计阶段的估价，层次的划分就应该很细。

例如，要对某条河上的拟建桥梁进行造价估算，投资匡算是对每个潜在的方案进行估算，如是采用拱桥方案还是悬臂桁架桥方案。当桥的类型确定后，比如选定拱形桥而不是其他形式的桥，这时就要基于拱形桥的平面布置，在初步或概念设计的基础上做初步估算。当详细设计进行到一定阶段，最根本的详细设计已经完成时，就要基于项目的明确范围进行详细估算。当完成了详细施工计划和施工指导说明后，就可以根据各项工作和其工程量进行工程师估算了。

- 投标估价

对于承包商来说，提交给业主的投标估价的目的是为竞争的需要或者是与业主谈判的需要，投标估价中包括直接施工成本(包括现场监督以及在此基础上增加一笔总体管理费)和利润。用于投标估价中的直接施工成本常用以下几种方法组合计算：

(1) 根据分包商的报价。
(2) 估计的工程量。
(3) 施工方案。

承包商的投标估价常常反映了承包商对完成投标工程的期望值，也反映了其所采用的估价工具。有些承包商拥有良好的估价程序，而有些则没有。由于在大多数工程招标中一般都是最低价中标，所以对于未中标者来说，在投标估价过程中的任何投入都是浪费。因此，如果一个承包商认为自己胜出的机会不是很大，他就会花费尽可能少的精力来进行成本估价。

如果一个总承包商在设施的建设过程中希望将工程进行分包，他有可能要求各个专业分包商提交分包报价单，所以总承包商将把成本估算的任务转移到分包商头上。如果所有的工程或部分工程由总承包商来施工，投标估计就要根据业主提出的计划和工程量或由承包商提供的施工组织计划来进行编制。例如，某类房屋某种基础的成本可以从某些商业出版物中找到其单价，再根据工程量就可以算出成本。但是，项目的实际情况可能导致实际施工程序与一般设计要求不同，在这种情况下承包商就要想办法估算其真实的成本和相关的费用。因此，为完成不同任务所需要的劳动力、材料和设备等就应该作为成本估算的参数。

- 控制估价

为在施工过程中进行管理和控制，需要基于以下信息编制一个控制性的估价：

(1) 财务预算。

(2) 签订合同后在开工前的预算。

(3) 在施工过程中所做的对完工前的成本估算。

在施工过程中，业主和承包商都会有一个成本的基准来控制实际成本。对业主来说，必须尽早明确预算(budget estimate)用于项目的长期财务规划。因而，在工程师估算完成前的相当长时间里，只能用详细估算来作为控制预算，因为详细估算也能充分明确地反映项目的范围。在工程进行的过程中，必须对成本估算进行定期更新，以反映完工前的预测成本。由于在施工中业主可能提出变更要求，或者有不可预见的突破成本或节约成本的情况发生，对成本估算进行及时更新是很必要的。

对承包商来说，经常用投标估价作为预算，既可以进行成本控制，也可以进行施工期间的财务规划。该预算成本也要定期更新，以反映完工前的预测成本，并确保项目完工前的现金投入。

Unit 4　The Project Budget(1)

For cost control on a project, the construction plan and the associated cash flow estimates can provide the baseline reference for subsequent project monitoring and control. For schedules, progress on individual activities can be compared with the project schedule to monitor the progress of activities. Contract and job specifications provide the criteria by which to assess and assure the required quality of construction. The final or detailed cost estimate provides a baseline for the assessment of financial performance during the project. To the extent that costs are within the detailed cost estimate, then the project is thought to be under financial control. Overruns in particular cost categories signal the possibility of problems and give an indication of exactly what problems are being encountered. Expense oriented construction planning and control focuses upon the categories included in the final cost estimation.

For control and monitoring purposes, the original detailed cost estimate is typically converted to a project budget, and the project budget is used subsequently as a guide for management. Specific items in the detailed cost estimate become job cost elements. Expenses incurred during the course of a project are recorded in specific job cost accounts to be compared with the original cost estimates in each category. Thus, individual job cost accounts generally represent the basic unit for cost control. Alternatively, job cost accounts may be disaggregated or divided into work elements which are related both to particular scheduled activities and to particular cost accounts.

In addition to cost amounts, information on material quantities and labor inputs within each job account is also typically retained in the project budget. With this information, actual materials usage and labor employed can be compared to the expected requirements. As a result, cost overruns or savings on particular items can be identified as due to changes in unit prices, labor productivity or in the amount of material consumed.

The number of cost accounts associated with a particular project can vary considerably. For constructors, on the order of four hundred separate cost accounts might be used on a small project. These accounts record all the transactions associated with a budget. Thus, separate accounts might exist for different types of materials, equipment use, payroll, project office, etc. Both physical and non-physical resources are represented, including overhead items such as computer use or interest charges. Table 4-1 summarizes a typical set of cost accounts that might be used in building construction. Note that this set of accounts is organized hierarchically, with seven major divisions (accounts 201 to 207) and numerous subdivisions under each division. This hierarchical structure facilitates aggregation of costs into pre-defined categories; for example, costs associated with the superstructure (account 204) would be the sum of the underlying subdivisions (ie. 204.1, 204.2, etc.). The sub-division accounts in Table 4-1 could be further divided into personnel, material and other resource costs for the purpose of financial accounting.

Table 4-1 Illustrative Set of Project Cost Accounts

201	Clearing and Preparing Site
202	Substructure
202.1	Excavation and Shoring
202.2	Piling
202.3	Concrete Masonry
202.31	Mixing and Placing
202.32	Formwork
202.33	Reinforcing
203	Outside Utilities (water, gas, sewer, etc.)
204	Superstructure
204.1	Masonry Construction
204.2	Structural Steel
204.3	Wood Framing, Partitions, etc.
204.4	Exterior Finishes (brickwork, terra cotta, cut stone, etc.)
204.5	Roofing, Drains, Gutters, Flashing, etc.
204.6	Interior Finish and Trim
204.61	Finish Flooring, Stairs, Doors, Trim
204.62	Glass, Windows, Glazing
204.63	Marble, Tile, Terrazzo
204.64	Lathing and Plastering
204.65	Soundproofing and Insulation
204.66	Finish Hardware
204.67	Painting and Decorating
204.68	Waterproofing
204.69	Sprinklers and Fire Protection
204.7	Service Work
204.71	Electrical Work
204.72	Heating and Ventilating
204.73	Plumbing and Sewage
204.74	Air Conditioning
204.72	Fire Alarm, Telephone, Security, Miscellaneous
205	Paving, Curbs, Walks
206	Installed Equipment (elevators, revolving doors, mailchutes, etc.)
207	Fencing

In developing or implementing a system of cost accounts, an appropriate numbering or coding system is essential to facilitate communication of information and proper aggregation of cost information. Particular cost accounts are used to indicate the expenditures associated with specific projects and to indicate the expenditures on particular items throughout an organization. These are examples of different perspectives on the same information, in which the same information may be summarized in different ways for specific purposes. Thus, more than one aggregation of the cost information and more than one application program can use a particular cost account. Separate identifiers of the type of cost account and the specific project must be provided for project cost accounts or for financial transactions. As a result, a standard set of cost codes such as the MASTERFORMAT codes may be adopted to identify cost accounts along with project identifiers and extensions to indicate organization or job specific needs. Similarly the use of databases or, at a minimum, inter-communicating applications programs facilitate access to cost information.

Converting a final cost estimate into a project budget compatible with an organization's cost accounts is not always a straightforward task. Cost estimates are generally disaggregated into appropriate functional or resource based project categories. For example, labor and material quantities might be included for each of several physical components of a project. For cost accounting purposes, labor and material quantities are aggregated by type no matter for which physical component they are employed. For example, particular types of workers or materials might be used on numerous different physical components of a facility. Moreover, the categories of cost accounts established within an organization may bear little resemblance to the quantities included in a final cost estimate. This is particularly true when final cost estimates are prepared in accordance with an external reporting requirement rather than in view of the existing cost accounts within an organization.

One particular problem in forming a project budget in terms of cost accounts is the treatment of contingency amounts. These allowances are included in project cost estimates to accommodate unforeseen events and the resulting costs. However, in advance of project completion, the source of contingency expenses is not known. Realistically, a budget accounting item for contingency allowance should be established whenever a contingency amount was included in the final cost estimate.

A second problem in forming a project budget is the treatment of inflation. Typically, final cost estimates are formed in terms of real dollars and an item reflecting inflation costs is added on as a percentage. This inflation allowance would then be allocated to individual cost items in relation to the actual expected inflation over the period for which costs will be incurred.

Example 4.1 Project Budget for a Design Office.

An example of a small project budget is shown in Table 4-2.

This budget might be used by a design firm for a specific design project. While this budget might represent all the work for this firm on the project, numerous other organizations would be involved with their own budgets. In Table 4-2, a summary budget is shown as well as a detailed listing of costs for individuals in the Engineering Division. For the purpose of consistency with cost accounts and managerial control, labor costs are aggregated into three groups: the engineering, architectural and environmental divisions. The detailed budget shown in Table 4-2 applies only to the engineering division labor; other detailed budgets amounts for categories such as supplies and the other work divisions would also be prepared. Note that the salary costs associated with individuals are aggregated to obtain the total labor costs in the engineering group for the project. To perform this aggregation, some means of identifying individuals within organizational groups is required. Accompanying a budget of this nature, some estimate of the actual man-hours of labor required by project task would also be prepared. Finally, this budget might be used for internal purposes alone. In submitting financial bills and reports to the client, overhead and contingency amounts might be combined with the direct labor costs to establish an aggregate billing rate per hour.

Table 4-2 Example of a Small Project Budget for a Design Firm

Personnel	Budget Summary/dollar
Architectural Division	67 251.00
Engineering Division	45 372.00
Environmental Division	28 235.00
Total	140 858.00
Other Direct Expenses	
Travel	2 400.00
Supplies	1 500.00
Communication	600.00
Computer Services	1 200.00
Total	5 700.00
Overhead	175 869.60
Contingency and Profit	95 700.00
Total	418 127.60
Senior Engineer	
Associate Engineer	11 562.00
Engineer	21 365.00
Technician	12 654.00
Total	45 372.00

Example 4.2 Project Budget for a Constructor.

Table 4-3 illustrates a summary budget for a constructor. This budget is developed from a project to construct a wharf. As with the example design office budget above, costs are divided into direct and indirect expenses. Within direct costs, expenses are divided into material, subcontract, temporary work and machinery costs. This budget indicates aggregate amounts for the various categories. Cost details associated with particular cost accounts would supplement and support the aggregate budget shown in Table 4-3. A profit and a contingency amount might be added to the basic budget of $ 1 715 147 shown in Table 4-3 for completeness.

Table 4-3 An Example of a Project Budget for a Wharf Project

	Material Cost/$	Subcontract Work/$	Temporary Work/$	Machinery Cost/$	Total Cost/$
Steel Piling	292 172	129 178	16 389	0	437 739
Tie-rod	88 233	29 254	0	0	117 487
Anchor-Wall	130 281	60 873	0	0	191 154
Backfill	242 230	27 919	0	0	300 149
Coping	42 880	22 307	13 171	0	78 358
Dredging	0	111 650	0	0	111 650
Fender	48 996	10 344	0	1 750	61 090
Other	5 000	32 250	0	0	37 250
Sub-total	849 800	423 775	29 560	1 750	1 304 885
Summary					
Total of Direct Cost					$1 304 885
Indirect Cost					
Common Temporary Work					$19 320
Common Machinery					$80 934
Transportation					$15 550
Office Operating Costs					$294 458
Total of Indirect Cost					$ 410 262
Total Project Cost					$1 715 147

Questions

1. How is the original detailed cost estimate converted to a project budget?
2. What may job cost accounts be divided into?
3. In addition to cost amounts, what is also typically retained in the project budget?
4. List separate accounts that exist in different types.
5. What's the advantage of the hierarchical structure in cost accounts?
6. Converting a final cost estimate into a project budget compatible with an organization's cost accounts is not always a straightforward task, why?
7. How to treat the contingency amounts in forming a project budget in terms of cost accounts?
8. How to treat inflation in forming a project budget?
9. Say about the example of a small project budget for a design firm.
10. How is cost divided in the example of project budget for a contractor?

Vocabulary, Phrases and Expressions

project budget：项目预算
cost control：成本控制
cash flow：现金流量
job specifications：施工(工作)规范
financial performance：财务状况
overruns：超支
job cost elements：工作成本要素
work elements：作业要素
database：数据库
separate accounts：专账
contingency allowance：应急准备金
unforeseen events：不可预见事件
inflation allowance：通货膨胀准备金
a summary budget：汇总预算
financial bills：财务单据
direct labor costs：直接人工成本
indirect costs：间接成本
overhead and contingency amounts：企业管理费用和应急费用总计

参 考 译 文

第4单元　项目预算(1)

　　对于项目的成本控制、项目计划和相关的现金流量估算可以为后续的项目监督和控制提供参照基准。对于进度控制，可以将项目活动的实际进度和项目的计划进度进行比较，以监督项目的进度实施。合同和工作标准则为建设项目的质量提供了评价和保证准则。最终的或详细的成本预算为项目期的财务状况提供了评价基准。如果实际成本没有超出详细的成本估算，我们便认为项目的财务控制做得较好。特殊成本项次的超支发出了可能存在问题的信号，并且对所面临问题给出确切的指示。以费用为导向的建设项目计划和控制，侧重包含在最终成本估算内的成本项次。

　　本着控制和监督的目的，初始的详细成本估算通常被转化为项目预算，并被用来作为随后成本管理的指南。详细成本估算中的具体项次成为工作成本要素。在项目实施过程中所发生的支出被记录在具体的工作成本报告中，以用来在每一成本项次下和原始成本估算相比较。这样一来，个别的工作成本报告通常就被称为成本控制的基本单位。同时，工作成本报告还可分解成与具体的进度活动及具体的成本报告都有关的作业要素。

除了成本报告之外，项目预算中还应保留每项工作报告有关材料数量和劳动力投入的信息。有了这些信息，就可将实际的材料用量和人工消耗与预期的标准进行比较，这样就可以识别出具体活动成本超支或节约的原因，即是由于单价变化还是由于劳动生产率或材料消耗量上的变化所引起的。

一个具体项目上的成本报告数字差异很大。对于建设项目，一个小项目也可能有多达400多个独立的成本报告。这些报告记录了项目上的所有交易活动。因此，存在不同类型的专账，例如，有原材料报告、设备使用报告、工资报告、办公室报告等。同时，诸如计算机使用或利息支出之类的有形或无形的费用支出都要表示在报告当中。表4-1总结了一套用在建设项目上的成本报告。注意，这套报告被划分为7个主要部分(报告201到报告207)，同时每部分又包括了大量子目。这种等级式的报告结构有利于把成本按预先确定好的类别进行汇总。例如，主体结构的成本(报告204)是由其下的各子项目汇总而来的(即204.1、204.2等)。表4-1中的子目报告又可进一步被分解成人工、材料和其他资源成本，以方便财务会计工作。

表4-1 项目成本报告说明

201	清理和准备现场
202	地下结构
202.1	钻孔和支护
202.2	打桩
202.3	混凝土浇筑
202.31	搅拌
202.32	成型
202.33	养护
203	场外设施(水、气、排污等)
204	主体结构
204.1	混凝土施工
204.2	钢筋工程
204.3	砌体工程
204.4	室外工程
204.5	屋面工程
204.6	室内装饰
204.61	楼地面
204.62	玻璃和窗户
204.63	大理石
204.64	板条拌灰
204.65	隔音与绝缘
204.66	五金
204.67	喷涂
204.68	防水

续表

204.69	消防
204.7	服务设施
204.71	电器照明
204.72	供热通风
204.73	管道与排污
204.74	空调工程
204.75	火警、电话、安全和其他
205	铺坡道地砖
206	设备安全(电梯、旋转门等)
207	围墙

在开发和运用成本报告系统时，适当的编码或译码体系有利于信息沟通和成本信息的汇总。特定的成本报告既可用来显示有关具体项目的费用，也可以显示组织中具体事项的开支，这就是相同的信息有不同角度应用的例子，即相同的信息因为特定的目的可以用不同的方法被计算和汇总。因而，一个成本报告可能被多个成本信息汇总应用程序所使用。具体项目中的项目成本报告或财务交易的每一类成本报告必须有独立的标识符。这样一来，就可以采用主格式编码这样一套标准成本编码，连同项目识别符来识别成本报告及显示组织或工作需求的工作范围。同样地，还可以通过使用数据库，或至少通过使用内部联络应用程序来进行成本信息的获取。

把最终的成本估算转化成与组织的成本报告兼容的项目预算并不是一项简单的工作。成本估算通常被分解到基于项目范畴的功能或资源上。例如，项目的任何一个实体分部都会包括人工或材料的消耗量，从成本会计的角度出发，在统计人工和材料的消耗量时，是按照其类型而不考虑其具体被使用在哪个实体分部上。也就是说，同一类型的人工或材料可能在建筑产品的许多实体分部上都被使用过。此外，建立在组织内部的成本报告种类同详细的成本估算中的数量很少有相似之处。当详细的成本估算是按照外部的汇报要求而不是按照组织内部现有的成本报告来编制时，其情况就更加如此。

在按照成本报告来形成项目预算时所面临的一个具体问题是如何对待意外事件。为了应付不可预见事件和由此产生的成本，通常在项目成本估算中要安排一定数量的储备金。然而，在项目完工前，应急储备金的动用与否是根据意外事件是否发生来确定的。在实际操作当中，无论详细的成本估算中是否包括了意外事件，项目预算都应列支一笔应急储备金。

在形成项目预算时遇到的第二个问题是如何对待通货膨胀。典型地，详细成本估算是按照美元现价来编制的，同时追加一个以百分比形式出现的反应通货膨胀成本的列项，即通常所说的通货膨胀准备金。这笔通货膨胀准备金根据通货膨胀的实际发生水平所引发的成本被分配至各个具体的成本项目上。

例4.1 一个设计事务所的项目预算。

一个小的项目预算示例见表4-2。这是一个为具体项目进行设计的设计公司的预算。尽管这个预算涵盖了这家设计公司在项目上的所有工作，然而其他的组织也应有其自己的项目预算。在表 4-2 当中，不但有一个汇总预算，同时还有一个设计部的人工费用明细表。

为了成本报告的连续性和便于管理上的控制，人工费按设计部、建筑部和环境部 3 个部门来进行汇总。表 4-2 中只列出了设计部的详细预算，而后勤等其他部门的详细预算理应同时列出，此表省略了。在设计部，总的劳动力成本是由为项目工作的所有人员的工资累加而得到的。为了完成这项工作，需要一些区分组织内部不同人员工资及绩效考评的方法，而通常我们会按项目各任务所需实际工时的估算来进行这项工作。最后，这个预算只能为组织内部的特定目标服务。在向客户提交财务单据和报告时，管理费和应急费在直接劳动力成本的基础上，以固定百分比汇总累加的形式出现。

表 4-2 一个设计事务所的项目预算示例

分类	预算汇总/美元
人员所在部门	
建筑学	67 251.00
设计部	45 372.00
环境部	28 235.00
合计	140 858.00
其他直接费用	
差旅	2 400.00
后勤	1 500.00
通信	600.00
计算机服务	1 200.00
合计	5 700.00
管理费	175 869.60
应急费与利润	95 700.00
合计	418 127.60
工程部人员明细	
高级工程师	11 562.00
工程师	21 365.00
技术人员	12 654.00
合计	45 372.00

例 4.2 一个承包商的项目预算。

表 4-3 显示了一个承包商的简单项目的预算。该项目为一个承建码头施工的项目。和前面的例子一样，这里把成本也分为直接成本和间接成本两种。在直接成本里面，又将支出划分为材料费、合同分包费、临时工作费和机械费。这个预算是按不同的项次来汇总的。具体成本报告中的成本数据可以对表 4-3 所示的汇总预算进行补充和支持。完工利润和应急费可在表 4-3 中 1 715 147 美元的基本预算上另行计算。

表 4-3 某码头项目预算示例

	材料费/$	合同分包费/$	暂定工作费/$	机械费/$	单项汇总/$
钢桩	292 172	129 178	16 389	0	437 739
连接杆	88 233	29 254	0	0	117 487
锚定墙	130 281	60 873	0	0	191 154
回填	242 230	27 919	0	0	300 149
压顶	42 880	22 307	13 171	0	78 358
疏浚	0	111 650	0	0	111 650
挡泥板	48 996	10 344	0	1 750	61 090
其他	5 000	32 250	0	0	37 250
分项汇总	849 800	423 775	29 560	1 750	1 304 885
			总计		
			总直接成本		$1 304 885
			间接成本		
			共用暂定工作		$19 320
			公用机械		$80 934
			交通运输		$15 550
			办公费用		$294 458
			总间接成本		$410 262
			总项目成本		$1 715 147

Unit 5　The Project Budget(2)——
Forecasting for Activity Cost Control

For the purpose of project management and control, it is not sufficient to consider only the past record of costs and revenues incurred in a project. Good managers should focus upon future revenues, future costs and technical problems. For this purpose, traditional financial accounting schemes are not adequate to reflect the dynamic nature of a project. Accounts typically focus on recording routine costs and past expenditures associated with activities. Generally, past expenditures represent sunk costs that cannot be altered in the future and may or may not be relevant in the future. For example, after the completion of some activity, it may be discovered that some quality flaw renders the work useless. Unfortunately, the resources expended on the flawed construction will generally be sunk and cannot be recovered for re-construction (although it may be possible to change the burden of who pays for these resources by financial withholding or charges; owners will typically attempt to have constructors or designers pay for changes due to quality flaws). Since financial accounts are historical in nature, some means of forecasting or projecting the future course of a project is essential for management control. In this section, some methods for cost control and simple forecasts are described.

An example of forecasting used to assess the project status is shown in Table 5-1. In this example, costs are reported in five categories, representing the sum of all the various cost accounts associated with each category.

Table 5-1　Illustration of a Job Status Report

Factor	Budgeted Cost/$	Estimated Total Cost/$	Cost Committed/$	Cost Exposure/$	Cost To Date/$	Over or Under/$
Labor	99 406	102 342	49 596	—	52 746	2 936
Material	88 499	88 499	42 506	45 993	—	0
Subcontracts	198 458	196 323	83 352	97 832	15 139	(2 135)
Equipment	37 543	37 543	23 623	—	13 920	0
Other	72 693	81 432	49 356	—	32 076	8 739
Total	496 509	506 139	248 433	143 825	113 881	5 950

- Budgeted cost.

The budgeted cost is derived from the detailed cost estimate prepared at the start of the project. Examples of project budgets were presented in above section. The factors of cost would be referenced by cost account.

Unit 5 The Project Budget(2)—Forecasting for Activity Cost Control

- Estimated total cost.

The estimated or forecast total cost in each category is the current best estimate of costs based on progress and any changes since the budget was formed. Estimated total costs are the sum of cost to date, commitments and exposure. Methods for estimating total costs are described below.

- Cost to date.

The actual cost incurred to date is recorded in column 6 and can be derived from the financial record keeping accounts.

- Over or Under.

A final column in Table 5-1 indicates the amount over or under the budget for each category. This column is an indicator of the extent of variance from the project budget; items with unusually large overruns would represent a particular managerial concern. Note that variance is used in the terminology of project control to indicate a difference between budgeted and actual expenditures. The term is defined and used quite differently in statistics or mathematical analysis. In Table 5-1, labor costs are running higher than expected, whereas subcontracts are less than expected.

The current status of the project is a forecast budget overrun of $ 5 950, with 23 percent of the budgeted project costs incurred to date.

For project control, managers would focus particular attention on items indicating substantial deviation from budgeted amounts. In particular, the cost overruns in the labor and in the other expense category would be worthy of attention by a project manager in Table 5-1. A next step would be to look in greater detail at the various components of these categories. Overruns in cost might be due to lower than expected productivity, higher than expected wage rates, higher than expected material costs, or other factors. Even further, low productivity might be caused by inadequate training, lack of required resources such as equipment or tools, or inordinate amounts of re-work to correct quality problems. Review of a job status report is only the first step in project control.

The job status report illustrated in Table 5-1 employs explicit estimates of ultimate cost in each category of expense. These estimates are used to identify the actual progress and status of an expense category. Estimates might be made from simple linear extrapolations of the productivity or cost of the work to date on each project item. Algebraically, a linear estimation formula is generally one of two forms. Using a linear extrapolation of costs, the forecast total cost, C_f, is:

$$C_f = \frac{C_t}{P_t} \qquad (5\text{-}1)$$

Where C_t is the cost incurred to time t and p_t is the proportion of the activity completed at time t. For example, an activity which is 50 percent complete with a cost of $40 000 would be estimated to have a total cost of $40 000/0.5 = $80 000. More elaborate methods of forecasting costs would disaggregate costs into different categories, with the total cost the sum of the forecast costs in each category.

Alternatively, the use of measured unit cost amounts can be used for forecasting total cost.

The basic formula for forecasting cost from unit costs is:

$$C_f = Wc_t \tag{5-2}$$

Where C_f is the forecast total cost, W is the total units of work, and c_t is the average cost per unit of work experienced up to time t. If the average unit cost is $50 per unit of work on a particular activity and 1 600 units of work exist, then the expected cost is $1\,600 \times 50 = \$80\,000$ for completion. The unit cost in Equation (5-2) may be replaced with the hourly productivity and the unit cost per hour (or other appropriate time period), resulting in the equation:

$$C_f = Wh_t u_t \tag{5-3}$$

where the cost per work unit c_t is replaced by the time per unit, h_t, multiplied by the cost per unit of time, u_t.

More elaborate forecasting systems might recognize peculiar problems associated with work on particular items and modify these simple proportional cost estimates. For example, if productivity is improving as workers and managers become more familiar with the project activities, the estimate of total costs for an item might be revised downward. In this case, the estimating equation would become:

$$C_f = C_t + (W - W_t)c_t \tag{5-4}$$

where forecast total cost, C_f, is the sum of cost incurred to date, C_t, and the cost resulting from the remaining work $(W - W_t)$ multiplied by the expected cost per unit time period for the remainder of the activity, c_t.

As a numerical example, suppose that the average unit cost has been $50 per unit of work, but the most recent figure during a project is $45 per unit of work. If the project manager was assured that the improved productivity could be maintained for the remainder of the project (consisting of 800 units of work out of a total of 1 600 units of work), the cost estimate would be $50 \times 800 + 45 \times 800 = \$76\,000$ for completion of the activity. Note that this forecast uses the actual average productivity achieved on the first 800 units and uses a forecast of productivity for the remaining work.

In addition to changes in productivities, other components of the estimating formula can be adjusted or substituted. For example, the change in unit prices due to new labor contracts or material supplier's prices might be reflected in estimating future expenditures. In essence, the same problems encountered in preparing the detailed cost estimate are faced in the process of preparing exposure estimates, although the number and extent of uncertainties in the project environment decline as work progresses. The only exception to this rule is the danger of quality problems in completed work which would require re-construction.

Each of the estimating methods described above require current information on the state of work accomplishment for particular activities. There are several possible methods to develop such estimates, including:

● Units of work completed.

For easily measured quantities the actual proportion of completed work amounts can be measured. For example, the linear feet of piping installed can be compared to the required

Unit 5 The Project Budget(2)—Forecasting for Activity Cost Control

amount of piping to estimate the percentage of piping work completed.

- Incremental milestones.

Particular activities can be sub-divided or "decomposed" into a series of milestones, and the milestones can be used to indicate the percentage of work complete based on historical averages. For example, the work effort involved with installation of standard piping might be divided into four milestones.

① Spool in place: 20% of work and 20% of cumulative work.
② Ends welded: 40% of work and 60% of cumulative work.
③ Hangars and Trim Complete: 30% of work and 90% of cumulative work.
④ Hydrotested and Complete: 10% of work and 100% of cumulative work.

Thus, a pipe section for which the ends have been welded would be reported as 60% complete.

- Opinion.

Subjective judgments of the percentage complete can be prepared by inspectors, supervisors or project managers themselves. Clearly, this estimated technique can be biased by optimism, pessimism or inaccurate observations. Knowledgeable estimaters and adequate field observations are required to obtain sufficient accuracy with this method.

- Cost ratio.

The cost incurred to date can also be used to estimate the work progress. For example, if an activity was budgeted to cost $20 000 and the cost incurred at a particular date was $10 000, then the estimated percentage complete under the cost ratio method would be 10 000/20 000 = 0.5 or fifty percent. This method provides no independent information on the actual percentage complete or any possible errors in the activity budget: the cost forecast will always be the budgeted amount. Consequently, managers must use the estimated costs to complete an activity derived from the cost ratio method with extreme caution.

Systematic application of these different estimating methods to the various project activities enables calculation of the percentage complete or the productivity estimates used in preparing job status reports.

In some cases, automated data acquisition for work accomplishments might be instituted. For example, transponders might be moved to the new work limits after each day's activity and the new locations automatically computed and compared with project plans. These measurements of actual progress should be stored in a central database and then processed for updating the project schedule.

Example 5.1 Estimated total cost to complete an activity.

Suppose that we wish to estimate the total cost to complete piping construction activities on a project. The piping construction involves 1 000 linear feet of piping which has been divided into 50 sections for management convenience. At this time, 400 linear feet of piping has been installed at a cost of $40 000 and 500 man-hours of labor. The original budget estimate was

$90 000 with a productivity of one foot per man-hour, a unit cost of $60 per man hour and a total material cost of $ 30 000. Firm commitments of material delivery for the $30 000 estimated cost have been received.

The first task is to estimate the proportion of work completed. First, 400 linear feet of pipe is in place out of a total of 1 000 linear feet, so the proportion of work completed is 400/1 000 = 0.4 or 40%. This is the "units of work completed" estimation method. Second, the cost ratio method would estimate the work complete as the cost-to-date divided by the cost estimate or $40 000/$ 90 000 = 0.44 or 44%. Third, the "incremental milestones" method would be applied by examining each pipe section and estimating a percentage complete and then aggregating to determine the total percentage complete. For example, suppose the following quantities of piping fell into four categories of completeness:

complete (100%)	380 ft
hangars and trim complete (90%)	20 ft
ends welded (60%)	5 ft
spool in place (20%)	0 ft

Then using the incremental milestones shown above, the estimate of completed work would be $380 + 20 \times 0.9 + 5 \times 0.6 + 0 = 401$ ft and the proportion complete would be 401 ft/1 000 ft = 0.401 or 40% after rounding.

Once an estimate of work completed is available, then the estimated cost to complete the activity can be calculated. First, a simple linear extrapolation of cost results in an estimate of $40 000/0.4 = $100 000 for or the piping construction using the 40% estimate of work completed. This estimate projects a cost overrun of 100 000−90 000 = $10 000.

Second, a linear extrapolation of productivity results in an estimate of (1 000 ft)(500 hrs/400 ft)($60/hr) + 30 000 = $105 000 for completion of the piping construction. This estimate suggests a variance of 105 000−90 000 = $15 000 above the activity estimate. The source of the variance can also be identified in this calculation: compared to the original estimate, the labor productivity is 1.25 hours per foot or 25% higher than the original estimate.

Example 5.2 Estimated Total Cost for Completion.

The forecasting procedures described above assumed linear extrapolations of future costs, based either on the complete experience on the activity or the recent experience. For activities with good historical records, it can be the case that a typically non-linear profile of cost expenditures and completion proportions can be estimated. Figure 5.1 illustrates one possible non-linear relationships derived from experience in some particular activity. For example, point A in Figure 5.1 suggests a higher expenditure than is normal for the completion proportion. This point represents 40% of work completed with an expenditure of 60% of the budget. Since the historical record suggests only 50% of the budget should be expended at time of 40% completion, a 60%−50%=10% overrun in cost is expected. If comparable cost overruns continue to accumulate, then the cost-to-complete will be even higher.

Unit 5 The Project Budget(2)—Forecasting for Activity Cost Control

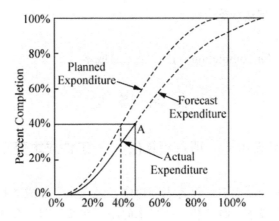

Figure 5.1 Illustration of Proportion Completion versus Expenditure for an Activity

Questions

1. What's the disadvantage of traditional financial accounting schemes?
2. What does the term "sunk costs" mean?
3. How to calculate the estimated total cost?
4. For project control, managers would focus particular attention on items indicating substantial deviation from budgeted accounts, why?
5. Which factors may cause overruns in cost?
6. How many methods can be used to get the forecast total cost? What are they?
7. What does the term "units of work completed" mean?
8. How to understand the term "incremental milestone"?
9. How to calculate cost ratio?
10. In some cases, automated data acquisition for work accomplishments might be instituted, why?

Vocabulary, Phrases and Expressions

financial accounting: 财务计算；财务会计
sunk cost: 沉没成本；已支付成本
forecasting for activity cost: 工作成本预测
cost to date: 完工成本
cost committed: 承诺成本
cost exposure: 附加成本
project control: 项目控制
job status report: 工作状况报告
units of work completed: 完工劳动单元
incremental milestones: 里程碑累计

field observations：现场观察

cost ratio：成本率

estimated total cost for completion：预计完工总成本

参 考 译 文

第 5 单元　项目预算(2)——工作成本预测

对于项目的管理和控制而言，仅考虑项目中已经发生了的成本和收益是不够的。好的项目经理还会关注未来成本、收益和一些技术问题。传统的财务会计计划无法反映出项目的动态特征，而只能集中在对日常性成本和已发生的各项工作开支的记录上。通常把过去已经发生且在未来无法再改变的支出称为"沉没成本"。例如，当某些工作完成后，有时会发现由于存在质量缺陷而使得产品毫无用处。遗憾的是，耗费在缺陷的建筑产品上的各种资源通常就"沉没了"，并且无法通过重建而得到恢复(尽管可以根据责任的归属来确定由谁承担所造成的损失，业主也会要求承包商或设计方来负担由于质量缺陷而产生的费用)。由于财务报告的历史局限性，为了进行有效的管理和控制，有必要使用一些预测和规划项目未来进程的方法和手段。下面将介绍一些有关成本控制和预测的方法。

一个用来预测和评价项目状况的例子见表 5-1。在这个例子当中，成本按 5 个项次进行统计，每个项次再按不同口径进行汇总。

表 5-1　工作状况报告示例

要素	预算成本/$	预计总成本/$	承诺成本/$	附加成本	完工成本/$	超支或节约/$
人工	99 406	102 342	49 596	—	52 746	2 936
材料	88 499	88 499	42 506	45 993	—	0
合同分包	198 458	196 323	83 352	97 832	15 139	(2 135)
设备	37 543	37 543	23 623	—	13 920	0
其他	72 693	81 432	49 356	—	32 076	8 739
总计	496 509	506 139	248 433	143 825	113 881	5 950

● 预算成本。

预算成本由项目初始阶段的详细成本估算得来。项目预算的例子在上一部分已经介绍过。成本要素可参考成本报告。

● 预计总成本。

每一项次的预计总成本是根据预算形成后项目的实际进展和变化对当前成本的最为精确的估算。预计总成本由完工成本、承诺成本和附加成本累加得到。估算总成本的方法将在下面介绍。

● 完工成本。

已完工的实际成本记录在表 5-1 的第 6 栏里，它可由财务记录报告得到。

- 超支或节约。

表 5-1 的最后一栏显示了每一项次预算超支或节约的数值,这一栏也是预算偏差的指示器。那些超出合理范围的成本偏差应当引起管理上的关注。注意,被用在项目控制中的"偏差"一词指的是预算值和实际值之间的差异。在统计学和数学分析中,这个术语的定义和使用是完全不同的。在表 5-1 中,人工成本比预期的高,而分包合同成本却比预期的低。

项目目前的状况是预计总成本相对于预算成本超支 5 950 美元,同时完工成本占预算成本的比例为 23%。

从项目控制的角度而言,项目经理应对那些和预算成本有重大偏差的项次给予特殊的关注。具体地说,在表 5-1 中,"人工"和其他两个项次都出现了超支的现象,应当引起注意。而下一步则要具体分析这些项次的不同组成部分的具体情况。例如,成本的超支可能是由于劳动生产率的降低、工资的提高、材料涨价或其他原因等引起的。进一步讲,劳动生产率的降低又有可能源于新来的工人未经培训、缺乏机器和设备等生产所需的资源、纠正质量问题的重复工作不当等原因。分析工作状况报告只是项目控制的第一步。

表 5-1 所示的工作状况报告对每一个费用项次都给出了较为精确的最终成本估算。这个估算被用来判别项目的实际进展和某成本项次的状况。这个估算值可以用每一项次的劳动生产率或完工成本进行简单的线性推演得到。在代数学中,一个线性估算的方程通常有两种形式。用成本的线性推演可得预测总成本 C_f,即

$$C_f = \frac{C_t}{P_t} \tag{5-1}$$

其中,C_t 为某工作在 t 时刻所发生的成本,P_t 为 t 时刻某工作完工的百分比。例如,某花费 40 000 美元且已完工 50%的工作其预测总成本为 40 000 美元/0.5=80 000 美元。更为精确的方法是将成本分解成不同的项次,再将每一项次的预测成本汇总得到总预测成本。

此外,还可以用单位成本数来得到预测总成本。其公式为

$$C_f = Wc_t \tag{5-2}$$

其中,C_f 为预测总成本,W 为总劳动单元数,而 c_t 为已完工劳动单元的平均成本。如果某项具体工作包含 1 600 个劳动单元,而每个劳动单元的平均成本为 50 美元,则完工时的预测总成本为 1 600×50 美元=80 000 美元,方程(5-2)中的单位成本可用每小时劳动生产率和每小时(或其他合适的时间段)单位成本的乘积代替,即

$$C_f = Wh_t u_t \tag{5-3}$$

其中,h_t 为每一劳动单元所耗时间,u_t 为每一单位时间所耗成本。

一些更为精确的方法可以反映出某项具体工作中与劳动有关的特殊问题,并适当调整成本预测的比例。例如,如果由于工人和项目经理更加熟悉项目工作而使得劳动生产率得以提高,那么项目工作的预测总成本应向下调整。在这种情况下,预测方程就变为

$$C_f = C_t + (W - W_t)c_t \tag{5-4}$$

其中,预测总成本 C_f 等于完工成本 C_t 加上剩余工作($W-W_t$)和剩余工作的预测期单位成本 c_t 的乘积。

在前面的例子当中,曾经假定每劳动单元的平均成本为 50 美元,但项目近期劳动单元成本为 45 美元。如果项目经理确信项目的剩余工作能够将改进了的生产率保持下去(在 1 600 个劳动单元中,有 800 个剩余劳动单元),那么项目完成的预测成本应为 50×800 美

元+45×800 美元=76 000 美元。注意，这里面分别用到了已完工 800 个劳动单元的实际平均生产率和剩余劳动单元的预计生产率。

除了生产率的变化之外，预测方程中的其他组成部分也可以进行替换或调整。例如，由于新的劳动合同或材料价格所引起的单元上的变化也可以在预测总成本中得以反映。实际上，在计算附加成本时也会遇到同样的问题，尽管随着项目的不断进展，项目当中不确定性的量和度都呈下降趋势。这个规则的唯一例外是完工产品因为严重质量问题而需返修重建的情形。

上面所介绍的每一种预测方法都需要具体工作的劳动量完成状态信息。下面的几种方法有助于进行成本的预测。

● 完工劳动单元。

对于易于测量的劳动数量，可直接得到实际完工劳动量占总劳动量的比例。例如，将已安装的直线管道和需要安装的管道数量进行比较便可测算出已完工管道劳动量的百分比。

● 里程碑累计。

某项具体工作可被分解成一系列的里程碑，而这些里程碑可用来显示完工劳动量基于历史平均值的百分比。例如，某标准管道安装工作的劳动可被划分为如下 4 个里程碑。

① 管轴就位：20%的劳动量和 20%的累计劳动量。
② 管道焊接：40%的劳动量和 60%的累计劳动量。
③ 支座和清理：30%的劳动量和 90%的累计劳动量。
④ 热压测试和完工：10%的劳动量和 100%的累计劳动量。

从这里可以看出，管缝焊接完工时，工作总劳动量的 60%已经完成。

● 判断。

对于完工百分比的主观判断可由监督方、监理方或项目经理自己做出。显然，由于乐观、悲观或观察不够细致等主观原因，会使上面所做出的判断有所偏颇。因此，使用这种方法要想保证相当的准确性，就要求预测者不但具有丰富的知识，还应有足够的现场观察。

● 成本率。

完工成本也能用来预测工作进度。例如，如果某工作的预算成本为 20 000 美元而截止某特定日期已发生的成本为 10 000 美元，那么用成本率来表示预测完工百分率就是 10 000/20 000=0.5 或 50%。然而，用这种方法来准确地反映工作实际完工比例还需依靠其他信息，并且会产生工作预算上的一些错误，因为在这里，预测成本始终等于预算成本。因此，项目经理在用成本率导出的预测成本来完成某工作时必须极其审慎。

通过对各种项目工作系统地运用不同的预测方法，可以计算出工作状况报告要用到的完工百分比和生产率的估算值。

在有些情况下，需要构建一个自动读取完工数据的系统。例如，在当天工作完成之后，读取器会自动移向新的工作表及其地址进行运算并和项目计划进行比较。项目的实际进度会被存储到中央数据库中，经过处理后用以更新项目计划。

例 5.1　完成某项工作的预计总成本。

假定欲估算某项目直线管道铺设工程的总成本。该管道工程是总长为 1 000 英尺(1 英尺=0.304 8 米)的直线管道铺设，为了方便管理被划分成 50 段。此时，已有 400 英尺的直线管道以 40 000 美元的成本和 500 人工时的劳动力进行了铺设。初始预算约为 90 000 美元，其中生产率为 1 英尺/工时，每工时的单位成本为 60 美元，且总的材料成本为 30 000 美元。

材料的运输已得到保证。

第一项工作是估算完工劳动的比例。首先,已对总长度为 1 000 英尺的直线管道中的 400 英尺进行了铺设,所以已完工劳动的百分比为 400/1 000=0.4 或 40%。这里用到的是完工劳动单元估算法。其次,用成本率法来估算完工劳动率,即用完工成本除以估算成本,亦即 40 000 美元/90 000 美元=0.44 或 44%。最后,用"里程碑累计"法来核对管道的每一分项工程,估算其完工百分比并进行逐项累计,以确定总完工百分比。例如,假定把管道工程的完成按 4 个类别进行划分。

全部完成(100%):380 英尺。

完成了支座和清理(90%):20 英尺。

完成了管缝焊接(60%):5 英尺。

完成了管轴就位(20%):0 英尺。

根据上面的里程碑累计,完工劳动的估算应当为(380+20×0.9+5×0.6+0)英尺=401 英尺,完工比例为 401 英尺/1 000 英尺=0.401,或近似取 0.4。

一旦得到了完工劳动量的估算值,就可以进行工作完工成本的计算。首先,由于管道工程已完成了约 40%,所以用线性推演得到的预计成本为 40 000 美元/0.4=100 000 美元。这意味着按当前状态项目将会出现(100 000-90 000)美元=10 000 美元的成本超支。

其次,如果用生产率进行线性推演,可得管道工程的完工估算成本为 1 000 英尺×500 小时/400 英尺×60 美元/小时+30 000 美元=105 000 美元。在这种情况下,预计有(105 000-90 000)美元=15 000 美元的成本偏差。偏差的原因也可以理解为和初始估算相比,劳动生产率为 1.25 小时/英尺或比初始估算中的劳动生产率在每英尺管道上多用了 0.25 小时。

例 5.2 完工项目的预计总成本。

上例中的预测程序是在对工作有完全的或近期的经验基础上,用线性方法来推断未来的成本。而对有些历史数据完整的工作,即使数据之间成非线性关系,仍可预测其成本超支和完工百分比。图 5.1 所示为成本和完工百分比呈非线性关系的某工作。例如,图 5.1 中的 A 点表示在对应的完工百分比上其成本却有所超支,即在该点劳动量完成了 40%,但成本支出却占到了预算成本的 60%。而根据历史统计,当劳动量完成 40%时,成本支出应占预算成本的 50%,因此出现了 60%-50%=10%的成本偏差。如果这种可比的成本超支继续累计下去,那么完工成本将变高。

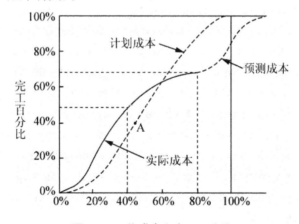

图 5.1 工作成本和完工百分比

Unit 6　The Contractor

The Contractor's General Obligations

The Contractor shall design, execute and complete the Works in accordance with the Contract, and shall remedy any defects in the Works. When completed, the Works shall be fit for the purposes for which the Works are intended as defined in the Contract.

The Contractor shall provide the Plant and Contractor's Documents specified in the Contract, and all contractor's Personnel, Goods, consumables and other things and services, whether of a temporary or permanent nature, required in and for this design, execution, completion and remedying of defects.

The Works shall include any work which is necessary to satisfy the Employer's Requirements, or is implied by the Contract, and all works which (although not mentioned in the Contract) are necessary for stability or for the completion, or safe and proper operation, of the Works.

The Contractor shall be responsible for the adequacy, stability and safety of all Site operations, of all methods of construction and of all the Works.

The Contractor shall, whenever required by the Employer, submit details of the arrangements and methods which the Contractor proposes to adopt for the execution of the Works. No significant alteration to these arrangements and methods shall be made without this having previously been notified to the Employer.

Performance security

The Contractor shall obtain (at his cost) a Performance Security for proper performance, in the amount and currencies stated in the Particular Conditions if an amount is not stated in the Particular Conditions, this Sub-Clause shall not apply.

The Contractor shall deliver the Performance Security to the Employer within 28 days after both Parties have signed the Contract Agreement. The Performance Security shall be issued by an entity and from within a country (or other jurisdiction) approved by the Employer, and shall be in the form annexed to the Particular Conditions or in another form approved by the Employer.

The Contractor shall ensure that the Performance Security is valid and enforceable until the Contractor has executed and completed the Works and remedied any defects. If the terms of the Performance Security specify its expiry date, and the Contractor has not become entitled to receive the Performance Certificate by the date 28 days prior to the expiry date, the Contractor shall extend the validity of the Performance Security until the Works have been completed and any defects have been remedied.

The Employer shall not make a claim under the Performance Security, except for amounts to which the Employer is entitled under the Contract in the event of:

(1) failure by the Contractor to extend the validity of the Performance Security as described in the preceding paragraph, in which event the Employer may claim the full amount of the Performance Security.

(2) failure by the Contractor to pay the Employer an amount due, as either agreed by the Contractor or determined under Sub-Clause 2.5 [Employer's Claims] or Clause 20 [Claims, Disputes and Arbitration], within 42 days after this agreement or determination.

(3) failure by the Contractor to remedy a default within 42 days after receiving the Employer's notice requiring the default to be remedied.

(4) circumstances which entitle the Employer to termination under Sub-Clause 15.2 [Termination by Employer], irrespective of whether notice of termination has been given.

The Employer shall indemnify and hold the Contractor harmless against and from all damages, losses and expenses (including legal fees and expenses) resulting from a claim under the Performance Security to the extent to which the Employer was not entitled to make the claim.

The Employer shall return the Performance Security to the Contractor within 21 days after the Contractor has become entitled to receive the Performance Certificate.

Contractor's Representative

The Contractor shall appoint the Contractor's Representative and shall give him all authority necessary to act on the Contractor's behalf under the Contract.

Unless the Contractor's Representative is named in the Contract, the Contractor shall, prior to the Commencement Date, submit to the Employer for consent the name and particulars of the person the Contractor proposes to appoint as Contractor's Representative. If consent is withheld or subsequently revoked, or if the appointed person fails to act as Contractor's Representative, the Contractor shall similarly submit the name and particulars of another suitable person for such appointment.

The Contractor shall not, without the prior consent of the Employer, revoke the appointment of the Contractor's Representative or appoint a replacement.

The Contractor's Representative shall, on behalf of the Contractor, receive instructions under Sub-Clause 3.4 [Instructions].

The Contractor's Representative may delegate any powers, functions and authority to any competent person, and may at any time revoke the delegation. Any delegation or revocation shall not take effect until the Employer has received prior notice signed by the Contractor's Representative, naming the person and specifying the powers, functions and authority being delegated or revoked.

The Contractor's Representative and all these persons shall be fluent in the language for communications defined in Sub-Clause 1.4 [Law and Language].

Subcontractors

The Contractor shall not subcontract the whole of the Works.

The Contractor shall be responsible for the acts or defaults of any Subcontractor, his agents or employees, as if they were the acts or defaults of the Contractor. Where specified in the Particular Conditions, the Contractor shall give the Employer not less than 28 days' notice of:

(1) the intended appointment of the Subcontractor, with detailed particulars which shall include his relevant experience.

(2) the intended commencement of the Subcontractor's work.

(3) the intended commencement of the Subcontractor's work on the Site.

Nominated Subcontractors

In this Sub-Clause, "nominated Subcontractor" means a Subcontractor whom the Employer, under Clause 13 [Variations and Adjustments], instructs the Contractor to employ as a Subcontractor. The Contractor shall not be under any obligation to employ a nominated Subcontractor against whom the Contractor raises reasonable objection by notice to the Employer as soon as practicable, with supporting particulars.

Co-operation

The Contractor shall, as specified in the Contract or as instructed by the Employer, allow appropriate opportunities for carrying out work to:

- the Employer's personnel
- any other contractors employed by the Employer
- the personnel of any legally constituted public authorities

who may be employed in the execution on or near the Site of any work not included in the Contract.

Any such instruction shall constitute a variation if and to the extent that it causes the Contractor to incur Cost in an amount which was not reasonably foreseeable by an experienced contractor by the date for submission of the Tender. Services for these personnel and other contractors may include the use of Contractor's Equipment, Temporary Works or access arrangements which are the responsibility of the Contractor.

The Contractor shall be responsible for his construction activities on the Site, and shall co-ordinate his own activities with those of other contractors to the extent (if any) specified in the Employer's Requirements.

If, under the Contract, the Employer is required to give to the Contractor possession of any foundation, structure, plant or means of access in accordance with Contractors Documents, the Contractor shall submit such documents to the Employer in the time and manner stated in the Employer's Requirements.

Setting Out

The Contractor shall set out the Works in relation to original points, lines and levels of reference specified in the Contract. The Contractor shall be responsible for the correct positioning of all parts of the works, and shall rectify any error in the positions, levels, dimensions or alignment of the Works.

Safety Procedures

The Contractor shall:

(1) comply with all applicable safety regulations.

(2) take care for the safety of all persons entitled to be on the Site.

(3) use reasonable efforts to keep the Site and Works clear of unnecessary obstruction so as to avoid danger to these persons.

(4) providing fencing, lighting, guarding and watching of the Works until completion and taking over under Clause 10 [Employer's Taking Over].

(5) provide any Temporary Works (including roadways, footways, guards and fences) which may be necessary, because of the execution of the Works, for the use and protection of the public and of owners and occupiers of adjacent land.

Quality Assurance

The Contractor shall institute a quality assurance system to demonstrate compliance with the requirements of the Contract. The system shall be in accordance with the details stated in the Contract. The Employer shall be entitled to audit any aspect of the system.

Details of all procedures and compliance documents shall be submitted to the Employer for information before each design and execution stage is commenced. When any document of a technical nature is issued to the Employer, evidence of the prior approval by the Contractor himself shall be apparent on the document itself.

Compliance with the quality assurance system shall not relieve the Contractor of any of his duties, obligations or responsibilities under the Contract.

Site Data

The Employer shall have made available to the Contractor for his information, prior to the Base Date, all relevant data in the Employer's possession on subsurface and hydrological conditions at the Site, including environmental aspects. The Employer shall similarly make available to the Contractor all such data which come into the Employer's possession after the Base Date.

The contractor shall be responsible for verifying and interpreting all such data. The Employer shall have no responsibility for the accuracy or completeness of such data, except as stated in Sub-Clause 5.1 [General Design Responsibilities].

Sufficiency of the Contract Price

The Contractor shall be deemed to have satisfied himself as to the correctness and sufficiency of the Contract Price.

Unless otherwise stated in the Contract, the Contract price covers all the Contractor's obligations under the Contract (including those under Provisional Sums, if any) and all things necessary for the proper design, execution and completion of the Works and the remedying of any defects.

Unforeseeable Difficulties

Except as otherwise stated in the Contract:

(1) the Contractor shall be deemed to have obtained all necessary information as to risks, contingencies and other circumstances which may influence or affect the Works.

(2) by signing the Contract, the Contractor accepts total responsibility for having foreseen all difficulties and costs of successfully completing the Works.

(3) the Contract Price shall not be adjusted to take account of any unforeseen difficulties or costs.

Rights of Way and Facilities

The Contractor shall bear all costs and charges for special and/or temporary rights-of-way which he may require, including those for access to the Site. The Contractor shall also obtain, at his risk and cost, any additional facilities outside the Site which he may require for purposes of the Works.

Avoidance of Interference

The Contractor shall not interfere unnecessarily or improperly with:

(1) the convenience of the public.

(2) the access to and use and occupation of all roads and footpaths, irrespective of whether they are public or in the possession of the Employer or of others.

The Contractor shall indemnify and hold the Employer harmless against and from all damages, losses and expenses (including legal fees and expenses) resulting from any such unnecessary or improper interference.

Access Route

The Contractor shall be deemed to have been satisfied as to the suitability and availability of access routes to the Site. The Contractor shall use reasonable efforts to prevent any road or bridge from being damaged by the Contractor's traffic or by the Contractor's Personnel. These efforts shall include the proper use of appropriate vehicles and routes.

Except as otherwise stated in these Conditions:

(1) the Contractor shall (as between the Parties) be responsible for any maintenance which may be required for his use of access routes.

(2) the Contractor shall provide all necessary signs or directions along access routes, and shall obtain any permission which may be required from the relevant authorities for his use of routes, signs and directions.

(3) the Employer shall not be responsible for any claims which may arise from the use or otherwise of any access route.

(4) the Employer does not guarantee the suitability or availability of particular access routes.

(5) Costs due to non-suitability or non-availability, for the use required by the Contractor, of access routes shall be borne by the Contractor.

Transport of Goods

Unless otherwise stated in the Particular Conditions.

(1) the Contractor shall give the Employer not less than 21 days' notice of the date on which any Plant or a major item of other Goods will be delivered to the Site.

(2) the Contractor shall be responsible for packing, loading, transporting, receiving, unloading, storing and protecting all Goods and other things required for the Works.

(3) the Contractor shall indemnify and hold the Employer harmless against and from all damages, losses and expenses (including legal fees and expenses) resulting from the transport of Goods, and shall negotiate and pay all claims arising from their transport.

Contractor's Equipment

The Contractor shall be responsible for all Contractor's Equipment. When brought on to the Site, Contractor's Equipment shall be deemed to be exclusively intended for the execution of the Works.

Protection of the Environment

The Contractor shall take all reasonable steps to protect the environment (both on and off the Site) and to limit damage and nuisance to people and property resulting from pollution, noise and other results of his operations.

The Contractor shall ensure that emissions, surface discharges and effluent from the Contractor's activities shall not exceed the values indicated in the Employer's Requirements, and shall not exceed the values prescribed by applicable Laws.

Electricity, Water and Gas

The Contractor shall, except as stated below, be responsible for the provision of all power, water and other services he may require.

The Contractor shall be entitled to use for the purposes of the Works such supplies of electricity, water, gas and other services as may be available on the Site and of which details and prices are given in the Employer's Requirements. The Contractor shall, at his risk and cost, provide any apparatus necessary for his use of these services and for measuring the quantities consumed.

The quantities consumed and the amounts due (at these prices) for such services shall be agreed or determined in accordance with Sub-Clause 2.5 [Employer's Claims] and Sub-Clause 3.5 [Determinations]. The Contractor shall pay these amounts to the Employer.

Employer's Equipment and Free-Issue Material

The Employer shall make the Employer's Equipment (if any) available for the use of the Contractor in the execution of the Works in accordance with the details, arrangements and prices stated in the Employer's Requirements. Unless otherwise stated in the Employer's Requirements:

(1) the Employer shall be responsible for the Employer's Equipment, except that stated in (2).

(2) the Contractor shall be responsible for each item of Employer's Equipment whilst any of the Contractor's Personnel is operating it, driving it, directing it or in possession or control of it.

The appropriate quantities and the amounts due (at such stated price) for the use of Employer's Equipment shall be agreed or determined in accordance with Sub-Clause 2.5 [Employer's Claims] and Sub-Clause 3.5 [Determinations]. The Contractor shall pay these amounts to the Employer.

The Employer shall supply, free of charge, the "free-issue material" (if any) in accordance with the details stated in the Employer's Requirement. The Employer shall, at his risk and cost, provide these materials at the time and place specified in the contractor. The Contractor shall then visually inspect them, and shall promptly give notice to the Employer of any shortage, defect or default in these materials. Unless otherwise agreed by both Parties, the Employer shall immediately rectify the notified shortage, defect or default.

After this visual inspection, the free-issue materials shall come under the care, custody and control of the Contractor. The Contractor's obligations of inspection, care, custody and control shall not relieve the Employer of liability for any shortage, defect or default not apparent from a visual inspection.

Progress Reports

Unless otherwise stated in the Particular Conditions, monthly progress reports shall be prepared by the Contractor and submitted to the Employer in six copies. The first report shall cover the period up to the end of the first calendar month following the Commencement Date. Reports shall be submitted monthly thereafter, each within 7 days after the last day of the period to which it relates.

Reporting shall continue until the Contractor has completed all work which is known to be outstanding at the completion date stated in the Taking-Over Certificate for the Works.

Each report shall include:

(1) charts and detailed descriptions of progress, including each stage of design, Contractor's Documents, procurement, manufacture, delivery to Site, construction, erection, testing, commissioning and trial operation.

(2) photographs showing the status of manufacture and of progress on the Site.

(3) for the manufacture of each main item of Plant and Materials, the name of the manufacturer, manufacture location, percentage progress, and the actual or expected dated of:

- commencement of manufacture.
- Contractor's inspections.
- test.
- shipment and arrival at the Site.

(4) the details described in Sub-Clause 6.10 [Records of Contractor's personnel and Equipment].

(5) copies of quality assurance document documents, test results and certificates of Materials.

(6) list of Variations, notices given under Sub-Clause 2.5 [Employer's Claims] and notices given under Sub-Clause 20.1 [Contractor's Claims].

(7) safety statistic, including details of any hazardous incidents and activities relating to environmental aspect and public relations.

(8) comparisons of actual and planned progress, with details of any events or circumstances which may jeopardize the completion in accordance with the Contract, and the measures being (or to be) adopted to overcome delays.

Security of the Site

Unless otherwise stated in the Particular Conditions:
(1) the Contractor shall be responsible for keeping unauthorized persons off the Site.
(2) authorized persons shall be limited to the Contractor's Personnel and the Employer's Personnel; and to any other personnel notified to the Contractor, by (or on behalf of) the Employer, as authorized personnel of the Employer's other contractors on the Site.

Contractor's Operations on Site

The Contractor shall confine his operations to the Site, and to any additional areas which may be obtained by the Contractor and agreed by the Employer as working areas. The Contractor shall take all necessary precautions to keep Contractor's Equipment and Contractor's Personnel within the Site and these additional areas, and to keep them off adjacent land.

During the execution of the Works, the Contractor shall keep the Site free from all unnecessary obstruction, and shall store or dispose of any Contractor's Equipment or surplus materials. The Contractor shall clear away and remove from the Site any wreckage, rubbish and Temporary Works which are no longer required.

Upon the issue of the Taking-Over Certificate for the Works, the Contractor shall clear away and remove all Contractor's Equipment, surplus material, wreckage, rubbish and Temporary Works. The Contractor shall leave the Site and the Works in a clean and safe condition. However, the Contractor may retain on Site, during the Defects Notification Period, such goods as are required for the Contractor to fulfill obligations under the Contract.

Fossils

All fossils, coins, articles of value or antiquity, and structures and other remains or items of geological or archaeological interest found on the Site shall be placed under the care and authority of the Employer. The Contractor shall take reasonable precautions to prevent Contractor's Personnel or other persons from removing or damaging any of these findings.

The Contractor shall, upon discovery of any such finding, promptly give notice to the Employer, who shall issue instructions for dealing with it. If the Contractor suffers delay and/or incurs cost from complying with the instructions, the Contractor shall give a further notice to the

Employer and shall be entitled subject to Sub-Clause 20.1[Contractor's Claims] to:

(1) an extension of time for any such delay, if completion is or will be delayed, under Sub-Clause 8.4 [Extension of Time for Completion].

(2) payment of any such cost, which shall be added to the Contract Price.

After receiving this further notice, the Employer shall proceed in accordance with Sub-Clause 3.5[Determinations] to agree or determine these matters.

Questions

1. What shall contractor do according to the contractor's general obligations?
2. By whom shall the performance security be issued?
3. In what event may the employer claim the full amount of the performance security?
4. When shall the employer return the performance security to the contractor?
5. Who shall appoint the contractor's representative, the contractor or the employer?
6. Shall the contractor be responsible for the acts or defaults of any subcontractor, his agents or employees, as if they were the acts or defaults of the contractor?
7. Of what notice shall the contractor give the employer not less than 28 day's ?
8. Who shall set out the works in relation to original points, lines and levels of reference specified in the contract?
9. Who shall be responsible for the correct positioning of all parts of the works?
10. Shall the employer be entitled to audit any aspect of the quality assurance system?

Vocabulary, Phrases and Expressions

performance security：履约担保

expiry date：有效期限；满期日；终止日期

contractor's representative：承包商代表

subcontractor：分包商

agents：代理(商)

nominated subcontractor：指定的分包商

variation：变更；变化

set out：放线

safety procedures：安全程序

quality assurance system：质量保证体系

base date：基准日期

site data：现场数据

contract price：合同价格

rights-of-way：道路通行权

additional facilities outside the site：现场以外的附加设施

access routes：进场通路

permission：许可

transport of goods：货物运输

negotiate：谈判；协商

protection of the environment：环境保护

contractor's equipment：承包商设备

employer's equipment：雇主设备

free-issue material：免费供应材料

progress reports：进度报告

security of the site：现场保安

contractor's operations on site：承包商的现场作业

temporary works：临时工程

taking-over certificate：接收证书

参 考 译 文

第6单元 承 包 商

承包商的一般义务

承包商应按照合同设计、实施和完成工程，并修补工程中的任何缺陷。完成后，工程应能满足合同规定的工程预期目的。

承包商应提供合同规定的生产设备和承包商文件，以及设计、施工、竣工和修补缺陷所需的所有临时性或永久性的承包商人员、货物、消耗品及其他物品和服务。

工程应包括为满足雇主要求或合同隐含要求的任何工作，以及(合同虽未提及但)为工程的稳定或完整、安全和有效运行所需的所有工作。

承包商应对所有现场作业、所有施工方法和全部工程的完备性、稳定性和安全性承担责任。

当雇主提出要求时，承包商应提交其建议采用的工程施工安排和方法的细节。若事先未通知雇主，对这些安排和方法不得做重要改变。

履约担保

承包商应对严格履约(自费)取得履约担保，保证金额与币种应符合专用条件中的规定。专用条件中没有提出保证金额的，本款应不适用。

承包商应在双方签署合同协议书后28天内，将履约担保交给雇主。履约担保应由雇主批准的国家(或其他司法管辖区)内的实体提供，并采用专用条件所附格式或采用雇主批准的其他格式。

承包商应确保履约担保直到其完成工程的施工、竣工和修补完任何缺陷前持续有效和可执行。如果在履约担保的条款中规定了其期满日期，而承包商在该期满日期28天前尚无权拿到履约证书，承包商应将履约担保的有效期延至工程竣工和修补完任何缺陷时为止。

除出现以下情况雇主根据合同有权获得赔偿金额外，雇主不应根据履约担保提出索赔：

(1) 承包商未能按前一段所述延长履约担保的有效期，这时雇主可以索赔履约担保的全部金额。

(2) 承包商未能在商定或决定后 42 天内，将承包商同意的，或根据第 2.5 款［雇主的索赔］或第 20 条［索赔、争端和仲裁］的规定确定的承包商应付金额付给雇主。

(3) 承包商未能在收到雇主要求纠正违约的通知后 42 天内进行纠正。

(4) 根据第 15.2 款［由雇主终止］的规定，雇主有权终止的情况，不管是否已发出终止通知。

雇主应保障并保持承包商免受因雇主根据履约担保提出的超出雇主有权索赔范围的索赔引起的所有损害赔偿费、损失和开支(包括法律费用和开支)的伤害。

雇主应在承包商有权获得履约证书后 21 天内，将履约担保退还承包商。

承包商代表

承包商应任命承包商代表，并授予他代表承包商根据合同采取行动所需要的全部权力。除非合同中已写明承包商代表的姓名，承包商应在开工日期前，将其拟任命为承包商代表的人员姓名和详细资料提交给雇主，以取得同意。如果未获同意，或随后撤销了同意，或任命的人不能担任承包商代表，承包商应同样地提交另外适合人选的姓名、详细资料，以取得该项任命。

未经雇主事先同意，承包商不应撤销承包商代表的任命，或任命替代人员。

承包商代表应代表承包商受理根据第 3.4 款［指示］规定的指示。

承包商代表可向任何胜任的人员托付任何职权、任务和权力，并可随时撤销托付。任何托付或撤销，应在雇主收到承包商代表签发的指明人员姓名并说明托付或撤销的职权、任务和权力的事先通知后生效。

承包商代表和所有这些人员应能流利地使用第 1.4 款［法律和语言］规定的交流语言。

分包商

承包商不得将整个工程分包出去。

承包商应对任何分包商、其代理人或雇员的行为或违约，如同承包商自己的行为或违约一样地负责。对专用条件中有规定的，承包商应在不少于 28 天前向雇主通知以下事项。

(1) 拟雇用的分包商，并附包括其相关经验的详细资料。

(2) 分包商承担工作的拟定开工日期。

(3) 分包商承担现场工作的拟定开工日期。

指定的分包商

在本款中，"指定的分包商"系指雇主根据第 13 条［变更和调整］的规定，指示承包商雇用的分包商。如果承包商对指定的分包商尽快向雇主发出通知，提出合理的反对意见，并附有详细的依据资料，承包商不应有任何雇用义务。

合作

承包商应依据合同的规定或雇主的指示，为可能被雇用在现场或其附近从事本合同未包括的任何工作的下列人员进行工作提供适当的机会：
- 雇主人员
- 雇主雇用的任何其他承包商
- 任何合法建立的公共当局的人员

如果任何此类指示导致承包商增加费用，达到一个有经验的承包商在提交投标书时不能合理预见的数额时，该指示应构成一项变更。为这些人员和其他承包商的服务可包括使用承包商设备以及由承包商负责的临时工程或进入的安排。

承包商应对其在现场的施工活动负责，并应按照雇主要求中规定的范围(如果有)协调其自己与其他承包商的活动。

如果根据合同，要求雇主按照承包商文件向承包商提供任何基础、结构、生产设备或进入手段的占用权，承包商应按雇主要求中提出的时间和方式，向雇主提交此类文件。

放线

承包商应根据合同中规定的原始基准点、基准线和基准标高，给工程放线。承包商应负责对工程的所有部分正确定位，并纠正在工程的位置、标高、尺寸或定线中出现的任何差错。

安全程序

承包商应：
(1) 遵守所有适用的安全规则。
(2) 照料有权在现场的所有人员的安全。
(3) 尽合理的努力保持现场和工程没有不需要的障碍物，以避免对这些人员造成危险。
(4) 在工程竣工和按照第 10 条[雇主的接收]的规定移交前，提供围栏、照明、保卫和看守。
(5) 因实施工程为公众和临近土地的所有人、占用人使用和提供保护，提供可能需要的任何临时工程(包括道路、人行路、防护物和围栏等)。

质量保证

承包商应建立质量保证体系，以证实符合合同要求。该体系应符合合同的详细规定。雇主有权对体系的任何方面进行审查。

承包商应在每一设计和实施阶段开始前，向雇主提交所有程序和如何贯彻要求的文件的细节，供其参考。向雇主发送任何技术性文件时，文件本身应有经承包商本人事先批准的明显证据。

遵守质量保证体系，不应解除合同规定的承包商的任何任务、义务和职责。

现场数据

雇主应在基准日期前，将其取得的现场地下和水文条件及环境方面的所有有关资料提交给承包商。同样地，雇主在基准日期后得到的所有此类资料也应提交给承包商。

承包商应负责核实和解释所有此类资料。除第 5.1 款[设计义务一般要求]提出的情况以外，雇主对这些资料的准确性、充分性和完整性不承担责任。

合同价格

承包商应被认为已确信合同价格的正确性和充分性。

除非合同另有规定,合同价格包括承包商根据合同所承担的全部义务(包括根据暂列金额所承担的义务,如果有),以及为正确设计、实施和完成工程并修补任何缺陷所需的全部有关事项。

不可预见的困难

除合同另有说明外:
(1) 承包商应被认为已取得了对工程可能产生影响和作用的有关风险、意外事件和其他情况的全部必要资料。
(2) 通过签署合同,承包商接受对预见到的所有困难和成功完成工程所需的费用所负的全部责任。
(3) 对于任何未预见到的困难和费用不应考虑调整合同价格。

道路通行权与设施

承包商应为其所需要的专用和(或)临时道路包括进场道路的通行权承担全部费用和开支。承包商还应自担风险和费用,取得为工程目的可能需要的现场以外的任何附加设施。

避免干扰

承包商应避免对以下事项产生不必要或不当的干扰。
(1) 公众的方便。
(2) 所有道路和人行道的进入、使用和占用,不论他们是公共的,还是雇主或是其他人所有的。

承包商应保障并保持雇主免受因任何此类不必要或不当的干扰造成任何损害赔偿费、损失和开支(包括法律费用和开支)的伤害。

进场通路

承包商应被认为已对现场的进入道路的适宜性和可用性感到满意。承包商应尽合理的努力,防止任何道路或桥梁因承包商的通行或承包商人员受到损坏。这些努力应包括正确使用适宜的车辆和道路。

除本条件另有规定外:
(1) 承包商应(就双方而言)对因他使用现场通路而需要的任何维护负责。
(2) 承包商应提供进场道路的所有必需的标志或方向指示,还应为他使用这些道路、标志和方向指示取得必要的有关当局的许可。
(3) 雇主不应对由于任何进场通路的使用或其他原因引起的索赔负责。
(4) 雇主不保证特定进场通路的适宜性和可用性。
(5) 因进场通路对承包商的使用要求不适宜、不能用而发生的费用应由承包商负担。

货物运输

除非专用条件中另有规定:
(1) 承包商应在不少于 21 天前,将任何工程设备或每项其他主要货物将运到现场的日期通知给雇主。

(2) 承包商应负责工程需要的所有货物和其他物品的包装、装货、运输、接收、卸货、存储和保护。

(3) 承包商应保障并保持雇主免受因货物运输引起的所有损害赔偿费、损失和开支(包括法律费用和开支)的伤害，并应协商和支付由于货物运输引起的所有索赔。

承包商设备

承包商应负责所有承包商设备。承包商设备运到现场后，应视作准备为工程施工专用。

环境保护

承包商应采取一切适当措施，保护(现场内外)环境，限制由其施工作业引起的污染、噪音和其他后果对公众和财产造成的损害和妨害。

承包商应确保因其活动产生的气体排放、地面排水及排污等不超过雇主要求中规定的数值，也不超过适用法律规定的数值。

电、水和燃气

除下述情况外，承包商应负责供应其所需的所有电、水和其他服务。

承包商应有权因工程的需要使用现场可供的电力、水、燃气和其他服务，其详细规定和价格见雇主要求。承包商应自担风险和费用，提供他使用这些服务和计量所需要的任何仪器。

这些服务的耗用数量和应付金额(按其价格)应根据第2.5款[雇主的索赔]和第3.5款[确定]的要求商定或确定。承包商应向雇主支付此金额。

雇主设备和免费供应的材料

雇主应准备雇主设备(如果有)，供承包商按照雇主要求中提出的细节、安排和价格，在工程实施中使用。除非在雇主要求中另有说明：

(1) 除(2)所列情况外，雇主应对雇主设备负责。

(2) 当任何承包商人员操作、驾驶、指挥或占用或控制某项雇主设备时，承包商应对该项设备负责。

使用雇主设备的适当数量和应付费用金额(按规定价格)应按第2.5款[雇主的索赔]和第3.5款[确定]的要求商定或确定。承包商应按此金额付给雇主。

雇主应按照雇主要求中规定的细节免费提供"免费供应的材料"(如果有)。雇主应自行承担风险和费用，按照合同规定的时间和地点供应这些材料。随后，承包商应对其进行目视检查，并将这些材料的短少、缺陷或缺项迅速通知给雇主。除非双方另有协议，雇主应立即改正通知指出的短少、缺陷或缺项。

目视检查后，这些免费供应的材料应由承包商照管、监护和控制。承包商的检查、照管、监护和控制的义务，不应解除雇主对目视检查难发现的任何短少、缺陷或缺项所负的责任。

进度报告

除非专用条件中另有规定，承包商应编制月进度报告，一式六份，提交给雇主。第一次报告所包括的期间,应自开工日期起至当月的月底止。以后应每月报告一次,在每次报告期最后一天后 7 日内报出。

报告应持续到承包商完成在工程移交证书上注明的竣工日期时所有未完扫尾工作为止。每份报告应包括:

(1) 设计、承包商文件、采购、制造、货物运达现场、施工、安装、试验、投产准备和试运行等每一阶段进展情况的图表和详细说明。

(2) 反映制造情况和现场进展情况的照片。

(3) 关于每项主要工程设备和材料的生产、制造商名称、制造地点、进度百分比,以及下列事项的实际或预计日期。

- 开始制造。
- 承包商检验。
- 试验。
- 发货和运抵现场。

(4) 第 6.10 款[承包商的人员和设备的记录]中所述的细节。

(5) 材料的质量保证文件、试验结果及合格证的副本。

(6) 变更、根据第 2.5 款[雇主的索赔]的规定发出的通知和根据第 20.1 款[承包商的索赔]的规定发出的通知的清单。

(7) 安全统计,包括对环境和公共关系有危害的任何事件与活动的详细情况。

(8) 实际进度与计划进度的对比,包括可能影响按合同竣工的任何事件或情况的详情,以及为消除延误正在(或准备)采取的措施。

现场保安

除非专用条件中另有规定,否则:

(1) 承包商应负责阻止未经授权的人员进入现场。

(2) 授权人员应仅限于承包商人员和雇主人员,以及由(或代表)雇主通知承包商,作为雇主在现场的其他承包商的授权人员的任何其他人员。

承包商的现场作业

承包商应将其作业限制在现场,以及承包商可得到并经雇主同意作为工作场地的任何附加区域内。承包商应采取一切必要的预防措施,以保持承包商设备和承包商人员处在现场和此类附加区域内,避免他们进入邻近地区。

在工程施工期间,承包商应保持现场没有一切不必要的障碍物,并应妥善存放和处置承包商设备或多余的材料。承包商应从现场清除并运走任何残物、垃圾和不再需要的临时工程。

在颁发工程接收证书后,承包商应清除并运走所有承包商设备、剩余材料、残物、垃圾和临时工程。承包商应使现场和工程处于清洁和安全的状况。但在缺陷通知期限内,承包商可在现场保留其根据合同完成规定义务所需要的此类货物。

化石

在现场发现的所有化石、硬币、有价值的物品或文物,以及具有地质或考古意义的结构物和其他遗迹或物品，应置于雇主的照管和权限下。承包商应采取合理的预防措施，防止承包商人员或其他人员移动或损坏任何这类发现物。

一旦发现任何上述物品，承包商应立即通知雇主。雇主应就处理上述物品发出指示。如果承包商因执行这些指示遭受延误和(或)招致费用，承包商应向雇主再次发出通知，有权根据第 20.1 款[承包商的索赔]的规定提出：

(1) 根据第 8.4 款[竣工时间的延长]的规定，如果竣工已或将受到延误，对任何此类延误给予延长期。

(2) 任何上述费用应加入合同价格，给予支付。

雇主收到进一步的通知后，应按照第 3.5 款[确定]的要求商定或确定这些事项。

Unit 7　Types of Construction Contracts

While construction contracts serve as a means of pricing construction, they also structure the allocation of risk to the various parties involved. The owner has the sole power to decide what type of contract should be used for a specific facility to be constructed and to set forth the terms in a contractual agreement. It is important to understand the risks of the contractors associated with different types of construction contracts.

- Lump Sum Contract.

In a lump sum contract, the owner has essentially assigned all the risk to the contractor, who in turn can be expected to ask for a higher markup in order to take care of unforeseen contingencies. Beside the fixed lump sum price, other commitments are often made by the contractor in the form of submittal such as a specific schedule, the management reporting system or a quality control program. If the actual cost of the project is underestimated, the underestimated cost will reduce the contractor's profit by that amount. An overestimate has an opposite effect, but may reduce the chance of being a low bidder for the project.

- Unit Price Contract.

In a unit price contract, the risk of inaccurate estimation of uncertain quantities for some key tasks has been removed from the contractor. However, some contractors may submit an "unbalanced bid" when it discovers large discrepancies between its estimates and the owner's estimates of these quantities. Depending on the confidence of the contractor on its own estimates and its propensity on risk, a contractor can slightly raise the unit prices on the underestimated tasks while lowering the unit prices on other tasks. If the contractor is correct in its assessment, it can increase its profit substantially since the payment is made on the actual quantities of tasks; and if the reverse is true, it can lose on this basis. Furthermore, the owner may disqualify a contractor if the bid appears to be heavily unbalanced. To the extent that an underestimate or overestimate is caused by changes in the quantities of work, neither error will affect the contractor's profit beyond the markup in the unit prices.

- Cost Plus Fixed Percentage Contract.

For certain types of construction involving new technology or extremely pressing needs, the owner is sometimes forced to assume all risks of cost overruns. The contractor will receive the actual direct job cost plus a fixed percentage, and have little incentive to reduce job cost. Furthermore, if there are pressing needs to complete the project, overtime payments to workers are common and will further increase the job cost. Unless there are compelling reasons, such as the urgency in the construction of military installations, the owner should not use this type of contract.

- Cost Plus Fixed Fee Contract.

Under this type of contract, the contractor will receive the actual direct job cost plus a fixed fee, and will have some incentive to complete the job quickly since its fee is fixed regardless of the duration of the project. However, the owner still assumes the risks of direct job cost overrun while the contractor may risk the erosion of its profits if the project is dragged on beyond the expected time.

- Cost Plus Variable Percentage Contract.

For this type of contract, the contractor agrees to a penalty if the actual cost exceeds the estimated job cost, or a reward if the actual cost is below the estimated job cost. In return for taking the risk on its own estimate, the contractor is allowed a variable percentage of the direct job-cost for its fee. Furthermore, the project duration is usually specified and the contractor must abide by the deadline for completion. This type of contract allocates considerable risk for cost overruns to the owner, but also provides incentives to contractors to reduce costs as much as possible.

- Target Estimate Contract.

This is another form of contract which specifies a penalty or reward to a contractor, depending on whether the actual cost is greater than or less than the contractor's estimated direct job cost. Usually, the percentages of savings or overrun to be shared by the owner and the contractor are predetermined and the project duration is specified in the contract. Bonuses or penalties may be stipulated for different project completion dates.

- Guaranteed Maximum Cost Contract.

When the project scope is well defined, an owner may choose to ask the contractor to take all the risks, both in terms of actual project cost and project time. Any work change orders from the owner must be extremely minor if at all, since performance specifications are provided to the owner at the outset of construction. The owner and the contractor agree to a project cost guaranteed by the contractor as maximum. There may be or may not be additional provisions to share any savings if any in the contract. This type of contract is particularly suitable for turnkey operation.

Principles of Competitive Bidding

Competitive bidding on construction projects involves decision making under uncertainty where one of the greatest sources of the uncertainty for each bidder is due to the unpredictable nature of his competitors. Each bid submitted for a particular job by a contractor will be determined by a large number of factors, including an estimate of the direct job cost, the general overhead, the confidence that the management has in this estimate, and the immediate and long-range objectives of management. So many factors are involved that it is impossible for a particular bidder to attempt to predict exactly what the bids submitted by its competitors will be.

It is useful to think of a bid as being made up of two basic elements:

(1) the estimate of direct job cost, which includes direct labor costs, material cost, equipment costs, and direct filed supervision.

(2) the markup or return, which must be sufficient to cover a portion of general overhead

costs and allow a fair profit on the investment.

A large return can be assured simply by including a sufficiently high markup. However, the higher the markup, the less chance there will be of getting the job. Consequently a contractor who includes a very large markup on every bid could become bankrupt from lack of business. Conversely, the strategy of bidding with very little markup in order to obtain high volume is also likely to lead to bankruptcy. Somewhere in between the two extreme approaches to bidding lies an "optimum markup" which considers both the return and the likelihood of being low bidder in such a way that, over the long run, the average return maximized.

From all indications, most contractors confront uncertain bidding conditions by exercising a high degree of subjective judgment, and each contractor may give different weights to various factors. The decision on the bid price, if a bid is indeed submitted, reflects the contractor's best judgment on how well the proposed project fits into the overall strategy for the survival and growth of the company, as well as the contractor's propensity to risk greater profit versus the chance of not getting a contract.

One major concern in bidding competitions is the amount of "money left on the table" of the difference between the winning and the next best bid. The winning bidder would like the amount of "money left on the table" to be as small as possible. For example, if a contractor wins with a bid of $200 000, and the next lowest bid was $225 000 (representing $25 000 of "money left on the table"), then the winning contractor would have preferred to have bid $220 000 (or perhaps $224 999) to increase potential profits.

Some of the major factors impacting bidding competitions include:

- Exogenous Economic Factors.

Contractors generally tend to specialize in a submarket of construction and concentrate their work in particular geographic locations. The level of demand in a submarket at a particular time can influence the number of bidders and their bid prices. When work is scarce in the submarket, the average number of bidders for projects will be larger than at times of plenty. The net result of scarcity is likely to be the increase in the number of bidders per project and downward pressure on the bid price for each project in the submarket. At times of severe scarcity, some contractors may cross the line between segments to expand their activities, or move into new geographic locations to get a larger share of the existing submarket. Either action will increase the risks incurred by such contractors as they move into less familiar segments or territories. The trend of market demand in construction and of the economy at large may also influence the bidding decisions of a contractor in other ways. If a contractor perceives drastic increases in labor wages and material prices as a result of recent labor contract settlements, it may take into consideration possible increases in unit prices for determining the direct project cost. Furthermore, the perceptions of increase in inflation rates and interest rates may also cause the contractor to use a higher markup to hedge the uncertainty. Consequently, at times of economic expansion and/or higher inflation rate, contractors are reluctant to commit themselves to long-term fixed price contracts.

Unit 7 Types of Construction Contracts

- Characteristics of Bidding Competition.

All other things being equal, the probability of winning a contract diminishes as more bidders participate in the competition. Consequently, a contractor tries to find out as much information as possible about the number and identities of potential bidders on a specific project. Such information is often available in the Dodge Bulletin [Dodge Bulletin (daily publication), F. W. Dodge Corp., New York, N.Y.] or similar publications which provide data of potential projects and names of contractors who have taken out plans and specifications. For certain segments, potential competitors may be identified through private contacts, and bidders often confront the same competitor's project after project since they have similar capabilities and interests in undertaking the same type of work, including size, complexity and geographical location of the projects. A general contractor may also obtain information of potential subcontractors from publications such as Credit Reports (Credit Reports, Building Construction Division, and Bradstreet, Inc., New York, N.Y.) published by Dun and Bradstreet, Inc. However, most contractors form an extensive network with a group of subcontractors with whom they have had previous business transactions. They usually rely on their own experience in soliciting subcontract bids before finalizing a bid price for the project.

- Objectives of General Contractors in Bidding.

The bidding strategy of some contractors is influenced by a policy of minimum percentage markup for general overhead and profit. However, the percentage markup may also reflect additional factors stipulated by the owner such as high retention and slow payments for completed work, or perceptions of uncontrollable factors in the economy. The intensity of a contractor's efforts in bidding a specific project is influenced by the contractor's desire to obtain additional work. The winning of a particular project may be potentially important to the overall mix of work in progress or the cash flow implications for the contractor. The contractor's decision is also influenced by the availability of key personnel in the contractor organization. The company sometimes wants to reserve its resources for future projects, or commits itself to the current opportunity for different reasons.

- Contractor's Comparative Advantages.

A final important consideration in forming bid prices on the part of contractors is the possible special advantages enjoyed by a particular firm. As a result of lower costs, a particular contractor may be able to impose a higher profit markup yet still have a lower total bid than competitors. These lower costs may result from superior technology, greater experience, better management, better personnel or lower unit costs. A comparative cost advantage is the most desirable of all circumstances in entering a bid competition.

Questions

1. Who has the sole power to decide what type of contract should be used for a specific facility to be constructed and to set forth the terms in a contractual agreement?

2. In a lump sum contract, who will bear all the risks?
3. When may some contractors submit an "unbalanced bid"?
4. What may the owner do if the bid appears to be heavily unbalanced?
5. Unless there are compelling reasons, such as the urgency in the construction of military installations, the owner should not use cost plus fixed percentage contract, why?
6. How shall the risks be shared between the contractor and the employer under the cost plus fixed fee contract?
7. How shall the risks be shared between the contractor and the employer under the cost plus variable percentage contract?
8. What are the principles of competitive bidding?
9. What are the major factors impacting bidding competitions?
10. What will influence the bidding strategy of some contractors?

Vocabulary, Phrases and Expressions

construction contract：工程承包合同
a lump sum contract：总价合同
a low bidder：低价投标人
a unit price contract：单价合同
unbalanced bid：不平衡报价
a cost plus fixed percentage contract：成本加固定百分比费用合同
a cost plus fixed fee contract：成本加固定费用合同
a cost plus variable percentage contract：成本加变动比例费用合同
a target estimate contract：目标估算合同
a guaranteed maximum cost contract：保证最大成本合同
decision making：决策
optimum markup：最优增加值
exogenous economic factors：外部经济因素
potential competitors：潜在的竞争者
comparative advantages：相对优势；比较优势

参 考 译 文

第 7 单元 工程承包合同的类型

工程承包合同作为工程定价工具的同时，还规定了风险在参与各方之间的分配。业主拥有单独的权利决定应该为建设一个特定的工程而采用哪种合同形式，并在合同中用条款阐明。掌握各种不同合同形式中承包商的风险是非常重要的。

- 总价合同。

在总价合同中，业主本质上是将所有的风险赋予了承包商，可以料想，承包商继而会寻求更大的增加值以覆盖不可预见的费用。除固定总价外，承包商通常以提供其他文件的形式做出另外的承诺，例如，某一特定的进度计划、管理报告系统或质量控制计划。如果工程的真实费用被低估，那么被低估的费用将减少承包商的利润。被高估的费用具有相反的结果，但可能减小成为工程低价投标人的机会。

- 单价合同。

在单价合同中，承包商不再因某些主要分项工程量的不明确而承担估算不准确的风险。但是，一些承包商在发现自己的工程量估算与业主的估算之间存在很大差距时，可能提交"不平衡报价"。基于对自己估算的信心以及对风险承担的态度，承包商可能在被低估数量的分项工程上略微提高相应单价，而将其他分项工程的单价降低。如果承包商的估算是正确的，承包商就可以增加相当的利润，因为业主的支付是根据实际工程量来确定的；如果业主的估算是对的，承包商的利润则可能据此而减少。此外，如果投标报价过于不平衡，业主可能将该承包商排除在外。就由工程量变化引起的低估或高估这种情况而言，不管估算错误与否，都不会影响承包商所报单价增加值之外的利润。

- 成本加固定百分比费用合同。

对于一些采用新技术或有急迫需求的特定工程，业主有时候被迫承担成本超支的所有风险。承包商将得到实际成本以及固定比例的酬金，因而没有降低工程成本的动力。而且，如果对工程完成时间有急迫的要求，则工人超时工作费用的支付是普遍的，这也将进一步提高工程成本。除非有特殊的原因，例如，紧急军事工程的建造，业主不应采用这种形式的合同。

- 成本加固定费用合同。

在这种合同形式下，承包商将得到实际成本加上固定的酬金，并得到激励而尽快完成工程，因为不管工程历时多久，酬金是固定的。但是，业主仍然要承担工程成本超支的风险，承包商则承担工程实际工期超过预计时间而导致利润减少的风险。

- 成本加变动比例费用合同。

对于这种合同形式，承包商同意在实际成本超过估算成本时接受处罚，或者在实际成本低于估算成本时获得奖励。作为承担自己估算成本风险的回报，承包商被允许以直接成本的变动比例作为报酬。此外，项目工期通常是明确规定的，承包商必须按期限完成工程。这类合同将相当的成本超支风险分配给业主，但也给予承包商激励，尽可能地降低成本。

- 目标估算合同。

这是根据实际成本高于或低于承包商估算的直接成本而给予承包商惩罚或奖励的另一种合同形式。通常，由业主和承包商分担节约或超支部分的比例事先约定，项目工期在合同中明确规定。奖金或罚金根据不同的工程完成日期来确定。

- 保证最大成本合同。

当工程范围清楚定义后，业主可能选择要求承包商承担所有的风险，既包括实际工程成本，也包括工期。任何来自业主方的工程变更想必十分微小，因为项目的功能说明在施工开始前就提供给业主。业主和承包商同意由承包商保证的一个工程成本值作为最大值。在合同中可能有也可能没有附加条款来分享可能的节约额。这种合同形式特别适合于交钥匙工程。

竞争性投标的原则

建设工程的竞争性投标包括在不确定的情况下进行决策，对每一个投标人而言这种不确定的根源之一在于竞争者的不可预知性。承包商为某一特定工程提交的投标将取决于很多因素，包括直接成本的估算、总管理费用、管理者对这一估算的信心以及短期和长期的管理目标。如此之多的因素，使得一个特定的投标人试图准确预测竞争者的投标是不可能的。

将投标分为两个基本组成要素是有用的：

(1) 直接成本的估算，包括直接人工费、材料费、机械费和直接现场管理费。

(2) 增加值或回报，其必须足以覆盖总管理费部分，以及获得相当的投资利润。

只要简单地添加一个足够高的增加值，就能保证高回报。但是，增加值越高，获得工程的机会就越小。因此，在每一次投标中，增加值取得非常大的承包商会因接不到工程而破产。相反，为了获得大量工程而采用低增加值投标策略的承包商也可能导致破产。在两种极端投标方法中，存在一个"最优增加值"，它既考虑回报，也考虑成为低价投标人的可能性，从长远来看，采用这种方法的平均回报最大。

所以现象表明，大多数承包商面对不确定的投标条件，在很大程度上采用主观的判断来应对，每个承包商可能对不同的因素给予不同的权重。如果投标真正提交，投标价格的决策就反映了承包商如何使拟定的计划适合公司生存和发展的整体战略，以及反映承包商对待取得较大利润与失去合同机会这一风险的态度。

关于投标竞争的一个主要问题是"桌面上剩下的钱"为多少，获胜与次最佳投标之间的相差值是多少。获胜的投标人希望"桌面上剩下的钱"越少越好。比如，如果一个承包商以 200 000 美元的投标价获胜，而次低的投标价为 225 000 美元（意味着"桌面上剩下的钱"是 25 000 美元），那么获胜的承包商就希望自己最好以 220 000 美元（也可能是 224 999 美元）投标，以增加潜在的利润。

影响投标竞争的主要因素包括如下几个。

- 外部经济因素。

承包商一般倾向于专注某一专业工程的承包市场以及将他们承包工程的范围集中于特定的区域。在一特定时间，市场的需求水平可以影响投标人的数量和投标价格。当承包市场上的工程稀少时，工程投标人的平均数目将比工程多的时候大。工程稀少的最终结果可能导致承包市场上参加每一工程投标的人数增加，工程投标价格面临向下的压力。当工程严重稀少时，一些承包商可能会越过专业界线以扩展自己的活动范围，或者迁移到一个新的地区谋求获得已有承包市场上的更大份额。任何一个这样的行动，都会增加承包商的风险，因为他们是进入一个不熟悉的专业领域或地区。工程的市场需求趋势和经济的变化趋势也可能以另一种方式影响承包商的投标决策。如果承包商感到按目前签订的人工合同的结果，工人工资和材料价格会大幅度提高，则其在确定直接成本时可能考虑适当提高单价。此外，如果预感通货膨胀率和利率会提高，也可能会引起承包商采用较高的增加值来规避不确定性。因此，当在经济膨胀和/或通货膨胀率较高时，承包商不愿意签订工期较长的固定价格合同。

Unit 7　Types of Construction Contracts

- 投标竞争的特征。

与所有其他情形一样，如果有许多人参加竞争，赢得合同的可能性就会减小。因此，承包商总是试图获得尽可能多的有关某一特定工程潜在投标人数目和投标人特点的信息。这种信息常常可以在 Dodge 报告(Dodge 报告（每日出版），F. W. Dodge 公司，纽约)中获取，或是从提供拟招标工程的数据和已经取得计划和说明书的承包商的名单的类似出版物中得到。对于某些特殊的专业，潜在竞争者的情况可能通过秘密方法确定，投标人经常在一个接一个的工程上与相同竞争者相遇，因为他们对承担同一类型的工程，包括规模、复杂性以及地理位置都有相同的能力和兴趣。总承包商也可以从由 Dun & Bradstreet 公司出版的 Credit 报告(Credit 报告，Building Construction Division，Bradstreet 公司，纽约)这样的出版物中得到潜在分包商的信息。但是，大部分总承包商是通过与以前有过交易的分包商群建立的广泛网络，从中获取潜在分包商的信息的。在最后确定工程投标价格之前，他们通常是根据自己的经验来选择分包商的。

- 投标中总承包商的目标。

一些承包商的投标战略受增加值比例最小这样的投标方针的影响，以此获得总管理费和利润。但是，增加值比例也可能反映业主规定的其他因素，例如，承包商对已完工工程较高的保管率及其业主缓慢的支付，或对经济中不可控制因素的预计。对投标某一特定工程的努力程度，受承包商对获得更多工程渴望程度的影响。对于承包商来说，获得某一特定工程对所有进行中的工程或在隐含的现金流方面可能具有潜在的重要性。承包商的决策还受到能否从承包商自己的组织中获得关键人员的影响。公司有时候需要为将来的工程储备资源，或由于其他不同的原因而集中关注于目前的机会。

- 承包商的比较优势。

承包商在确定投标报价时考虑的最重要的因素是来自公司可能的特殊优势。作为低成本的结果，某一承包商就可能加上一个有较高利润的增加值而使总的投标价格仍比其他竞争者低。这些更低的成本可能来自于先进的技术、丰富的经验、优秀的管理、出色的员工或者较低的单位成本。比较成本优势是参与投标竞争时在所有的措施中最有价值的。

Unit 8　Tendering Procedure(1)

The FIDIC Conditions of Contract envisage that a contractor will be selected by the Employer following competitive tendering.

Experience has shown that, for major projects and those involving international tendering, prequalification of tenderers is desirable since it enables the Employer /Engineer to establish, in advance, the competence of firms subsequently invited to tender. It also ensures that invitations are addressed to leading companies who would not necessarily participate in open or unrestricted tendering. Such unrestricted tendering does not always facilitate appropriate competition because the number of tenderers may be so great as to make the odds against tendering successfully unacceptable. Additionally, prequalification has the advantage of reducing the inflationary effect which must arise where firms incur unproductive expense in submitting a large number of tenders in the knowledge that a high proportion of these must be unsuccessful.

The documents issued to tenderers (the Tender documents) normally comprise Conditions of Contract, Specification, Drawings, Bill of Quantities and form of Tender, together with Instructions to Tenderers. All except Instructions to Tenderers become Contract documents on award of Contract. It is usual to send the Tender documents to tenderers under cover of a letter which should be limited to identifying the documents and giving the recipient an invitation to tender.

Conditions of Contract

The Conditions of Contract will consist of Part I and Part II of the Red Book. The Conditions set out the legal /contractual arrangements that will apply to the Contract.

Specification

The Specification will define the scope and the technical requirements of the Contract. The quality of materials and the standards of workmanship to be provided by the Contractor must be clearly described, together with the extent, if any, to which the Contractor will be responsible for the design of the permanent works. Details must be included of samples to be provided and tests to be carried out by the Contractor during the course of the Contract. Any limitations on the Contractor's freedom of choice in the order,timing or methods of executing the work or sections of the works must be clearly set out and any restrictions in his use of the site of the works, such as the provision of access or space for other contractors, must be given.

Drawings

The Drawings must be in sufficient detail to enable tenderers to assess accurately, in conjunction with the Specification and the Bill of Quantities, the nature and scope of work included in the Contract. Only rarely is it possible to provide, at tender stage, a complete set of drawings so fully detailed that the work can be executed without any further drawings becoming necessary. On most contracts supplementary drawings will be issued after award as work proceeds.

Bill of Quantities

The Bill of Quantities is a list of items giving descriptions and estimated quantities of work to be executed under the Contract. The Red Book assumes a remeasurement form of contract, although that does not preclude the inclusion of a number of lump sum items in the Bill of Quantities provided that the scope of work to be covered by each lump sum item is adequately defined.

The Tender

It is highly desirable when inviting competitive offers from a number of tenderers, that the tenders received should be based as far as possible on equal terms and conditions and presented in a standardised manner. In this way evaluation and comparison between the tenders received can be made more simply and accurately with less risk of misunderstandings, errors and omissions.

The Tender is the most important single document submitted by the tenderer. It is here that each tenderer confirms that he has read and understood the requirements of the Tender documents and based on such requirements. It is here that he states his tender sum for undertaking and fulfilling all his obligations under the Contract. It is therefore essential for the Employer that all Tenders received are stated in identical terms and thus it is necessary for the Employer, when inviting Tenders, to provide tenderers with a standard form of tender which each tenderer is required to complete and sign.

The form of Tender which is included at the end of the first volume of the Red Book following Part I of the Conditions of Contract is recommended for this purpose. It is short, it is clear and when signed and submitted creates a legally binding and valid offer.

It is common for Tenders to be identified by a tender reference or contract number which should be added to link the Tender to the project in question.

The organisation to which the Tender is being submitted must be stated in the appropriate space on the form.

The sum to be entered under paragraph 1 of the Tender is the tenderer's total Tender sum, which should be the same as the total from the summary page of the Bill of Quantities. The amount shall be entered in words and in figures and in the event of a discrepancy between the two it is common practice in most countries that the written amount shall prevail over the amount expressed in figures.

The sum agreed may vary during the execution of the project depending on what circumstances occur, e. g. the instruction of variations, the occurrence of unforeseen events, which in accordance with the Conditions of Contract entitle the Contractor to additional (or reduced) payment.

Under paragraph 4 the Employer must state the time during which he requires the Tender to remain valid and open to acceptance. This time should be adequate to permit proper evaluation and award procedures to be completed.

In the event that the stated time proves to be insufficient, the Employer may ask tenderers to extend the period of validity of their Tenders for a further named period. At the same time tenderers should be asked to extend the validity of any tender bond accordingly. Tenderers are free to extend or not, if so requested, and in the event that they choose not to do so, the Employer has no right to cash or hold their tender bond.

Instructions to Tenderers

Instructions to Tenderers must be prepared to meet the requirements of individual contracts. Their purpose is to convey information and instructions which apply during the tendering period. Any material on which it is intended to rely after award must be included elsewhere, e. g. in the Conditions of Contract or the Specification.

The following notes provide a guide to subjects to be covered, but they are not necessarily exhaustive.

(1) General. Under this heading should be included brief details of the organisation (Government, Ministry, Department, Authority, etc.) calling for Tenders, together with an outline of the project to be covered by the Contract.

Any stipulations regarding firms and persons qualified to tender, such as prior prequalification and/or requirements in the event of formation of joint ventures, should be stated, together with details of any special requirements to establish the validity of the Tender and the authority of the signatory, e. g. Power of Attorney.

Tenderers must be advised if the successful tenderer will be required to establish a locally registered company for the purpose of the Contract.

(2) Documents. A list of documents issued to tenderers should be included together with instructions as to which of these documents must be completed by the tenderer and handed in on the submission date.

If the Tender documents are not issued free of charge then the sum required for the original set and for any additional sets should be stated and whether payment is to be made in local or equivalent foreign currency. Tenderers should be advised as to how the extra sets of documents can be obtained and also of procedures to be followed for the return of the documents by unsuccessful tenderers.

(3) Completion and Submission of Tenders. Concise instructions as to the time, date and place for the submission of Tenders should be given.

It should also be made clear to tenderers that all entries and signatures should be in indelible

Unit 8 Tendering Procedure (1)

ink and that no erasures or additions are permitted other than those necessary to correct errors. All such corrections must be initialled.

It is normal to ask for more than one copy of the Tender, in which case tenderers should be instructed as to the manner in which the Tenders are to be packaged.

It is usual to stipulate that one set of documents should be clearly marked "Original Tender" and others marked "Copy" , and that if there are discrepancies the Original Tender takes precedence. Photocopies of the Original Tender minimize the risk of discrepancies.

The tenderer should be told whether, if he has handed in his Tender before the formal submission date or has sent it by post, he has the right to withdraw, modify or correct it after dispatch. This would normally be permitted, provided that a request for modification, etc. , has been received by the Employer either in writing or by cable, telex or facsimile transmission before the time set for receiving Tenders. The Original Tender as amended would then be considered as the official offer.

(4) Supplementary Information Required. Tenderers should be advised of any supplementary information to be submitted with the Tender documents , such as details of the proposed sureties for any performance security, general terms of insurance, the constitution of the tenderer's organization together with the address to be used for the purposes of the Contract, a preliminary programme of work (the Instructions to Tenderers should give an indication of what is required) and a list of major items of Contractor's Equipment required for the purpose of executing the works.

A forecast of labour and staff, local and foreign, may be requested. Where a Tender sum has been requested on the basis that it is adjustable by reason of changes in the cost of labour, materials and transport, the tenderer should, unless the particulars are given by the Employer in the Tender documents, be requested to indicate the formula or formulae which he wishes to use as the basis for adjusting the sum. If his formula is to be index based, officially published indices should be used. These would normally be indices published in the country where the project is to be located. The Tenderer should also provide the names of any subcontractors he proposes to employ, together with details of those parts of the works proposed to be subcontracted.

It must also be made clear in the Instructions to Tenderers to what extent the supplementary information is required by the Employer purely to demonstrate that the tenderer has understood the extent and nature of the work and the programme required and to what extent, if at all, the supplementary information is required as a part of the offer for inclusion in the Contract documents on award.(to be continued.)

Questions

1. Why is prequalification necessary for major projects and those involving international tendering?

2. What should be included in the specification?
3. Is it possible to provide a detailed complete set of drawings at tender stage? Why?
4. What is the bill of quantities?
5. Why is the tender the most important single document submitted by the tenderer?
6. Why dose the tender sum agreed may vary during the execution of the project?
7. What is the purpose of "instructions to tenderers"?
8. What should be included or stated under the heading "general" in "instructions to tenderers"?
9. On what condition is the tenderer permitted to withdraw, modify or correct his tender after dispatch?
10. What are the supplementary information required to be submitted with the tender documents?

Vocabulary, Phrases and Expressions

tender：招标；投标
competitive tendering：竞争性招标
prequalification：资格预审
conditions of contract：合同条件
specification：规范；详述；说明书
drawings：图纸
bill of quantities：工程量表
instructions to tenderers：投标者须知；投标者指令
contract documents：合同文件
permanent works：永久性工程
standards of workmanship：工艺标准
supplementary drawings：补充图纸
tender reference number：投票参考编号
contract number：合同编号
award procedures：授予程序
period of validity of tenders：投标书的有效期
tender bond：投标保函；投标保证金
original tender：投标书正本
official offer：正式报价
supplementary information：补充信息

参 考 译 文

第8单元　招标程序(1)

　　FIDIC合同条件设想由雇主采用竞争性招标方式选择承包商。

　　经验表明，对于大型的和涉及国际招标的项目来说，对投标者的资格预审是必须的。因为，通过资格预审可以使雇主(或工程师)提前了解应邀投标的公司的能力。同时，也保证了向不一定愿意参加公开或无限制投标的大公司发出邀请。那种无限制招标并不总是有利于合理竞争，因为投标者数量可能太多以致影响到成功的投标反而不能被接受。此外，如果各公司明知大部分投标不可能中标仍递交大量投标，它们将为此付出无效的费用从而导致大量的多余投标，而资格预审就具有减少上述多余投标的优点。

　　颁发给投标者的文件(招标文件)一般包括合同条件、规范、图纸、工程量表、投标书格式以及投标者须知。除投标者须知外，上述全部文件在授予合同时构成为合同文件。通常，把招标文件连同一封信函送给投标者，信函仅限于说明上述文件并发给收件人一份投标邀请书。

合同条件

　　合同条件由红皮书第一部分和第二部分组成。条件说明了适用于合同的法律(或契约)安排。

规范

　　规范将规定合同的范围和技术要求。对承包商提供的材料的质量和工艺标准，以及承包商对永久性工程的设计所负责的程度(如有时)，必须做出明确规定。规范还应包括合同期间承包商提供的样品及其进行的试验的细节；对承包商实施工程或区段的顺序、时间安排或方法的选择自由如有任何限制时，都需明确规定；同时还需给出对承包商使用工程现场的任何限制，例如，为其他承包商提供通道和空间。

图纸

　　图纸必须足够详细，以使投标者在参考了规范和工程量表后，能准确确定合同所包括的工作性质和范围。在投标阶段，极少可能提供出一整套完备的图纸，从而也极少可能在不需要提供任何进一步的图纸的情况下进行工作。对于大多数合同来说，补充图纸将在授予合同之后的工作中发放。

工程量表

　　工程量表是一个项目清单，载有按照合同实施的工作的说明以及估算的工程量。红皮书采用合同重新计量的方式，虽然这并不排除工程量表中包含有若干个包干项目，只要每一包干项目包含的工作范围有详细的规定即可。

投标书

　　当邀请众多投标者参与竞争性报价时，所收到的标书应尽可能地基于平等的条款和条件，并应以标准格式提交，这一点是十分必要的。因为，这样做有利于更为简单、准确地对收到的投标进行评价和比较，并能减少出现误解、错误和遗漏的可能。

投标书是投标者提交的最重要的单项文件。在此文件中，每位投标者确认他已阅读了招标文件并理解了其中的要求，基于这些要求，在此文件中，他申明了用于承担和完成合同规定的全部义务的投标金额。因而，对雇主来说，收到的所有标书应是根据统一条件制定的，招标时，雇主有必要为投标者提供统一标准的标书格式，要求每位投标者全部填写和签字。

为此目的，建议采用附在红皮书第一卷后面紧接合同条件第一部分的投标书格式。它既简短又明确，一经签字和提交，报价即生效，并具有法律约束力。

通常，为了将投标书与有关工程项目联系在一起，投标书应标明投标参考编号或合同号码。

在投标书格式的适当位置，必须标明将标书送交的机构的名称。投标书第一段填写的金额为投标者的投标书总金额，该金额必须与工程量表之一览表中所列的总价一致。该金额应同时用文字和数字填写，如文字和数字之间存在差异，大多数国家的一般惯例是，文字标明的金额应优先于数字表达的金额。

双方同意的金额可能在项目实施过程中根据发生的情况而变化。如变更指示，出现不可预见事件。对此，应根据合同条件使承包商能够得到增加或减少的付款。

在投标书第四段中，雇主必须注明其要求投标书保持有效和同意被接受的时间。这一时间应能满足用来完成适当的评估和授予合同的程序的要求。

倘若发现注明的时间不能满足要求，雇主可要求投标者将其投标书的有效期再延长一段指明的时间。同时，还应要求投标者相应的延长任何投标保函的有效期。投标者在接到此类要求后，有权决定是否延长。倘若他们决定不予延长，则雇主无权将他们的投标保函兑换成现金或持有该保函。

投标者须知

必须编制投标者须知以满足每一具体合同的需要。"须知"的目的在于，把招标期间适用的信息和指令传递出去，但在授标之后需作为依据的任何资料都必须被包括在另外的文件中，如包括在合同条件或技术规范中。

以下解释提供了一个"须知"内容的指南，但不一定很全面。

(1) 概述。在此标题下，应包括对招标机构(政府、部、部门、当局等)的简短的具体介绍，以及合同所包含的项目的概况。

涉及有资格投标的公司或个人的任何规定，诸如提前资格预审和(或)对组成联营体的要求以及有关确定投标书有效性和签署人的权利(如代理人的权利)的任何特殊规定的详细情况，应予申明。

如果要求中标者因合同建立一个在当地注册的公司，须告之投标者。

(2) 文件。颁发给投标者的文件中应包括一份文件清单，此类文件清单应说明其中哪些文件应由投标者填写并在规定的提交日期提交。

如果招标文件不是免费发放的，则应说明一套正本和任何附加套数的应收金额，并说明是否使用当地货币或等值外币支付。还应告诉投标者如何获得额外的各套文件，以及未中标的投标者退还这些文件时应遵循的程序。

(3) 投标书的完成与递交。应给出有关提交投标书的时间、日期和地点的简明指示。

还应向投标者说明所有条目和签字均应使用不褪色墨水,除非必须改正的错误,否则,不允许任何的删减或增加,所有的改正均须草签。

通常,均要求一份以上的投标书副本。在此情况下,应对投标者装订投标书的方法加以指导。

通常规定,一套文件应清楚地标明"投标书正本",其他均应标明"副本",如出现差异,投标书正本优先。投标书正本的影印本可将出现差异的风险降至最低程度。

应告诉投标者,如果在正式提交日期之前他已提交或邮寄出投标书,他是否拥有在发送之后撤回、修正或更改投标书的权力。如果在收到投标书的规定时间之前,雇主已收到以书面或以电报、电传、传真等方式进行修改的请求,一般是允许的。修改后的投标书正本被认为是正式的报价。

(4) 要求提供的补充信息。应将随投标文件同时提交的任何补充信息告之投标者,例如,为任何履约担保所拟用的保证人的详情;保险的一般条件;投标者的机构组成和为合同所使用的地址;工作的初步进度计划(投标者须知中应说明要求);以及为施工日的所需要的承包商的设备的主要项目一览表。

可能需要对当地和外国的劳务与职员的需求量进行预测。当要求投标书的金额可以因劳务、材料和运输成本的变化进行调整时,应要求所有投标者,说明他希望使用的作为调价基础的一种或几种计算公式,除非招标文件中已含有雇主给出的详细说明。如果其公式以指数为基础,那么,就应使用正式发布的指数。这些指数一般是项目所在国已公开发布的。投标者还须提供其拟雇用的任何分包商的姓名及其准备分包的那部分工程的细节。

同时还须在投标者须知中说明,完全为表明投标者对工作范围和性质以及所要求的进度计划的理解,雇主所需的补充信息的程度,以及在进行合同授予时,作为包含在合同文件内的报价的一部分所需的补充信息的程度。(未完待续。)

Unit 9　Tendering Procedure(2)

5) Amendments to Tender Documents

It is possible that explanations, revisions, additions or deletions to the documents issued to tenderers may be necessary during the tendering period. Tenderers should be told how these will be dealt with, the normal method being by formal addenda. If a tenderer is in doubt about the meaning of some item in the Tender documents, he should be advised to notify the Engineer not later than a given number of days (e. g. 42 days) before the Tender submission date. The Engineer will then issue to all tenderers an explanation in the form of an addendum. Each addendum should be accompanied by a receipt form which must be returned so that the Employer and the Engineer have confirmation that each tenderer has received all the necessary information. Failure to acknowledge receipt of an addendum may result in rejection of a Tender. The addenda become part of the Tender documents and the numbers issued should be inserted by tenderers in the space provided in paragraph 1 of the form of Tender.

Tenderers would normally be required to submit their offers strictly in accordance with the requirements of the Tender documents. If tenderers are permitted to offer an alternative Tender, any departure from the documents issued to tenderers should be clearly identified and detailed. The option to submit alternative Tenders may make the evaluation process difficult.

6) Currency Requirements and Exchange Rates

Tenderers should be required to give notice to the Employer of the various currencies in which they may wish to be paid if the Contract is awarded to them. This information should be supplied as soon as possible after invitations to tender have been issued and not less than a given number of days (e. g. 42 days) before the Tender submission date.

The Employer may wish to specify in the Instructions to Tenderers that payments will be made only in the currencies of the countries from which the goods and services are to be acquired.

The Tender documents should include a schedule in which tenderers record the sums in the various approved currencies that together constitute their total Tender sum. This schedule becomes part of the Contract when awarded.

It is common practice to require tenderers to submit their Tenders in a single currency—usually of the country in which the Works are to be executed. If this is the case it is necessary to define the rates of exchange which have been used to convert the various currencies, in which payment is required, into a single currency unit. As more than one tenderer may request part payment in one particular currency, it is preferable that the exchange rates to be used should be consistent and, therefore, that they should be defined by the Employer and notified by him, or the Engineer on his behalf, to each tenderer a reasonable time before the date of submission. In accordance with Sub-Clause 72.2 of the Conditions of Contract, these rates shall be stated in Part II or if not so stated, shall be those prevailing, as determined by the Central Bank of the country in which the works are to be executed, on the date 28 days prior to the latest date for the submission of Tenders or as provided for in the Tender. The rates quoted are incorporated in the Contract when awarded.

In order to assist in forward budgeting it is useful to request tenderers to provide an estimate of the payments to be made by the Employer to the Contractor during the period of the Contract, preferably in quarterly periods.

The estimate of payments referred to above does not become a part of the Contract and should not be regarded as binding. The figures may have to be reviewed and adjusted as the work proceeds. Expenditure under Provisional Sums will affect the figures, and so also will changes in the source of supply of materials and modifications to the programme or variations of the Works.

7) Site Visits

It is customary to expect tenderers to visit the site of the project during the tender period. Details should be given of the date and arrangements for visiting when staff of the Employer and the Engineer will be on site to answer questions and when any exploratory work carried out will be available for inspection, e. g. borehole cores laid out and exploratory adits lit. A summary of all questions and answers thereto should be issued to all tenderers. Tenderers should not be restricted in their site visits and details of who to contact for further visits should be given.

8) Tender Bond

If a tender bond is required, a pro forma version of such bond should be included in the Tender documents. The amount of the bond should be stated and the currency or currencies required. In all cases the surety or sureties must be satisfactory to the Employer. If a tender bond has been requested, any Tender that has not been so secured will be rejected unless otherwise indicated.

Tenderers should be advised that the bond will be released after a specified period, or earlier if one of the Tenders has, within the period, been accepted by the Employer and an acceptable performance security has been submitted by the successful tenderer. It should also be made clear what will happen to the tender bond if the tenderer who has been accepted fails to provide a performance security within a specified number of days after being requested to do so. Usually the tender bond will be forfeited.

9) Bonus

If a bonus in relation to early completion is to be included in the Contract, tenderers should be reminded to state in the space provided in the Appendix to Tender what proportions of local and foreign currencies they wish to receive if they earn it.

10) Local Legislation

If there are any local laws or decrees or any special arrangements which the Employer wishes the tenderers to note particularly, these should be listed in the Instructions to Tenderers. It should be made clear that the list is not comprehensive.

11) Examination of Tenders

Tenderers should be advised that the Employer, or the Engineer on behalf of the Employer, may ask any tenderer for clarification of his Tender, but that no tenderer will be permitted to alter his Tender sum after Tenders have been opened. Clarifications that do not change the Tender sum may, if they are acceptable, be incorporated in the Contract. It should be made clear that all Tenders must remain valid for a specified validity period and any extension thereto agreed to by the respective tenderer.

Tenderers should be advised if any factors other than the Tender sum, such as foreign currency proportions, are to be taken into account when evaluating Tenders.

12) Acceptance of Tender

The Employer will normally state that he does not bind himself to award the Contract to the tenderer submitting the lowest tender or to any tenderer.

Evaluation of Tenders

Tenders for major and international contracts are generally opened in public when the names of the tenderers are announced together with the Tender sum. No other details are given at that time. Thereafter the Tenders are checked and studied by the Engineer on behalf of the Employer.

One of the first tasks of the Engineer is to establish whether the Tenders are arithmetically correct and, if they are not, how to overcome any errors. Another task is to check that the Tenders are responsive, that all the required information has been provided and that everything is consistent with the terms of the Tender documents.

If errors, omissions or inconsistencies are apparent a meeting should be held with the lowest tenderer, and possibly with one or two other tenderers, to clarify the position and to agree how to deal with the points in the event of an award. At such meetings, tenderers should not be permitted to change the substance of their Tenders. If it does not prove possible to clarify and agree how differences are to be resolved, the particular Tender should be treated as unresponsive and no further consideration should be given to that Tender.

Award of Contract

When the Engineer has completed the evaluation of tenders, and has obtained any necessary clarifications, he will make a recommendation to the Employer on the award of the Contract. If the Employer agrees with the Engineer's recommendation and is in a position to award the Contract immediately he will issue a Letter of Acceptance to the successful tenderer.

On occasions certain steps may still be necessary before the Employer can award the Contract, e. g. Government approval or ratification of a loan agreement. In such a case, the Employer may decide to issue to the potential Contractor a letter of intent. Such a letter should state the conditions that must be met before the award can be made. In most cases letters of intent are worded in such a way as to create no commitment on the part of the Employer and the potential Contractor carries out any preliminary work or incurs costs at his own risk. Sometimes a letter of intent gives instructions to the potential Contractor to take some action, such as to order materials and plant or to carry out limited work. In this case, it is necessary for the letter of intent to be clear about how, and to what extent, the potential Contractor will be paid for what he does if, for any reason, the Contract is not ultimately entered into.

In most cases it is the Employer's Letter of Acceptance which, together with tenderer's Tender, will form a binding Contract between the two parties. valid from the date of issue of the Letter. If on account of errors, omissions or inconsistencies in the Tender, or for any other reason, any changes have been tentatively agreed at a meeting of clarification, the Employer's letter may constitute only a counter-offer and the Contract will only be binding on the date that the Contractor acknowledges and confirms, in writing, agreement to the terms of the Letter of Acceptance.

Contract Agreement

The Conditions of Contract, Sub-Clause 9.1, make provision for the execution of a Contract Agreement between the parties which will record all the terms of the Contract between them. However, the execution of this document is not normally necessary to create a legally binding contract.

Nevertheless, in some countries a Contract Agreement is a requirement of law to create a binding Contract irrespective of the existence of a Tender and a Letter of Acceptance. In such cases, in particular, the Contract Agreement must be carefully prepared to comply with the requirements of the relevant law.

It is important to ensure that the exact wording of the Contract Agreement, including the documents listed as forming part thereof, properly records what has been agreed. The parties must ensure that the signatories and method of signature are in accordance with all the applicable laws.

Questions

1. What is the normal method for dealing with the explanations, revisions, additions or deletions to the documents issued to tenderers?
2. Why does the option to submit alternative tender make the evaluation process difficult?
3. What are the tenders required to do in terms of currency/currencies they intent to use to submit their tender and payment they will receive?
4. What is preferable if terderers request part payment in one particular currency?
5. What will happen to the tender bond if the tenderer fails to provide a performance security within a specified number of days?
6. What are the tasks of the engineer in the evaluation of tenders?
7. What should be the engineer do if errors, omissions or inconsistencies are apparent in tenders?
8. What should a letter of intent contain in most cases?
9. What makes a binding contract between the employer and the potential contractor in most cases?
10. Why is the contract agreement a requirement in some countries?

Vocabulary, Phrases and Expressions

formal addenda：正式补遗
receipt：回执；收据
an alternative tender：含替代方案的投标书
currency requirements：货币要求
exchange rates：汇率
tender submission date：投标书提交日期
provisional sums：暂定金额
site visits：现场考察
appendix to tender：投标书附录
a bonus in relation to early completion：提前完工奖金
local laws or decrees：当地法律或法令
acceptance of tender：中标
evaluation of tenders：评标
award of the Contract：授予合同
a letter of acceptance：中标函
contract agreement：合同协议
signatories：签署人

参 考 译 文

第9单元 招标程序(2)

5) 招标文件的修正

在招标期间可能有必要对发给投标者的文件进行解释、修正、增加或删减。应告诉投标者处理这些问题的方式，一般采用正式补遗的方式。如果投标者对招标文件中的某一条目的含义存有疑问，应建议他在投标书提交日期前某一确定的期限(例如42天)内通知工程师。然后，由工程师以补遗的方式向所有投标者进行解释。每项补遗必须附有回执，以便雇主与工程师确信每位投标者均已收到所有必要的信息。如未能告知收到补遗，可能导致投标书被拒绝。补遗成为招标文件的一部分，发出的编号应由投标者填入投标书第一段所预留的空白处。

通常，要求投标者严格按照招标文件的要求提交报价。如果投标者被允许提交一个含有替代方案的投标书，则其中与颁发给投标者的文件任何相偏离的地方均应清楚地标明并详细说明。允许提交替代方案的投标书的做法可能使评标过程更困难。

6) 货币要求与汇率

如果将合同授予投标者，就应要求他们通知雇主，他们希望雇主支付何种货币。此类信息应在招标文件颁发之后，并于投标书提交日期之前不迟于某一特定的期限(如42天)内

Unit 9 Tendering Procedure(2)

尽快提供。

雇主可能希望，在投标者须知中规定仅使用获得货物和服务的国家的货币进行支付。

招标文件应包括一份计划表，表中由投标者记载构成投标总金额的各种经批准的货币金额。授予合同时，此类计划表构成合同的一部分。

通常的做法是，要求投标者提交标书时使用单一货币，一般为工程实施所在国的货币。在此类情况下，有必要确定把要求支付的各种货币兑换成单一货币而采用的汇率。由于不止一位投标者可能要求部分支付使用某一特定货币，采用的汇率以一致为宜。所以，上述汇率须由雇主确定，并在提交投标书前的一段合理时间内，由雇主或由工程师代表雇主通知每位投标者。根据合同条件第 72.2 款，此类汇率应在"第二部分"中规定。如果没有这样的规定，则采用提交投标书截止日期前 28 天当天，或按投标书中规定的日期，由工程实施所在国中央银行确定的通行汇率。授予合同时，此类汇率应载入合同中。

为了有助于提前预算，要求投标者提供一个在合同期间(以每季度为宜)雇主应支付给承包商款项的估算额是必要的。

上述付款的估算额不构成合同的一部分，因而不应被认为具有约束力。其数额在工作进程中可能不得不加以复查和调整。暂定金额下的支出将对数额产生影响，同样，材料来源的变化、进度计划的修正或工程变更也将影响此类数额。

7) 现场考察

投标期间常期望投标者前往现场考察。当雇主的职员和工程师可在现场回答问题并可将已进行的任何勘探工作(如展示钻到的岩芯和有照明的勘探平洞)提供视察时，则应安排考察的具体日期和相关事宜。上述所有有关问题和回答的概要情况，应发给所有投标者。投标者的现场考察不应受到限制，同时，还应给出再次考察时与何人联系的细节。

8) 投标保函

如果需要投标保函，保函的形式文本应被包括在招标文件中，并需要说明保函的金额及所要求的一种或几种货币。在所有情况下，担保人必须使雇主满意。如果要求提交投标保函，则未附保函的任何投标书将会被拒绝，除非另有说明。

应通知投标者，在规定的一个时间段后保函将被送还。如果其中一份投标书在该时间段内被雇主接收，且中标者已提供了一个可接受的履约保证，则该保函将被提前送还。同时还应说明，如发生上述情况，投标保函将面临的问题，即如果已被接受的投标者在被要求提供履约保证之后未能于规定的时间内提交履约保证，通常，投标保函将被没收。

9) 奖金

如果合同中包括有关提前竣工的奖金，假如投标者能够获得此类奖金，则应提醒他们，在投标书附件中预留的空白处，标明他们希望收到的当地货币与外币的比例。

10) 地方法规

如果有任何地方法律或条例，或雇主希望投标者格外注意的任何特殊协议，则应将它们列入投标者须知中，但应说明，所列文件并不全面。

11) 对投标书的审查

应告知投标者，雇主或代表雇主的工程师也许会要求任何投标者阐明其投标书，但在开标之后则不允许任何投标者改变其投标金额。未改变投标金额的投标书说明如被接受，则可纳入合同中。

应当说明，所有投标书必须在规定的有效期内保持有效，或在每位投标者同意的任何延长期内保持有效。

评标时，如果考虑投标金额以外的任何其他因素，如外币比例，则应告知投标者。

12) 中标

雇主一般将正式声明，他自己不受将合同授予报价最低的投标者或任何投标者的约束。

评标

大型国际合同的投标一般均采用公开开标的形式，届时公布投标者姓名及其投标金额。此时，不公布其他任何细节。随后，由工程师代表雇主对投标书进行审查和研究。

工程师的首要任务之一是核实投标书的计算是否正确，若不正确，应怎样纠正每一个错误。另一任务是检查投标书是否全部填写，所有要求的资料是否已提交以及所有事项是否与招标文件条款相一致。

如果有明显的错误、遗漏或不一致，可召开一次标价最低的投标者以及另外一两位其他投标者可能参加的会议，就一旦签订合同时如何解决上述问题表明态度并达成一致意见。在会议期间，不允许投标者改变其投标书的内容。如果无法就怎样解决差异表明态度并取得一致意见，则此类投标书应按没有全部填写的投标书处理，且对此类投标书不再予以考虑。

授予合同

工程师完成评标并得到必要的澄清之后，他将就授予合同之事向雇主提出建议。如果雇主同意工程师的建议并准备立即授予合同，他将向中标者颁发中标函。

在雇主授予合同之前，有时某些步骤可能仍然是必要的，如政府对贷款协议的批准或认可。在此情况下，雇主可以决定向有望中标的承包商颁发一意向书。此类意向书应说明，在能够被授予合同之前必须达到的条件。在大多数情况下，在意向书的措辞中雇主一方不做任何许诺。因此，有望中标的承包商只能自担风险进行任何准备工作或支付各类费用。有时，意向书能够指示有望中标的承包商采取某种行动，如订购材料和设备或进行有限的工作。在此情况下，意向书有必要阐明，如果由于任何原因没有最终缔结合同，对该有望中标的承包商所做的工作应如何支付，以及支付的程度。

在大多数情况下，雇主的中标函连同投标者的投标书组成一个对双方都具有约束力的合同，并自中标函颁发之日起生效。如果由于投标书中的错误、遗漏或不一致，或因任何其他原因，在澄清问题的会议上已对任何变动暂时达成协议，则雇主的信函仅作为一个还价，在承包商回函并以书面形式确认同意中标函的条件之日起，合同才具有约束力。

合同协议

合同条件第 9.1 款对记录双方全部合同条款的合同协议书的实施作了规定，然而，此文件的实施一般并不一定产生具有法律约束力的合同。

在一些国家，尽管已有投标书和中标函，然而，要产生一个具有约束力的合同，法律仍要求有一个合同协议书。在此情况下，尤其需要细心编制合同协议书以符合有关法律的要求。

保证合同协议书(包括构成协议书一部分的文件)的准确措辞严格地记录业已达成的协议，这是很重要的。

双方必须保证签署人和签署方法符合所有适用的法律。

Unit 10 Project Finance

More and more major construction projects involve project financing. Contractors, engineers and designer-builders are finding their work, compensation and risks are shaped by this method of financing. The following guide is provided to help them understand the overall process, their role in it and the risks involved.

Introduction

1) Definition

Project financing involves non-recourse financing of the development and construction of a particular project in which the lender looks principally to the revenues expected to be generated by the project for the repayment of its loan and to the assets of the project as collateral for its loan rather than to the general credit of the project sponsor.

Project financing is commonly used as a financing method in capital-intensive industries for projects requiring large investments of funds, such as the construction of power plants, pipelines, transportation systems, mining facilities, industrial facilities and heavy manufacturing plants. The sponsors of such projects frequently are not sufficiently creditworthy to obtain traditional financing or are unwilling to take the risks and assume the debt obligations associated with traditional financings. Project financing permits the risks associated with such projects to be allocated among a number of parties at levels acceptable to each party.

2) Principal Advantages and Objectives

(1) Non-recourse.

The typical project financing involves a loan to enable the sponsor to construct a project where the loan is completely "non-recourse" to the sponsor, i.e., the sponsor has no obligation to make payments on the project loan if revenues generated by the project are insufficient to cover the principal and interest payments on the loan. In order to minimize the risks associated with a non-recourse loan, a lender typically will require indirect credit supports in the form of guarantees, warranties and other covenants from the sponsor, its affiliates and other third parties involved with the project.

(2) Maximize leverage.

In a project financing, the sponsor typically seeks to finance the costs of development and construction of the project on a highly leveraged basis. Frequently, such costs are financed using 80 to 100 percent debt. High leverage in a non-recourse project financing permits a sponsor to put less in funds at risk, permits a sponsor to finance the project without diluting its equity investment in the project.

(3) Off-Balance-Sheet treatment.

Depending upon the structure of a project financing, the project sponsor may not be required to report any of the project debt on its balance sheet because such debt is non-recourse or of limited recourse to the sponsor. Off-balance-sheet treatment can have the added practical benefit of helping the sponsor comply with covenants and restrictions relating to borrowing funds contained in other indentures and credit agreements to which the sponsor is a party.

(4) Maximize tax benefits.

Project financings should be structured to maximize tax benefits and to assure that all available tax benefits are used by the sponsor or transferred, to the extent permissible, to another party through a partnership, lease or other vehicle.

3) Disadvantages

Project financings are extremely complex. It may take a much longer period of time to structure, negotiate and document a project financing than a traditional financing, and the legal fees and related costs associated with a project financing can be very high. Because the risks assumed by lenders may be greater in a non-recourse project financing than in a more traditional financing, the cost of capital may be greater than with a traditional financing.

4) Project Financing Participants and Agreements

(1) Sponsor/Developer.

The sponsor(s) or developer(s) of a project financing is the party that organizes all of the other parties and typically controls, and makes an equity investment in, the company or other entity that owns the project. If there is more than one sponsor, the sponsors typically will form a corporation or enter into a partnership or other arrangement pursuant to which the sponsors will form a "project company" to own the project and establish their respective rights and responsibilities regarding the project.

(2) Additional equity investors.

In addition to the sponsor(s), there frequently are additional equity investors in the project company. These additional investors may include one or more of the other project participants.

(3) Construction Contractor.

The construction contractor enters into a contract with the project company for the design, engineering and construction of the project.

(4) Operator.

The project operator enters into a long-term agreement with the project company for the day-to-day operation and maintenance of the project.

(5) Feedstock supplier.

The feedstock supplier(s) enters into a long-term agreement with the project company for the supply of feedstock (i.e., energy, raw materials or other resources) to the project (e.g., for a power plant, the feedstock supplier will supply fuel; for a paper mill, the feedstock supplier will supply wood pulp).

(6) Product offtaker.

The product offtaker(s) enters into a long-term agreement with the project company for the purchase of all of the energy, goods or other product produced at the project.

(7) Lender.

The lender in a project financing is a financial institution or group of financial institutions that provide a loan to the project company to develop and construct the project and that take a security interest in all of the project assets.

First Step in a Project Financing: The Feasibility Study

1) Generally

As one of the first steps in a project financing the sponsor or a technical consultant hired by the sponsor will prepare a feasibility study showing the financial viability of the project. Frequently, a prospective lender will hire its own independent consultants to prepare an independent feasibility study before the lender will commit to lend funds for the project.

2) Contents

The feasibility study should analyze every technical, financial and other aspect of the project, including the time-frame for completion of the various phases of the project development, and should clearly set forth all of the financial and other assumptions upon which the conclusions of the study are based. The more important items contained in a feasibility study are:

- Description of project.
- Description of sponsor(s).
- Sponsors' Agreements.
- Project site.
- Governmental arrangements.
- Source of funds.
- Feedstock Agreements.
- Offtake Agreements.
- Construction Contract.
- Management of project.
- Capital costs.
- Working capital.
- Equity sourcing.
- Debt sourcing.
- Financial projections.
- Market study.

The Project Company

1) Legal Form

Sponsors of projects adopt many different legal forms for the ownership of the project. The specific form adopted for any particular project will depend upon many factors, including:

- The amount of equity required for the project.
- The concern with management of the project.
- The availability of tax benefits associated with the project.

- The need to allocate tax benefits in a specific manner among the project company investors.

(1) Corporations.

This is the simplest form for ownership of a project. A special purpose corporation may be formed under the laws of the jurisdiction in which the project is located, or it may be formed in some other jurisdiction and be qualified to do business in the jurisdiction of the project.

(2) General partnerships.

The sponsors may form a general partnership. In most jurisdictions, a partnership is recognized as a separate legal entity and can own, operate and enter into financing arrangements for a project in its own name. A partnership is not a separate taxable entity, and although a partnership is required to file tax returns for reporting purposes, items of income, gain, losses, deductions and credits are allocated among the partners, which include their allocated share in computing their own individual taxes. Consequently, a partnership frequently will be used when the tax benefits associated with the project are significant. Because the general partners of a partnership are severally liable for all of the debts and liabilities of the partnership, a sponsor frequently will form a wholly owned, single-purpose subsidiary to act as its general partner in a partnership.

(3) Limited partnerships.

A limited partnership has similar characteristics to a general partnership except that the limited partners have limited control over the business of the partnership and are liable only for the debts and liabilities of the partnership to the extent of their capital contributions in the partnership. A limited partnership may be useful for a project financing when the sponsors do not have substantial capital and the project requires large amounts of outside equity.

(4) Limited Liability Companies.

They are a cross between a corporation and a limited partnership.

2) Project Company Agreements

Depending on the form of project company chosen for a particular project financing, the sponsors and other equity investors will enter into a stockholder agreement, general or limited partnership agreement or other agreement that sets forth the terms under which they will develop, own and operate the project. At a minimum, such an agreement should cover the following matters:

- Ownership interests.
- Capitalization and capital calls.
- Allocation of profits and losses.
- Accounting.
- Governing body and voting.
- Day-to-day management.
- Budgets.
- Transfer of ownership interests.

- Admission of new participants.
- Default.
- Termination and dissolution.

Principal Agreements in a Project Financing

1) Construction Contract

Some of the more important terms of the construction contract are:

(1) Project description.

The construction contract should set forth a detailed description of all of the work necessary to complete the project.

(2) Price.

Most project financing construction contracts are fixed-price contracts although some projects may be built on a cost-plus basis. If the contract is not fixed-price, additional debt or equity contributions may be necessary to complete the project, and the project agreements should clearly indicate the party or parties responsible for such contributions.

(3) Payment.

Payments typically are made on a "milestone" or "completed work" basis, with a retainage. This payment procedure provides an incentive for the contractor to keep on schedule and useful monitoring points for the owner and the lender.

(4) Completion date.

The construction completion date, together with any time extensions resulting from an event of force majeure, must be consistent with the parties' obligations under the other project documents. If construction is not finished by the completion date, the contractor typically is required to pay liquidated damages to cover debt service for each day until the project is completed. If construction is completed early, the contractor frequently is entitled to an early completion bonus.

(5) Performance guarantees.

The contractor typically will guarantee that the project will be able to meet certain performance standards when completed. Such standards must be set at levels to assure that the project will generate sufficient revenues for debt service, operating costs and a return on equity. Such guarantees are measured by performance tests conducted by the contractor at the end of construction. If the project does not meet the guaranteed levels of performance, the contractor typically is required to make liquidated damages payments to the sponsor. If project performance exceeds the guaranteed minimum levels, the contractor may be entitled to bonus payments.

2) Feedstock Supply Agreements

The project company will enter into one or more feedstock supply agreements for the supply of raw materials, energy or other resources over the life of the project. Frequently, feedstock supply agreements are structured on a "put-or-pay" basis, which means that the supplier must either supply the feedstock or pay the project company the difference in costs incurred in obtaining the feedstock from another source. The price provisions of feedstock supply agreements must assure that the cost of the feedstock is fixed within an acceptable range and consistent with the financial projections of the project.

3) Product Offtake Agreements

In a project financing, the product offtake agreements represent the source of revenue for the project. Such agreements must be structured in a manner to provide the project company with sufficient revenue to pay its project debt obligations and all other costs of operating, maintaining and owning the project. Frequently, offtake agreements are structured on a "take-or-pay" basis, which means that the offtaker is obligated to pay for product on a regular basis whether or not the offtaker actually takes the product unless the product is unavailable due to a default by the project company. Like feedstock supply arrangements, offtake agreements frequently are on a fixed or scheduled price basis during the term of the project debt financing.

4) Operations and Maintenance Agreement

The project company typically will enter into a long-term agreement for the day-to-day operation and maintenance of the project facilities with a company having the technical and financial expertise to operate the project in accordance with the cost and production specifications for the project. The operator may be an independent company, or it may be one of the sponsors. The operator typically will be paid a fixed compensation and may be entitled to bonus payments for extraordinary project performance and be required to pay liquidated damages for project performance below specified levels.

5) Management Agreement

6) Loan and Security Agreement

The borrower in a project financing typically is the project company formed by the sponsor(s) to own the project. The loan agreement will set forth the basic terms of the loan and will contain general provisions relating to maturity, interest rate and fees. The typical project financing loan agreement also will contain provisions such as these:

(1) Disbursement controls.

These frequently take the form of conditions precedent to each drawdown, requiring the borrower to present invoices, builders' certificates or other evidence as to the need for and use of the funds.

(2) Progress reports.

The lender may require periodic reports certified by an independent consultant on the status of construction progress.

(3) Covenants not to amend.

The borrower will covenant not to amend or waive any of its rights under the construction, feedstock, offtake, operations and maintenance, or other principal agreements without the consent of the lender.

(4) Completion covenants.

These require the borrower to complete the project in accordance with project plans and specifications and prohibit the borrower from materially altering the project plans without the consent of the lender.

(5) Dividend restrictions.

These covenants place restrictions on the payment of dividends or other distributions by the borrower until debt service obligations are satisfied.

(6) Debt and guarantee restrictions.

The borrower may be prohibited from incurring additional debt or from guaranteeing other obligations.

(7) Financial covenants.

Such covenants require the maintenance of working capital and liquidity ratios, debt service coverage ratios, debt service reserves and other financial ratios to protect the credit of the borrower.

(8) Subordination.

Lenders typically require other participants in the project to enter into a subordination agreement under which certain payments to such participants from the borrower under project agreements are restricted (either absolutely or partially) and made subordinate to the payment of debt service.

(9) Security.

The project loan typically will be secured by multiple forms of collateral, including:
- Mortgage on the project facilities and real property.
- Assignment of operating revenues.
- Pledge of bank deposits.
- Assignment of any letters of credit or performance or completion bonds relating to the project under which borrower is the beneficiary.
- Liens on the borrower's personal property.
- Assignment of insurance proceeds.
- Assignment of all project agreements.
- Pledge of stock in project company or assignment of partnership interests.
- Assignment of any patents, trademarks or other intellectual property owned by the borrower.

7) Site Lease Agreement

The project company typically enters into a long-term lease for the life of the project relating to the real property on which the project is to be located. Rental payments may be set in advance at a fixed rate or may be tied to project performance.

Insurance

The general categories of insurance available in connection with project financings are:

1) Standard Insurance

The following types of insurance typically are obtained for all project financings and cover

the most common types of losses that a project may suffer.
- Property Damage, including transportation, fire and extended casualty.
- Boiler and Machinery.
- Comprehensive General Liability.
- Worker's Compensation.
- Automobile Liability and Physical Damage.
- Umbrella or Excess Liability.

2) Optional Insurance

The following types of insurance often are obtained in connection with a project financing. Coverages such as these are more expensive than standard insurance and require more tailoring to meet the specific needs of the project.
- Business Interruption.
- Performance Bonds.
- Cost Overrun/Delayed Opening.
- Design Errors and Omissions.
- System Performance (Efficiency).
- Pollution Liability.

Questions

1. What is project financing?
2. Say the differences between project financing and traditional financing?
3. What are the principal advantages and disadvantages of project financing?
4. Say the main participants and the agreements in project financing?
5. What are main contents included in the feasibility study?
6. What legal forms are used by the project company?
7. Say the principal agreements in project financing?
8. What are the important items in the construction contract?
9. Interpret the feedstock supply agreements and the product offtake agreements.
10. What types of insurance typically are obtained for all project financings?

Vocabulary, Phrases and Expressions

project financing：项目融资
non-recourse：无追索权
traditional financing：传统融资
leverage：杠杆作用
limited recourse：有限追索权

off-balance-sheet treatment：资产负债表外处理
tax benefits：税收优惠
sponsor：发起方
Construction Contractor：建筑承包商
project operator：项目运营商
feedstock supplier：原材料供应商
product offtaker：产品承购商
lender：贷款人
feasibility study：可行性研究
general partnerships：普通合伙公司
file tax returns：报送纳税申报单位
wholly owned subsidiary：完全控股子公司
liquidated damages：违约赔偿金
financial projections：财务预算
put-or-pay：或供或付协议
owning cost：占有成本
take-or-pay contract：照付不议合同
on a regular basis：定期地
project performance：项目绩效
general provisions：一般条款
Financial Covenants：财务承诺
debt service coverage ratios：利息保障率
performance bonds：履约担保
completion bonds：完工担保
an assignment of：……提供的担保
assignment of interest：保险权益转让
intellectual property：知识产权
Comprehensive General Liability：公众责任险

参 考 译 文

第 10 单元　项 目 融 资

　　越来越多的大型建筑项目会涉及项目融资。承包商、工程师、设计师和设计建筑人员发现他们的工作、报酬和面临的风险正因这种融资方式而发生调整。以下的内容将帮助承包商、工程师和建筑设计师们理解项目融资的整个过程，以及他们在项目融资中的角色和所涉及的风险。

介绍

1) 定义

项目融资是某个特定项目发展和建设而涉及的融资方式,贷款者期望主要以项目本身产生的收入以及项目本身资产偿还贷款,而不是项目发起人的一般信用。

项目融资一般用于资金密集型产业中需要大量资金的项目,例如,建设发电站、运输管道、交通系统、采矿厂、工业设备和重工业。这些项目的发起人通常没有足够的信用进行传统融资,或是不愿意承担由传统融资引发的风险和债务责任。项目融资允许将该项目产生的风险在项目参与方之间以容许的水平进行分配。

2) 主要的优势和目的

(1) 无追索权。

典型的项目融资为发起方提供完全"无追索权"的贷款帮助项目建设。也就是说,当项目本身产生的收益不足以偿还贷款本金和利息时,项目发起方没有责任继续偿还贷款。为了极小化无追索贷款产生的风险,贷款人通常会要求间接信用支持,主要形式包括担保、保证、该项目发起方和其他参与方以及第三方之间的一些其他的契约。

(2) 极大化杠杆作用。

在项目融资中,项目发起方追求在很高的财务杠杆基础上为项目发展建设所需成本筹措资金。通常,这类成本资金中的80%~100%为债务资金。在无追索权的项目融资中,高的杠杆作用使得发起人的少量资金处于风险中,并且发起人无须削弱在该项目上的直接投资。

(3) 资产负债表外处理。

鉴于项目资金筹措结构,因为这样的债务对发起人是无追索权或有限追索权的,项目发起人可以不必将项目债务列于其资产负债表里。资产负债表外处理还有更多益处,即帮助项目发起人履行有关借款的契约和规定,而发起人是包含这些契约和规定的贷款协定和合同的签订方。

(4) 最大化税收优惠。

项目融资结构可以最大化税收优惠,保证所有的税收优惠被发起人利用,或者通过合伙契约、租约以及其他手段尽可能地将税收优惠转移给项目融资的其他方。

3) 劣势

项目融资极其复杂。与传统融资方式相比,项目融资需要更长的时间来组织、谈判和准备文件,并且项目融资的法律费用和相关成本相当高。因为在无追索的项目融资中贷款者所承担的风险比在传统融资方式中要大得多,所以资金成本也要高得多。

4) 项目融资参与者与协议

(1) 发起方/主办方。

项目融资发起方或主办方负责组织和调控各参与方,并且为项目公司或拥有该项目的其他实体提供直接投资。如果有多个发起方,则他们根据有限责任制,或是一个合伙制,或是其他形式的协议,组建一个"项目公司"拥有这个项目,并且根据项目设立各自的权利和责任。

(2) 其他权益投资者。

除发起方外,项目公司经常会有其他的权益投资者,其中可能包括一个或多个该项目的参与方。

(3) 建筑承包商。

建筑承包商与项目公司签订该项目设计、制造和施工合同。

(4) 运营商。

运营商与项目公司签订一份对项目进行日常运营与维护的长期的合同。

(5) 原材料供应商。

原材料供应商与项目公司签订一份长期的为该项目提供原材料(即能源、原材料或其他资源)的合同(例如，为发电厂提供燃料，为造纸厂提供木质纸浆)。

(6) 产品承购商。

产品承购商与项目公司签订一份长期的产品购买合同，用于购买项目公司生产的能源、货物或其他产品。

(7) 贷款方。

项目融资贷款方由一个金融机构或一组金融机构组成，为项目发展建设提供资金，并且拥有所有项目资产的担保物权。

项目融资第一步：可行性研究

1) 一般性

作为项目融资第一步，发起人或由发起人雇用的技术顾问要准备一份可行性研究报告，来陈述该项目的经济生存能力。

2) 内容

可行性报告应该研究该项目的全部技术、财务和其他问题，包括项目不同发展阶段的完工期限，还应该清晰地阐述作为研究报告基础的财务方面和其他方面的所有假设。一份可行性研究报告中包括的比较重要的内容有：

- 项目说明。
- 发起人说明。
- 发起人协议。
- 项目地址。
- 政府协议。
- 资金来源。
- 原材料供应协议。
- 承购协议。
- 建筑承包合同。
- 项目经营管理。
- 资金成本。
- 运营资金。
- 权益资金来源。
- 债务来源。
- 财务计划。
- 市场研究。

项目公司

1) 法律形式

项目发起方采用不同的法律形式拥有该项目。特殊的项目会采取特殊的法律形式,这依赖于以下因素:

- 项目所需的资产总量。
- 对项目管理的关注程度。
- 与项目相关的税收优惠的可用性。
- 在项目投资者之间明确地分配税收优惠的必要性。

(1) 法人公司。

这是一种最简单的项目所有权方式。根据项目所在地法律的管辖权建立具有特殊目的的项目公司,或是根据一些其他管辖权组建。项目公司有权在自己权限内营业。

(2) 普通合伙公司。

发起方可以组建一个普通合伙公司。合伙企业是公认的独立法人实体,它可以在最大权限范围内拥有、运营项目公司,并且可以以自己的名义为项目签订融资协议。合伙企业不是单独的纳税实体,尽管出于上报的目的,合伙企业也被要求报送纳税申报单,但是收入、利润、亏损、扣除和银行存款要在各方之间分配,然后各自计算税款,还要考虑各自分得的股份。因此,当与项目有关的税收优惠可观时,普通合伙公司的形式会被采用。因为合伙企业中负无限责任的合伙人分别对企业的全部债务负责,发起方通常会组建一个目的单一的、完全控股的子公司充当合伙公司的合伙人。

(3) 有限合伙公司。

有限合伙公司与普通合伙公司的基本特征相同,但是有限责任合伙人对公司事务具有有限控制权,并且只对他们为公司出资范围内的债务负责任。当发起人没有足够的资金,而项目需要大量的外部投资时,有限合伙公司的形式是有用的。

(4) 有限责任公司。

是结合合伙公司和法人公司的法律特征的法人团体。

2) 项目公司协议

根据为特定的项目融资选定的公司形式,发起方和其他权益投资者将会签订股东协议,普通合伙或有限合伙协议,或是其他协议,协议中阐明他们发展、拥有和运营该项目公司所根据的条款。协议中至少要包括以下事项:

- 所有者权益。
- 资本总额与资本需求。
- 利润与亏损的分配方案。
- 清算账目。
- 主管团体与选举机制。
- 日常管理。
- 项目预算。
- 所有权转让权益。

- 新参与者进入。
- 违约责任。
- 解除与终止规定。

项目融资中的主要协议

1) 建筑承包合同

建筑承包合同中的一些重要的条款包括：

(1) 项目描述。

建筑承包合同中应详细阐明完成项目所需的各项工作。

(2) 合同价格。

尽管一些项目使用成本加费用的合同价格，但大多数项目融资的建筑承包合同为固定价合同。如果不是固定价合同，可能需要投入额外的债务资本或权益资本来完成项目，项目协议中应该明确指出哪一方或哪些人对这些额外的投入负责。

(3) 支付。

支付通常以"工程转折点"或"已完工部分"为基础，留有部分工程保留款。这种支付方式可以激励承包商按进度施工，并且为业主和贷款方提供了有用的监测点。

(4) 完工日期。

建筑工程完工日期，以及由于不可抗力造成的时间延误，必须根据其他的项目文件与各方的责任联系在一起。如果在规定完工期限内没有完工，承包商需要缴纳规定的违约偿金，用以支付延误期内每天的债务费用，直到项目完工。如果提前完工，承包商有权获得提前完工的额外收入。

(5) 履约保证。

通常，承包商应该保证项目完工后达到一定的性能标准。这些标准必须保证项目可以产生足够的收入，用于贷款的还本付息，支付运营费用和权益资金报酬。

2) 原材料供应协议

在项目生命周期内，项目公司要签订一份或多份原材料供应协议，为项目提供原料、能源或其他资源。经常地，原材料供应协议是"或供或付"合同，即供应商或是提前供应原材料，或是支付因项目公司从其他来源购入原材料引起的成本差价。这种原材料供应合同中的价格条款可以将原材料成本控制在可接受范围内，并且符合项目财务预算。

3) 产品承购协议

在项目融资中，产品承购协议代表了项目收入的来源。签定这类协议必须能够为项目公司提供足够的收入，用以支付项目贷款债务和所有其他的运营、维护和占有费用。通常，产品承购协议是一种"照付不议"合同，即承购商不论是否取走了产品，都有责任定期地支付产品货款，除非因为项目公司违约而不能获得产品。如同原材料供应协议，在项目债务融资期间，产品承购协议通常建立在固定价格或预定价格基础上。

4) 运营维护协议

为了工程设施的日常运转与维护，项目公司通常会与一家具有技术和财务专长，并且能够根据项目成本和生产技术条件运营项目的公司签订一份长期协议。运营商可以是一个独立的公司，或是项目发起方之一。当项目绩效显著时，运营商通常会得到固定报酬，并且可能获得奖金。当项目绩效低于规定水平时，要求运营商支付规定的违约偿金。

5) 经营协议

6) 贷款和担保协议

借款人通常是拥有该项目公司的发起方。贷款协议应阐明基本条款，包括期限、利率和费用等一般条款。典型的贷款协议还应包括以下条款。

(1) 支出控制。

通常对每一笔资金采用先决条件的形式，需要借款方提供需求和使用资金的清单、建筑者证明或其他证据。

(2) 进度报告。

贷款方需要由独立顾问签订的、关于工程进展情况的定期报告。

(3) 不修改协议保证。

在没有经过贷款人同意的情况下，借款人保证不会修改建筑承包协议、原材料供应协议、运营与维护协议或其他主要协议，保证不会放弃自己的权利。

(4) 完工保证。

要求借款人按项目计划和规定完成项目，禁止借款人在没有取得贷款人同意的情况下对项目计划进行重大调整。

(5) 股息限制。

这类条款限制借款人在没有为贷款还本付息之前支付股息或进行其他分配。

(6) 债务和担保限制。

禁止借款人承受另外的债务，禁止借款人为其他债务做担保。

(7) 财务承诺。

这类承诺要求项目公司保持一定的营运资金、流动比率、利息保障率、偿债储备资金和其他的财务比率，以便保障借款人信用。

(8) 从属协议。

贷款人通常要求项目的其他参与者签订一份从属协议。根据这份从属协议，借款人依据项目合同应支付给这些参与方的确定的款项是受到限制的(或是完全限制，或是部分限制)，并且这些款项的支付应在项目公司还本付息之后。

(9) 担保。

项目公司为贷款提供多种抵押物担保，包括：
- 以项目设备和不动产做抵押。
- 营业收入提供的担保。
- 以银行存款做抵押。
- 与项目相关并且受益人为借款人的信用证、履约保函、完工保证提供的担保。
- 对借款人个人资产的留置权。
- 保险收益提供的担保。
- 以所有项目协议做担保。
- 以项目公司股票做抵押或转让参与方的保险权益。
- 以借款人拥有的专利权、商标或其他知识产权做担保。

7) 工地租用协议

通常，在项目生命周期内，项目公司要签订一份长期不动产租用协议，作为项目所在地。租金或是以固定比率提前支付，或是根据项目执行情况支付。

保险

项目融资涉及的有用的保险有以下类型。

1) 标准保险类

以下是在项目融资中被采用的典型的保险种类,并且覆盖了大部分项目公司可能普遍承受的损失。

- 财产损失保险,包括运输、火灾或其他范围内的伤亡。
- 锅炉和机械保险。
- 公共责任险。
- 劳工保险。
- 机动车责任险和车体损失险。
- 伞护式或超额责任险。

2) 可选择保险类

下面是项目融资中经常采用的保险种类。这些种类保险的费用比标准种类的保险费用要昂贵,并且需要做更多调整来适应项目的特殊需求。

- 营业中断保险。
- 履约保函。
- 成本超支保险/延期开工保险。
- 设计误差和疏忽保险。
- 系统执行效率保险。
- 污染责任保险。

Unit 11　The Critical Path Method

The most widely used scheduling technique is the critical path method (CPM) for scheduling, often referred to as critical path scheduling. This method calculates the minimum completion time for a project along with the possible start and finish times for the project activities. Indeed, many texts and managers regard critical path scheduling as the only usable and practical scheduling procedure. Computer programs and algorithms for critical path scheduling are widely available and can efficiently handle projects with thousands of activities.

The critical path itself represents the set or sequence of predecessor/successor activities which will take the longest time to complete. The duration of the critical path is the sum of the activities' durations along the path. Thus, the critical path can be defined as the longest possible path through the "network" of project activities, as described in Unit 9. The duration of the critical path represents the minimum time required to complete a project. Any delays along the critical path would imply that additional time would be required to complete the project.

There may be more than one critical path among all the project activities, so completion of the entire project could be delayed by delaying activities along any one of the critical paths. For example, a project consisting of two activities performed in parallel that each requires three days would have each activity critical for a completion in three days.

Formally, critical path scheduling assumes that a project has been divided into activities of fixed duration and well defined predecessor relationships. A predecessor relationship implies that one activity must come before another in the schedule. No resource constraints other than those implied by precedence relationships are recognized in the simplest form of critical path scheduling.

To use critical path scheduling in practice, construction planners often represent a resource constraint by a precedence relation. A constraint is simply a restriction on the options available to a manager, and a resource constraint is a constraint deriving from the limited availability of some resource of equipment, material, space or labor. For example, one of two activities requiring the same piece of equipment might be arbitrarily assumed to precede the other activity. This artificial precedence constraint insures that the two activities requiring the same resource will not be scheduled at the same time. Also, most critical path scheduling algorithms impose restrictions on the generality of the activity relationships or network geometries which are used.

In essence, these restrictions imply that the construction plan can be represented by a network plan in which activities appear as nodes in a network, and no two nodes can have the same number or designation. Two nodes are introduced to represent the start and completion of the project itself.

The actual computer representation of the project schedule generally consists of a list of activities along with their associated durations, required resources and predecessor activities. Graphical network representations rather than a list are helpful for visualization of the plan and to insure that mathematical requirements are met. The actual input of the data to a computer program may be accomplished by filling in blanks on a screen menu, reading an existing datafile, or typing data directly to the program with identifiers for the type of information being provided.

With an activity-on-branch network, dummy activities may be introduced for the purposes of providing unique activity designations and maintaining the correct sequence of activities. A dummy activity is assumed to have no time duration and can be graphically represented by a dashed line in a network. Several cases in which dummy activities are useful are illustrated in Figure 11.1. In Figure 11.1(a), the elimination of activity C would mean that both activities B and D would be identified as being between nodes 1 and 3. However, if a dummy activity X is introduced, as shown in part (b) of the figure, the unique designations for activity B (node 1 to 2) and D (node 1 to 3) will be preserved. Furthermore, if the problem in part (a) is changed so that activity E cannot start until both C and D are completed but that F can start after D alone is completed, the order in the new sequence can be indicated by the addition of a dummy activity Y, as shown in part (c). In general, dummy activities may be necessary to meet the requirements of specific computer scheduling algorithms, but it is important to limit the number of such dummy link insertions to the extent possible.

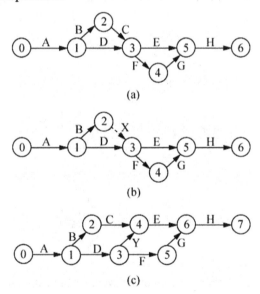

Figure 11.1 Dummy Activities in a Project Network

Many computer scheduling systems support only one network representation, either activity-on-branch or acitivity-on-node. A good project manager is familiar with either representation.

Example 11.1 Formulating a network diagram.

Suppose that we wish to form an activity network for a seven-activity network with the following precedences:

Activity	Predecessors
A	...
B	...
C	A, B
D	C
E	C
F	D
G	D, E

Forming an activity-on-branch network for this set of activities might begin with drawing activities A, B and C as shown in Figure 11.2(a). At this point, we note that two activities (A and B) lie between the same two event nodes; for clarity, we insert a dummy activity X and continue to place other activities as in Figure 11.2(b). Placing activity G in the figure presents a problem, however, since we wish both activity D and activity E to be predecessors. Inserting an additional dummy activity Y along with activity G completes the activity network, as shown in Figure 11.2(c). A comparable activity-on-node representation is shown in Figure 11.3, including project start and finish nodes. Note that dummy activities are not required for expressing precedence relationships in activity-on-node networks.

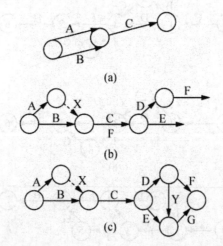

Figure 11.2 An Activity-on-Branch Network for Critical Path Scheduling

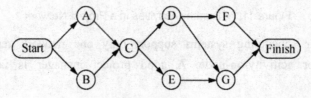

Figure 11.3 An Activity-on-Node Network for Critical Path Scheduling

Calculations for Critical Path Scheduling

With the background provided by the previous sections, we can formulate the critical path scheduling mathematically. We shall present an algorithm or set of instructions for critical path scheduling assuming an activity-on-branch project network. We also assume that all precedences are of a finish-to-start nature, so that a succeeding activity cannot start until the completion of a preceding activity. In a later section, we present a comparable algorithm for activity-on-node representations with multiple precedence types.

Suppose that our project network has $n+1$ nodes, the initial event being 0 and the last event being n. Let the time at which node events occur be $X_1, X_2, \cdots, X_n$, respectively. The start of the project at X_0 will be defined as time 0. Nodal event times must be consistent with activity durations, so that an activity's successor node event time must be larger than an activity's predecessor node event time plus its duration. For an activity defined as starting from event i and ending at event j, this relationship can be expressed as the inequality constraint, $X_j > X_i + D_{ij}$ where D_{ij} is the duration of activity (i,j). This same expression can be written for every activity and must hold true in any feasible schedule. Mathematically, then, the critical path scheduling problem is to minimize the time of project completion (X_n) subject to the constraints that each node completion event cannot occur until each of the predecessor activities have been completed:

Minimize

$$z = X_n \tag{11-1}$$

subject to

$$X_0 = 0$$
$$X_j - X_i - D_{ij} \geq 0 \text{ [for each activity}(i,j)]$$

This is a linear programming problem since the objective value to be minimized and each of the constraints is a linear equation.

Rather than solving the critical path scheduling problem with a linear programming algorithm (such as the Simplex method), more efficient techniques are available that take advantage of the network structure of the problem. These solution methods are very efficient with respect to the required computations, so that very large networks can be treated even with personal computers. These methods also give some very useful information about possible activity schedules. The programs can compute the earliest and latest possible starting times for each activity which are consistent with completing the project in the shortest possible time. This calculation is of particular interest for activities which are not on the critical path (or paths), since these activities might be slightly delayed or re-scheduled over time as a manager desires without delaying the entire project.

An efficient solution process for critical path scheduling based upon node labeling is shown in Table 11-1. Three algorithms appear in the table. The "event numbering algorithm" numbers the nodes (or events) of the project such that the beginning event has a lower number than the ending event for each activity. Technically, this algorithm accomplishes a "topological sort" of the activities. The project start node is given number 0. As long as the project activities fulfill the conditions for an activity-on-branch network, this type of numbering system is always possible. Some software packages for critical path scheduling do not have this numbering algorithm programmed, so that the construction project planners must insure that appropriate numbering is done.

Table 11-1 Critical Path Scheduling Algorithms (Activity-on-Branch Representation)

Event Numbering Algorithm

Step 1: Give the starting event number 0.
Step 2: Give the next number to any unnumbered event whose predecessor events are each already numbered.
Repeat Step 2 until all events are numbered.

Earliest Event Time Algorithm

Step 1: Let E(0) = 0.
Step 2: For $j = 1,2,3,\cdots,n$ (where n is the last event), let
$$E(j) = \text{maximum } \{E(i) + D_{ij}\}$$
where the maximum is computed over all activities (i,j) that have j as the ending event.

Latest Event Time Algorithm

Step 1: Let L(n) equal the required completion time of the project.
   Note: L(n) must equal or exceed E(n).
Step 2: For $i = n-1, n-2, \cdots, 0$, let
$$L(i) = \text{minimum } \{L(j) - D_{ij}\}$$
where the minimum is computed over all activities (i,j) that have i as the starting event.

The earliest event time algorithm computes the earliest possible time, E(i), at which each event, i, in the network can occur. Earliest event times are computed as the maximum of the earliest start times plus activity durations for each of the activities immediately preceding an event. The earliest start time for each activity (i,j) is equal to the earliest possible time for the preceding event E(i):

$$ES(I,j) = E(i) \qquad (11\text{-}2)$$

The earliest finish time of each activity (i,j) can be calculated by:

$$EF(i,j) = E(i) + D_{ij} \qquad (11\text{-}3)$$

Activities are identified in this algorithm by the predecessor node (or event) i and the successor node j. The algorithm simply requires that each event in the network should be examined in turn beginning with the project start (node 0).

The "latest event time algorithm" computes the latest possible time, L(j), at which each event j in the network can occur, given the desired completion time of the project, L(n) for the last event n. Usually, the desired completion time will be equal to the earliest possible completion time, so that E(n) = L(n) for the final node n. The procedure for finding the latest event time is analogous to that for the earliest event time except that the procedure begins with the final event and works backwards through the project activities. Thus, the earliest event time algorithm is often called a "forward pass" through the network, whereas the latest event time algorithm is the the "backward pass" through the network. The latest finish time consistent with completion of the

project in the desired time frame of L(n) for each activity (i,j) is equal to the latest possible time L(j) for the succeeding event:
$$LF(i,j)=L(j) \qquad (11\text{-}4)$$
The latest start time of each activity (i,j) can be calculated by:
$$LS(i,j)=L(j)- D_{ij} \qquad (11\text{-}5)$$
The earliest start and latest finish times for each event are useful pieces of information in developing a project schedule. Events which have equal earliest and latest times, $E(i) = L(i)$, lie on the critical path or paths. An activity (i,j) is a critical activity if it satisfies all of the following conditions:
$$E(i)=L(i) \qquad (11\text{-}6)$$
$$E(j)=L(j) \qquad (11\text{-}7)$$
$$E(j)+ D_{ij} = L(j) \qquad (11\text{-}8)$$
Hence, activities between critical events are also on a critical path as long as the activity's earliest start time equals its latest start time, $ES(i,j) = LS(i,j)$. To avoid delaying the project, all the activities on a critical path should begin as soon as possible, so each critical activity (i,j) must be scheduled to begin at the earliest possible start time, $E(i)$.

Example 11.2 Critical path scheduling calculations.

Consider the network shown in Figure 11.4 in which the project start is given number 0. Then, the only event that has each predecessor numbered is the successor to activity A, so it receives number 1. After this, the only event that has each predecessor numbered is the successor to the two activities B and C, so it receives number 2. The other event numbers resulting from the algorithm are also shown in the figure. For this simple project network, each stage in the numbering process found only one possible event to number at any time. With more than one feasible event to number, the choice of which to number next is arbitrary. For example, if activity C did not exist in the project for Figure 11.4, the successor event for activity A or for activity B could have been numbered 1.

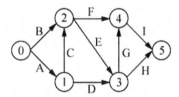

Figure 11.4 A Nine-Activity Project Network

Once the node numbers are established, a good aid for manual scheduling is to draw a small rectangle near each node with two possible entries. The left hand side would contain the earliest time the event could occur, whereas the right hand side would contain the latest time the event could occur without delaying the entire project. Figure 11.5 illustrates a typical box.

$$\boxed{E(i) \mid L(i)}$$

Figure 11.5 E(i) and L(i) Display for Hand Calculation of Critical Path for Activity-on-Branch Representation

For the network in Figure 11.4 with activity durations in Table 11-2, the earliest event time calculations proceed as follows:

Table 11-2 Precedence Relations and Durations for a Nine-Activity Project Example

Activity	Description	Predecessors	Duration
A	Site clearing	—	4
B	Removal of trees	—	3
C	General excavation	A	8
D	Grading general area	A	7
E	Excavation for trenches	B, C	9
F	Placing formwork and reinforcement for concrete	B, C	12
G	Installing sewer lines	D, E	2
H	Installing other utilities	D, E	5
I	Pouring concrete	F, G	6

Step 1 → $E(0) = 0$

Step 2

$j = 1$ → $E(1) = \text{Max}\{E(0) + D_{01}\} = \text{Max}\{0 + 4\} = 4$

$j = 2$ → $E(2) = \text{Max}\{E(0) + D_{02}; E(1) + D_{12}\} = \text{Max}\{0 + 3; 4 + 8\} = 12$

$j = 3$ → $E(3) = \text{Max}\{E(1) + D_{13}; E(2) + D_{23}\} = \text{Max}\{4 + 7; 12 + 9\} = 21$

$j = 4$ → $E(4) = \text{Max}\{E(2) + D_{24}; E(3) + D_{34}\} = \text{Max}\{12 + 12; 21 + 2\} = 24$

$j = 5$ → $E(5) = \text{Max}\{E(3) + D_{35}; E(4) + D_{45}\} = \text{Max}\{21 + 5; 24 + 6\} = 30$

Thus, the minimum time required to complete the project is 30 since $E(5) = 30$. In this case, each event had at most two predecessors.

For the "backward pass", the latest event time calculations are:

Step 1 → $L(5) = E(5) = 30$

Step 2

$j = 4$ → $L(4) = \text{Min}\{L(5) - D_{45}\} = \text{Min}\{30 - 6\} = 24$

$j = 3$ → $L(3) = \text{Min}\{L(5) - D_{35}; L(4) - D_{34}\} = \text{Min}\{30 - 5; 24 - 2\} = 22$

$j = 2$ → $L(2) = \text{Min}\{L(4) - D_{24}; L(3) - D_{23}\} = \text{Min}\{24 - 12; 22 - 9\} = 12$

$j = 1$ → $L(1) = \text{Min}\{L(3) - D_{13}; L(2) - D_{12}\} = \text{Min}\{22 - 7; 12 - 8\} = 4$

$j = 0$ → $L(0) = \text{Min}\{L(2) - D_{02}; L(1) - D_{01}\} = \text{Min}\{12 - 3; 4 - 4\} = 0$

In this example, $E(0) = L(0)$, $E(1) = L(1)$, $E(2) = L(2)$, $E(4) = L(4)$, and $E(5) = L(5)$. As a result, all nodes but node 3 are in the critical path. Activities on the critical path include A (0,1), C (1,2), F (2,4) and I (4,5) as shown in Table 11-3.

Table 11-3 Identification of Activities on the Critical Path for a Nine-Activity Project

Activity	Duration D_{ij}	Earliest start time $E(i)=ES(i,j)$	Latest finish time $L(j)=LF(i,j)$	Latest start time $LS(i,j)$
A (0,1)	4	0*	4*	0
B (0,2)	3	0	12	9
C (1,2)	8	4*	12*	4
D (1,3)	7	4	22	15
E (2,3)	9	12	22	13
F (2,4)	12	12*	24*	12
G (3,4)	2	21	24	22
H (3,5)	5	21	30	25
I (4,5)	6	24	30*	24

*Activity on a critical path since $E(i) + D_{ij} = L(j)$.

Questions

1. How to define the critical path?
2. What be assumed by critical path scheduling?
3. What is the simplest form of critical path scheduling?
4. What are the advantages of graphical network representation of the project schedule?
5. For what purpose to introduce dummy activities with an activity-on-branch network?
6. To tell the difference between an activity-on-branch network and an activity-on-node network.
7. How to calculate the earliest starting time and the latest starting time of an activity?
8. How to calculate the earliest finishing time and the latest finishing time of an activity?
9. How to identify the critical activities of the project schedule?
10. How to calculate the desired completion?

Vocabulary, Phrases and Expressions

the critical path method (CPM)：关键路径法
duration of the critical path：关键路径的持续时间
the longest possible path：最长可能路径
fixed duration：固定持续时间
precedence relationships：前后顺序关系
resource constraint：资源限制
precedence constraint：优先限制
a network plan：网络计划

nodes in a network：网络节点
predecessor activities：紧前工作
successor activities：紧后工作
graphical network：图解网络计划
an activity-on-branch network：有分支的网络计划
dummy activities：虚工作
an activity-on-branch network：双代号网络计划图
an activity-on-node network：单代号网络计划图
precedence of a finish-to-start nature：结束-开始型顺序
constraints：约束条件
a linear programming problem：线性规划问题
network structure：网络结构
the earliest starting time：最早开始时间
the latest starting time：最晚开始时间
the earliest finishing time：最早结束时间
the latest finishing time：最晚结束时间
event (or node)numbering algorithm：按节点编号算法
earliest event time algorithm：节点最早时间算法
latest event time algorithm：节点最晚时间算法
forward pass：顺向过程
backward pass：逆向过程
critical activities：关键工序

参 考 译 文

第 11 单元　关键路径法

　　关键路径法是使用最广的计划编制方法，也被称为关键路径计划。这种方法能推算出项目的最短完成时间和项目各项活动的可能开始和结束时间。确实，很多教材和管理人员都把关键路径法看作最实用的计划编制程序。关键路径法的计算机程序和运算法则已经被广泛应用，可以有效地处理包含数千活动的项目。

　　关键路径本身代表了一系列前继后续的活动，这些活动将会持续最长的时间，关键路径的持续时间等于关键线路上全部活动持续时间的总和。因此，关键路径就像在第 9 单元描述的那样，被定义为项目活动网络中最长的可能路径。关键路径的时间就代表了完成项目所需的最短时间。关键路径上的任何活动推迟都将导致项目完成时间的增加。

　　在全部的项目活动中，可能会有多条关键路径。所以，整个工程的完成时间会因任何一条关键路径上活动的推迟而延后。例如，一个项目由两个并列进行的活动组成，每个活动都需 3 天完成，那么就要求每个关键工作在 3 天内完成。

　　关键路径法在形式上假设项目已被分成具有固定持续时间和明确前后顺序关系的活

动。前后顺序关系在计划中意味着一个活动必须在另一个活动前开始。除了这种在时间上存在前后顺序的关系外，没有资源限制的关键路径计划被认为是最简单的形式。

在实际运用关键路径法时，工程计划者经常通过优先关系描述资源的限制。限制是对管理人员可能选择的一种约束，资源的限制来源于有限的可用资源，如设备、材料、空间或劳动力。例如，如果两个活动需要同样的设备，就可能假设任意一个活动优先于另一个。人为划分的优先限制确保两个需要同一资源的活动不被安排在同一时间。大部分关键路径的运算方法也利用了活动关系或所使用的网络几何学原则加以限制。

这些限制条件表明，工程计划能够用网络计划法表示。在网络计划中，用两个节点表示活动，节点要进行编号，两个节点不能用相同的号码，引入的两个节点表示一项工作的起始和终止。

工程进度计划的现行计算机表示法一般由一张表示工作以及这些工作相应的持续时间、所需的资源和紧前工作等内容的一览表组成。图解网络表示法不需要一览表，但提高了计划的可视性，也确保了满足数学条件。目前，计算机程序的数据输入可通过在屏幕菜单上填表完成，或读入现有数据文件，或将所需提供的信息以标识符形式直接向程序输入。

在一个有分支的网络图中，虚工作被用来提供特殊的工作安排和保持工作的正确顺序。一项虚工作的持续时间被假设为零，并且在作图时用网络中的一条虚线描述。使用虚工作的几种情况如图 11.1 所示。在图 11.1(a)中，如果去掉活动 C 就意味着活动 B 和 D 将位于节点 1 和 3 之间。但是，如果加入一个虚工作 X，如图 11.1(b)所示，特殊的工作 B(节点 1 到 2)和(节点 1 到 3)的特殊安排就能被保存下来。如果图 11.1(a)中的问题改变，活动 C 和 D 不完成，活动 E 便不能开始；只有活动 D 单独完成之后，F 才能开始。这种新顺序的安排可以通过增加虚工作 Y 来表示，如图 11.1(c)所示。通常必须用虚工作来满足具体的计算机进度算法的要求，但是在一定程度上尽可能限制插入虚工作的数量也同样是非常重要的。

网络图分为双代号网络图和单代号网络图两种，许多计算机进度程序只支持其中的一种。一个成功的项目经理对于这两种表示方法都要熟悉。

例 11.1 网络图的表述。

假设要根据下列逻辑关系绘制一个含有 7 项工作的双代号网络图：

工作代号	紧前活动
A	…
B	…
C	A，B
D	C
E	C
F	D
G	D，E

要对上面的一系列工作绘制双代号网络图，首先从工作 A、B、C 开始，如图 11.2(a)所示。A 和 B 两个工作位于两个相同的节点之间，为此需要增加一个虚拟工作 X，然后再依次绘制其余工作，如图 11.2(b)所示。但这时会出现一个问题：如何安排 G 工作？因为要使它满足前导工作为 D 和 E 的要求。解决这个问题就需要在 G 工作之前插入一个虚工作 Y，

如图 11.2(c)所示。

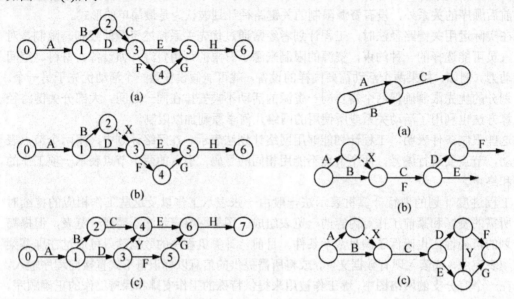

图 11.1 工程网络图中的虚拟工作　　图 11.2 双代号网络图关键路径表示法

同样地，可以绘制包括开始与结束节点的单代号网络图，如图 11.3 所示。注意在单代号网络图中并不需要添加虚工作来表示工作之间的逻辑关系。

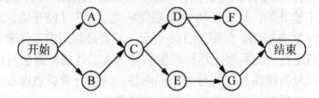

图 11.3 单代号网络图关键路径表示法

关键路径进度计划的计算

根据前面几部分所提供的背景，可以用数学公式描述关键路径进度计划。对一个假定项目的双代号网络图，应该制定一套关键路径进度计划的运算规则或说明。同时，还假定所有的工作顺序关系都是结束—开始型，所以只有当前导工作结束后，后续工作才能开始。下面将对具有多种前导工作类型的单代号网络图表示法也提出一套相应的运算规则。

下面介绍一套类似的针对有多种事件联系关系的双代号网络图的计算规则系统。

假设项目网络图中有 $n+1$ 个节点，起始节点为 0 而终止节点为 n。令各个节点的时间分别为 $X_1, X_2, \cdots, X_n$。项目的开始节点为 X_0 定义为时间的 0 点，节点时间必须与工作的持续时间相符合，故一项工作的终止节点时间必须大于其起始时间与该工作持续时间之和。对于一个开始节点为 i 而终止节点为 j 的活动，这种关系可以通过一个不等式约束条件表示出来：$X_j \geq X_i + D_{ij}$。这里，D_{ij} 为工作 (i,j) 的持续时间。每个工作都能够写出同样的表达式，并在任何可行的进度计划中都必须遵守这种约束。那么，从数学上看，关键路径进度计划要解决的问题就是在遵守每个节点事件只有在其前导工作完成后才能发生的约束条件下，使项目的完成时间 X_n 最小。

最小化，即

$$z = X_n \tag{11-1}$$

约束条件为

$$X_0 = 0$$
$$X_j - X_i - D_{ij} \geq 0 \text{ [对任何工作}(i,j)]$$

这是一个线性规划问题，因为目标值要求最小化，而每个约束条件都是线性方程。

除了运用线性规划算法(如单纯型法)解决关键路径进度外，还可以利用网络结构技术更有效地解决该问题。这种解法对于所需的计算很有效，因而即使是很大型的网络也可以用个人计算机进行运算，同时也对可行的工作进度计划提供了一些非常有用的信息。在保证项目在最短的可能时间内完成的条件下，计算每项工作的最早开始和最迟开始时间，这对于非关键路线上的工作尤为重要，因为这些工作可以按项目管理者的要求进行一定的推迟或随时调整，却不会影响整个项目的工期。

表 11-1 给出了以节点为标识求关键路径进度计划的解题过程。在表 11-1 中有 3 种运算法则。按节点编号法为项目的每个节点(或事件)进行编号，以保证每项工作开始节点的编号总是小于终止节点的编号。从技术上说，这个规则实现了对工作的"拓扑排序"。项目的起始节点编号为 0。只要项目的工作符合双代号网络图的条件，这种编号系统就可以实施。一些针对关键路径进度计划的软件没有这样的程序自动编号规则，那么工程项目的计划人员就必须进行合理的编号。

表 11-1 关键路径进度计划计算规则(以双代号网络图为例)

节点编号规则
第一步：令起始节点编号为 0
第二步：将下一个号码赋予任何一个前一节点已编号而自身未编号的节点。重复第二步直到所有的节点都完成编号
节点最早时间计算规则
第一步：令 $E(0) = 0$.
第二步：对 $j = 1,2,3,\cdots,n$ (n 为最后一个节点)，令 $$E(j) = \max\{E(i) + D_{ij}\},$$ 即对所有以 j 为终止节点的工作进行计算后，取大值
节点最迟时间计算规则
第一步：令 $L(n)$ 等于项目要求的工期 注意：$L(n)$ 必须等于或大于 $E(n)$
第二步：对 $i = n-1, n-2, \cdots, 0$，令 $$L(i) = \min\{L(j) - D_{ij}\}$$ 即对所有以 i 为开始节点的工作进行计算后，取最小值

节点最早时间计算规则用于计算网络图中每个节点事件发生的最早可能时间 $E(i)$。节点最早时间等于直接从前导事件引出的所有工作的最早开始时间与其持续时间之和的最大值。各项工作(i, j)的最早开始时间等于其起始节点的最早时间 $E(i)$，即

$$ES(i,j) = E(i) \tag{11-2}$$

每个工作(i, j)的最早结束时间可以按下面的公式计算：

$$EF(i,j) = E(i) + D_{ij} \tag{11-3}$$

在这一运算规则中，工作以开始节点 i 和终止节点 j 的编号标识，它只要求从项目起始节点(节点编号为0)开始依次计算网络图的每个节点的时间。

在给定完成项目要求的工期的情况下，L(n)作为节点 n 的最迟时间，节点最迟时间 L(j)是指网络图中的任何一个节点出现的最迟可能时间。通常要求工期等于可能的最早结束时间，这样对最后的节点 n 有 E(n)=L(n)。计算节点最迟时间的程序除了需要从最后一个节点开始起算和沿着项目工作从后面向前逆向进行之外，其他方面与计算最早节点时间的程序相同。因此，节点最早时间计算规则通常被称为网络图的顺向过程，而节点最迟时间计算规则则被称为网络图的逆向过程。工作最迟结束时间与完成该项目的要求工期 L(n)相对应，对每项工作(i, j)而言，其最迟结束时间就等于其终止节点的最迟时间。

$$LF(i,j) = L(j) \tag{11-4}$$

每项工作(i, j)的最迟开始时间可以按下面公式计算：

$$LS(i,j) = L(j) - D_{ij} \tag{11-5}$$

每个节点的最早时间和最迟时间是制定项目进度计划过程中非常有用的信息。那些最早时间和最迟时间相等的节点 E(i)=L(j)处于关键路线上。如果一项工作(i, j)满足全部下列条件，那么该工作为关键工作。

$$E(i) = L(i) \tag{11-6}$$
$$E(j) = L(j) \tag{11-7}$$
$$E(j) + D_{ij} = L(j) \tag{11-8}$$

因此，只要工作的最早开始时间等于其最迟开始时间 ES(i, j)=LS(i, j)，在关键节点之间的工作也处于关键路线上。为防止项目工期拖延，所有关键路线上的工作都必须尽早开始，所以每项关键工作(i, j)都应该安排在最早可能开始时间 E(i)启动。

例 11.2 关键路径进度计划的计算。

考虑图 11.4 中给出的网络图，其项目的起始点编号为0。之后，唯一的一个其全部紧前节点都被编号了的节点是 A 工作的终止节点，所以将它编号为 1。这之后，唯一的一个其全部前导节点都被编号了的节点是 B 和 C 两项工作共同的终止节点，所以将它编号为 2 号。其他节点的编号也按同样的规则得出，并标识于图上，在这张简单的网络图上，编号过程的每一个阶段都只能找到唯一的一个可选节点。如果有不止一个可选节点需要编号，那么任意选择哪一个都可以。举例来说，如果图 11.4 项目中的 C 工作不存在，A 工作或 B 工作的终止节点都可以被编为 1 号。

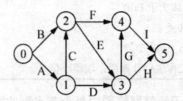

图 11.4 由 9 项工作组成的项目网络图

一旦节点编号确定以后，针对手工绘制进度计划的一项很好的辅助手段就是在每个节点旁边画上一个分成两个格子的小矩形框。左边格子里可以填入节点事件发生的最早时间，而右边的格子里可以填入在不推延整个项目工期的情况下，节点事件发生的最迟时间。图 11.5 是一个典型的矩形框。

$$\boxed{E(i) \mid L(i)}$$

图 11.5 双代号网络图关键路径法手工计算 E(i)和 L(i)图例

根据图 11.4 所示网络图和表 11-2 所示工作的持续时间，将节点最早时间计算如下：

表 11-2 由 9 项工作组成的项目实例中的工作关系与工作持续时间

工 作	描 述	前 导 工 作	持 续 时 间
A	现场清理	…	4
B	移走树木	…	3
C	场地平整	A	8
D	划分区域坡地	A	7
E	开挖基础地槽	B,C	9
F	混凝土支模与钢筋	B,C	12
G	安排排水管线	D,E	2
H	安排其他设备	D,E	5
I	浇筑混凝土	F,G	6

Step 1 → E(0) = 0

Step 2

j = 1 → E(1) = Max{E(0) + D_{01}} = Max{ 0 + 4 } = 4

j = 2 → E(2) = Max{E(0) + D_{02}; E(1) + D_{12}} = Max{0 + 3; 4 + 8} = 12

j = 3 → E(3) = Max{E(1) + D_{13}; E(2) + D_{23}} = Max{4 + 7; 12 + 9} = 21

j = 4 → E(4) = Max{E(2) + D_{24}; E(3) + D_{34}} = Max{12 + 12; 21 + 2} = 24

j = 5 → E(5) = Max{E(3) + D_{35}; E(4) + D_{45}} = Max{21 + 5; 24 + 6} = 30

所以，因为 E(5)=30，完成项目所需的最短时间为 30。在这个例子里，每个节点最多有两个前导节点。

而对于"逆向过程"，节点最迟时间计算如下：

Step 1 → L(5) = E(5) = 30

Step 2

j = 4 → L(4) = Min {L(5) − D_{45}} = Min {30 − 6} = 24

j = 3 → L(3) = Min {L(5) − D_{35}; L(4) − D_{34}} = Min {30 −5; 24 − 2} = 22

j = 2 → L(2) = Min {L(4) − D_{24}; L(3) − D_{23}} = Min {24 − 12; 22 − 9} = 12

j = 1 → L(1) = Min {L(3) − D_{13}; L(2) − D_{12}} = Min {22 − 7; 12 − 8} = 4

j = 0 → L(0) = Min {L(2) − D_{02}; L(1) − D_{01}} = Min {12 − 3; 4 − 4} = 0

在这个例子中，E(0) = L(0), E(1) = L(1), E(2) = L(2), E(4) = L(4), E(5) = L(5)。所以，除了节点 3，所有的节点都在关键路线上。关键路线上的工作包括 A (0,1)、C (1,2)、F (2,4) 和 I (4,5)，见表 11-3。

表 11-3 由 9 个工作组成的项目的关键路线上的工作

工作	持续时间 D_{ij}	最早开始时间 $E(i)=ES(i,j)$	最迟结束时间 $L(j)=LF(i,j)$	最迟开始时间 $LS(i,j)$
A (0,1)	4	0*	4*	0
B (0,2)	3	0	12	9
C (1,2)	8	4*	12*	4
D (1,3)	7	4	22	15
E (2,3)	9	12	22	13
F (2,4)	12	12*	24*	12
G (3,4)	2	21	24	22
H (3,5)	5	21	30	25
I (4,5)	6	24	30*	24

*在关键路径上的工作，因为 $E(i) + D_{ij} = L(j)$

Unit 12　Schedule Control(1)

Project Control Process

The project control process involves regularly gathering data on project performance, comparing actual performance to planned performance, and taking corrective actions if actual performance is behind planned performance. This process must occur regularly throughout the project.

Figure 12.1 illustrates the steps in the project control process. It starts with establishing a baseline plan that shows how the project scope (tasks) will be accomplished on time (schedule) and within budget (resources, costs). Once this baseline plan is agreed upon by the customer and the contractor or project team, the project can start.

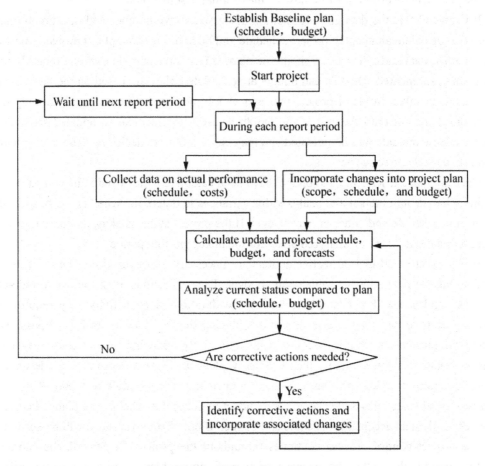

Figure 12.1　Project Control Process

A regular **reporting period** should be established for comparing actual progress with planned progress. Reporting may be daily, weekly, bi-weekly, or monthly, depending on the complexity or overall duration of the project. If a project is expected to have an overall duration of a month, the reporting period might be as short as a day. On the other hand, if a project is expected to run five years, the reporting period might be a month.

During each reporting period, two kinds of data or information need to be collected.

(1) Data on actual performance. This includes:
- the actual time that activities were started and/or finished.
- the actual costs expended and committed.

(2) Information on any changes to the project scope, schedule, and budget.

These changes could be initiated by the customer or the project team, or they could be the result of an unanticipated occurrence such as a natural disaster, a labor strike, or the resignation of a key project team member.

It should be noted that once changes are incorporated into the plan and agreed on by the customer, a new baseline plan has to be established. The scope, schedule, and budget of the new baseline plan may be different from those of the original baseline plan.

It is crucial that the data and information discussed above be collected in a timely manner and used to calculate an updated project schedule and budget. For example, if project reporting is done monthly, data and information should be obtained as late as possible in that monthly period so that when an updated schedule and budget are calculated, they are based on the latest possible information. In other words, a project manager should not gather data at the beginning of the month and then wait until the end of the month to use it to calculate an updated schedule and budget, because the data will be outdated and may cause incorrect decisions to be made about the project status and corrective actions.

Once an updated schedule and budget have been calculated, they need to be compared to the baseline schedule and budget and analyzed for variances to determine whether a project is ahead of or behind schedule and under or over budget. If the project status is okay, no corrective actions are needed; the status will be analyzed again for the next reporting period.

If it is determined that corrective actions are necessary, however, decisions must be made regarding how to revise the schedule or the budget. These decisions often involve a trade-off of time, cost, and scope. For example, reducing the duration of an activity may require either increasing costs to pay for more resources or reducing the scope of the task (and possibly not meeting the customer's technical requirements). Similarly, reducing project costs may require using materials of a lower quality than originally planned. Once a decision is made on which corrective actions to take, they must be incorporated into the schedule and budget. It is then necessary to calculate a revised schedule and budget to determine whether the planned corrective measures result in an acceptable schedule and budget. If not, further revisions will be needed.

The project control process continues throughout the project. In general, the shorter the reporting period, the better the chances of identifying problems early and taking effective corrective actions. If a project gets too far out of control, it may be difficult to achieve the project objective without sacrificing the scope, budget, schedule, or quality. There may be situations in which it is wise to increase the frequency of reporting until the project is back on track. For example, if a five-year project with monthly reporting is endangered by a slipping schedule or an increasing budget overrun, it may be prudent to reduce the reporting period to one week in order to monitor the project and the impact of corrective actions more closely.

The project control process is an important and necessary part of project management. Just establishing a sound baseline plan is not sufficient, since even the best laid plans don't always work out. Project management is a proactive approach to controlling a project, to ensure that the project objective is achieved even when things don't go according to plan.

Effects of Actual Schedule Performance

Throughout a project, some activities will be completed on time, some will be finished ahead of schedule, and others will be finished later than scheduled. Actual progress—whether faster or slower than planned—will have an effect on the schedule of the remaining, uncompleted activities of the project. Specifically, the **actual finish times** (AF) of completed activities will determine the earliest start and earliest finish times for the remaining activities in the network diagram, as well as the total slack.

Part (a) of Figure 12.2 is an AIB network diagram for a simple project. It shows that the earliest the project can finish is day 15 (the sum of the durations of the three activities, 7+5+3). Since the required completion time is day 20, the project has a total slack of +5 days.

Suppose that activity 1, "Remove Old Wallpaper" is actually finished on day 10, rather than on day 7 as planned, because it turns out to be more difficult than anticipated [See part (b) of Figure 12.2]. This means that the earliest start and finish times for activities 2 and 3 will be 3 days later than on the original schedule. Because "Remove Old Wallpaper" is actually finished on day 10, the ES for "Patch Walls" will be day 10 and its EF will be day 15. Following through with the forward calculations, we find that "Put Up New Wallpaper" will have an ES of day 15 and an EF of day 18. Comparing this new EF of the last activity to the required completion time of day 20, we find a difference of 2 days. The total slack got worse—it changed in a negative direction, from +5 days to +2 days. This example illustrates how the actual finish times of activities have a ripple effect, altering the remaining activities' earliest start and finish times and the total slack.

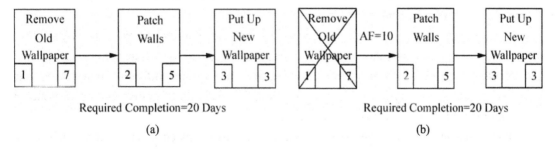

Figure 12.2   Effect of Actual Finish Times

It's helpful to indicate on the network diagram, in some manner, which activities have been completed. One method is to shade or crosshatch the activity box, as was done in part (b) of

Figure 12.2.

Incorporating Project Changes into The Schedule

Throughout a project, changes may occur that have an impact on the schedule. As was noted earlier, these changes might be initiated by the customer or the project team, or they might be the result of an unanticipated occurrence.

Here are some examples of changes initiated by the customer:
- A home buyer tells the builder that the family room should be larger and the bedroom windows should be relocated.
- A customer tells the project team developing an information system that the system must have the capability to produce a previously unmentioned set of reports and graphics.

These types of changes represent revisions to the original project scope and will have an impact on the schedule and cost. The degree of impact, however, may depend on when the changes are requested. If they're requested early in the project, they may have less impact on cost and schedule than if they're requested later in the project. For example, changing the size of the family room and relocating the bedroom windows would be relatively easy if the house were still being designed and the drawings being prepared. If the changes were requested after the framing was put up and the windows were installed, however, the impact on costs and schedule would be far greater.

When the customer requests a change, the contractor or project team should estimate the impact on the project budget and schedule and then obtain customer approval before proceeding. If the customer approves the proposed revisions to the project schedule and budget, any additional tasks, revised duration estimates, and material and labor costs should be incorporated.

An example of a change initiated by a project team is the decision by a team planning a town fair to eliminate all amusement rides for adults because of space limitations and insurance costs. The project plan would then have to be revised to delete or modify all those activities involving adult rides. Here is an example of a project manager-initiated change. A contractor, charged with developing an automated invoicing system for a customer, suggests that, rather than incorporate custom-designed software, the system use standard available software in order to reduce costs and accelerate the schedule.

Some changes involve the addition of activities that were overlooked when the original plan was developed. For example, the project team may have forgotten to include activities associated with developing training materials and conducting training for a new information system. Or the customer or contractor may have failed to include the installation of gutters and downspouts in the work scope for the construction of a restaurant.

Other changes become necessary because of unanticipated occurrences, such as a snowstorm that slows down construction of a building, the failure of a new product to pass quality tests, or the untimely death or resignation of a key member of a project team. These events will have an impact on the schedule and/or budget and will require that the project plan be modified.

Still other changes can result from adding more detail to the network diagram as the project moves forward. No matter what level of detail is used in the initial network diagram, there will be some activities that can be broken down further as the project progresses.

Any type of change—whether initiated by the customer, contractor, project manager, a team member, or an unanticipated event—will require a modification to the plan in terms of scope, budget, and/or schedule. When such changes are agreed upon, a new baseline plan is established and used as the benchmark against which actual project performance will be compared.

With respect to the project schedule, changes can result in the addition or deletion of activities, the resequencing of activities, the changing of activities' duration estimates or a new required completion time for the project.

Questions

1. What are involved in the project control process?
2. How to establish a regular project reporting period?
3. During each reporting period, which kinds of data or information to be collected?
4. On what condition must a new baseline be established?
5. If a project gets too far out of control, what's the wise method to solve that problem?
6. What will determine the earliest start and earliest finish times for the remaining activities in the network diagram, as well as the total slack?
7. What might initiate the changes that have an impact on the schedule?
8. The degree of impact may depend on when the changes are request, why?
9. When the customer request a change, who should estimate the impact on the project budget and schedule and obtain custom approval before proceeding?
10. With respect to the project schedule, what result can changes bring?

Vocabulary, Phrases and Expressions

project control process：项目控制过程
project scope：项目范围
baseline plan：基准计划
project team：项目团队
reporting period：报告期
data on actual performance：实际执行中的数据
variances：偏差；不一致
actual finish times：实际完成时间
total slack：总时差
project changes：项目变更

参考译文

第12单元 进度控制(1)

项目控制过程

项目控制过程包括定期收集项目完成情况的数据,并将实际完成情况数据与计划进程进行比较,一旦项目实际进程晚于计划进程,则采取纠正措施。这个过程在整个项目工期内必须定期进行。

图 12.1 说明了项目控制过程的步骤。这个过程以制定一个表明项目范围(任务)如何在预算(资源、成本)内按时完成的基准计划开始。一旦客户与承包商或者项目团队就基准计划达成一致,项目就可以开始了。

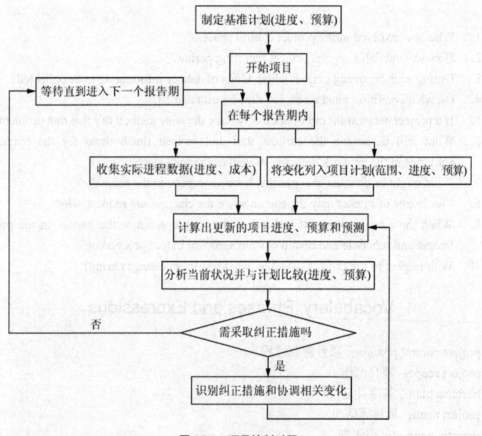

图 12.1 项目控制过程

应该确定一个固定的**报告期**(reporting period),将实际进程与计划进程进行比较。根据项目的复杂程度和完工期限,可以将报告期定为日、周、双周或月。如果项目预计在一个月内完成,报告期应该短至一天;另一方面,如果项目期为 5 年,则报告期可能是一个月。

在每个报告期内,需要收集两种数据或信息。

(1) 实际执行中的数据，它包括：
- 活动开始和/或结束的实际时间。
- 使用或投入的实际成本。

(2) 任何有关项目范围、进度计划和预算变更的信息。这些变更可能是由客户或项目团队引起的，或者是由某种不可预见的事情的发生引起的，如自然灾害、工人罢工或关键项目团队成员的辞职。

需要注意的是，一旦变更被列入计划并得到客户同意，就必须建立一个新的基准计划。这个计划的范围、进度和预算可能和最初的基准计划有所不同。

有一点很重要，上面讨论的数据或信息必须及时收集，以作为更新项目进度计划和预算的依据。例如，如果项目报告期是一个月，数据和信息应尽可能在该月的末期收集，这样才能保证在更新进度计划和预算时所依据的信息是最新的。换句话说，项目经理不应在月初收集信息，而到月末才利用它来更新进度和预算，因为月初的这些数据已过时，可能会引起在项目进展情况和纠正措施方面的决策失误。

最新的进度计划和预算一经形成，必须将它们与基准进度和预算进行比较，分析各种偏差，确定项目将提前还是延期完成，是低于还是超过预算。如果项目进展顺利，就不需要采取纠正措施，而在下一个报告期再对进展情况进行分析。

然而，如果认为需要采取纠正措施，必须就如何修订进度计划或预算做出决定，这些决定经常涉及时间、成本和项目范围的权衡。例如，缩减活动的工期可能需要增加资源，从而增大成本或缩小任务范围(并且可能达不到客户的技术要求)。同样，降低项目成本可能需要使用低于计划原定质量的材料。一旦决定采取某种纠正措施，就必须将其列入进度计划和预算，然后测算出一个新的进度计划和预算，以判定计划采取的纠正措施在进度和预算上能否接受；否则，还需进一步修改。

项目控制过程贯穿于整个项目。一般说来，报告期越短，提早发现问题并采取有效纠正措施的机会就越多。如果一个项目远远偏离了控制，就很难在不牺牲项目范围、预算、进度或质量的情况下实现项目目标。明智的做法是增加报告期的频率，直到项目按进度进行。例如，如果一个报告期为一个月的 5 年期项目偏离了进度或超出了预算，明智的做法是将报告期减至一周，以便更好地监控项目和纠正措施的效果。

项目控制过程是项目管理中重要而必备的部分，仅仅建立一个全面的基准计划是不够的，因为即使是最完善的计划也不能保证总是进展顺利。项目管理是控制项目的一种积极主动的方法，即使在项目不能按计划进展的情况下，也能确保项目目标的实现。

实际进度完成情况的影响

在整个项目进程中，一些活动会按时完成，一些活动会提前完成，而另一些活动则会延期完成。实际进展——无论比计划快还是慢——都会对项目余下部分的进度产生影响，特别是已完成活动的**实际完成时间**(actual finish times，AF)，不仅决定着网络图中其他未完成活动的最早开始与结束时间，而且决定着总时差。

图 12.2(a)是一个简单的 AIB 网络图，它表明项目的最早结束时间是第 15 天（即三项活动的工期之和，7+5+3）。因为要求项目的完工时间是第 20 天，所以项目共有 5 天的总时差。

假设活动 1，"除去旧墙纸"，由于比预计的难做，用了 10 天才完成，而不是预计的 7 天(参看图 12.2(b))。这意味着活动 2 和 3 的最早开始与结束时间比计划晚 3 天。由于"除去旧墙纸"实际上花费了 10 天，"修补墙纸"的最早开始时间将为第 10 天，最早结束时间将为第 15 天。以此类推，"粘贴新墙纸"的最早开始时间将为第 15 天，最早结束时间将为第 18 天。将最后一项活动新的最早结束时间与项目要求的完工时间相比较可以发现，有 2 天的时差，总时差变小——向着负方向转变，从+5 天减至+2 天。这个例子表明，活动的实际完成时间具有波形反应，将会改变未完成活动的最早开始和结束时间及总时差。

以某种方式在网络图上标明已完成的活动会很有帮助。一种方法就是如图 12.2(b)那样，在活动块上加阴影或者画"×"。

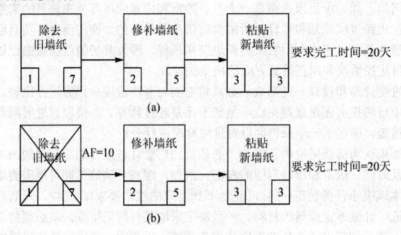

图 12.2　实际完成时间的影响

将项目变更纳入进度

在整个项目进程中，可能发生的变更会对进度计划产生影响。如前所述，这些变更可能是由客户或项目团队发起的，或者是由不可预见的事情的发生引起的。

下面是一些由客户引起变更的例子：

● 购房者向建筑商建议，房间应该更大些，卧室窗户的位置应重新设置。
● 客户要求信息系统开发项目团队增加信息系统的功能，以生成以前未提到过的报告和图表。

这类变更意味着对最初项目范围的修改将会对进度计划、成本产生影响。然而，影响程度却取决于做出变更的时间。发生在项目早期的变更对进度、成本的影响要比发生在晚期的变更小。例如，在房子的设计图纸尚未完成时，改变房子的大小和窗户的位置相对来说要容易些。然而，如果房子的框架已经搭起，窗户已安装好，这种变更对进度、成本的影响将会大得多。

当客户提出变更要求时，承包商或项目团队应该估计变更对项目预算和进度的影响。然后，在实施之前征得客户的同意。客户同意了对项目进度和预算的修改建议后，任何新增的任务、修改后的工期估计、原材料和劳动力成本均应列入计划。

下面是一个由项目团队引发变更的例子。在设计一个城镇展销会时，由于空间的限制

Unit 12　Schedule Control(1)

和保险费用的原因，项目团队决定取消供成年人娱乐的骑马设施。因此，项目计划必须改变，以去除或修改那些涉及供成年人骑马设施的活动。这里还有一个由项目经理引发变更的例子。一位负责为客户开发自动发票系统的承包商提出，为了减少成本，加快进度，自动发票系统应该使用现成的标准化软件，而不是再为客户专门设计软件。

一些变更是由最初制订计划时忽略了一些活动而引起的。例如，项目团队可能忘记将"开发培训教材"和"为新系统进行培训"列入计划，或者在建造饭店时，客户或承包商忘记将安装流水槽和下水道列入工作范围内了。

不可预见事件的发生使一些变更难以避免。比如说，暴风雪延缓了建筑施工过程，新产品未能通过质量检验，项目团队的关键成员突然死亡或辞职。这些事件对项目进度和/或预算都有影响，需要对项目计划进行修改。

然而，随着项目的进展，网络图上更多细节的增加也可能引起变更。无论最初的网络图详细到何种程度，在项目进展过程中一定也会分解出一些新的活动。

变更无论是由客户、承包商、项目经理、项目团队成员还是由不可预见事件的发生引起的，都要求对计划从范围、预算和/或进度的角度进行修改。一旦这些变更得到各方同意，就要生成一个新的基准计划，作为衡量项目进展情况的比较基准。

对于项目进度，变更可能会引起活动的增加或删除、活动的重新排序、活动工期估计的变更或者项目要求完工时间的更新。

Unit 13　Schedule Control(2)

Updating the Project Schedule

Network-based planning and scheduling allows project schedules to be dynamic. Because the network plan (diagram) and schedule (tabulation) are separate, they are much easier to update manually than a traditional Gantt chart. However, various project management software packages are available to assist with the automated generation of schedules, network diagrams, budgets, and even network-to-Gantt-chart conversions.

Once data have been collected on the actual finish times of completed activities and the effects of any project changes, an updated project schedule can be calculated. These calculations are based on the methodology explained in Unit 10:

- The earliest start and finish times for the remaining, uncompleted activities are calculated by working forward through the network, but they're based on the actual finish times of completed activities and the estimated durations of the uncompleted activities.
- The latest start and finish times for the uncompleted activities are calculated by working backward through the network.

Approaches to Schedule Control

Schedule control involves four steps:

(1) Analyzing the schedule to determine which areas may need corrective action.

(2) Deciding what specific corrective actions should be taken.

(3) Revising the plan to incorporate the chosen corrective actions.

(4) Recalculating the schedule to evaluate the effects of the planned corrective actions.

If the planned corrective actions do not result in an acceptable schedule, these steps need to be repeated.

Throughout a project, each time a schedule is recalculated—whether it's after actual data or project changes are incorporated or after corrective actions are planned—it is necessary to analyze the newly calculated schedule to determine whether it needs further attention. The schedule analysis should include identifying the critical path and any paths of activities that have a negative slack, as well as those paths where slippages have occurred (the slack got worse) compared with the previously calculated schedule.

A concentrated effort to accelerate project progress must be applied to the paths with negative slack. The amount of slack should determine the priority with which these concentrated efforts are applied. For example, the path with the most negative slack should be given top priority.

Corrective actions that will eliminate the negative slack from the project schedule must be identified. These corrective actions must reduce the duration estimates for activities on the negative-slack paths. Remember, the slack for a path of activities is shared among all the activities on that path. Therefore, a change in the estimated duration of any activity on that path will cause a corresponding change in the slack for that path.

When analyzing a path of activities that has negative slack, you should focus on two kinds of activities:

(1) Activities that are near term (that is, in progress or to be started in the immediate future). It's much wiser to take aggressive corrective action to reduce the durations of activities that will be done in the near term than to plan to reduce the durations of activities that are scheduled sometime in the future. If you postpone until the distant future taking corrective action that will reduce the durations of activities, you may find that the negative slack has deteriorated even further by that time. As the project progresses, there is always less time remaining in which corrective action can be taken.

Looking at Table 13-1, we can see that it would be better to try to reduce the durations of the near-term activities on the critical path, such as "Review Comments & Finalize Questionnaire" or "Print Questionnaire" than to put off corrective action until the last activity, "Prepare Report".

Table 13-1 Updated Schedule for Consumer Market Study Project

	Activity	Respon.	Dur. Estim	Earliest Start	Earliest Finish	Latest Start	Latest Finish	Total Slack	Actual Finish
1	Identify Target Consumers	Susan							2
2	Develop Draft Questionnaire	Susan							11
3	Pilot-Test Questionnaire	Susan							30
4	Review Comments & Finalize Questionnaire	Susan	15	30	45	25	40	−5	
5	Prepare Mailing Labels	Steve	2	45	47	48	50	3	
6	Print Questionnaire	Steve	10	45	55	40	50	−5	
7	Develop Data Analysis Software	Andy	12	45	57	88	100	43	
8	Develop Software Test Data	Susan	2	45	47	98	100	53	
9	Mail Questionnaire & get Responses	Steve	55	55	110	50	105	−5	
10	Test Software	Andy	5	57	62	100	105	43	
11	Input Response data	Jim	7	110	117	105	112	−5	
12	Analyze Results	Jim	8	117	125	112	120	−5	
13	Prepare Report	Jim	10	125	135	120	130	−5	
14	Order New Database for Labels	Steve	21	23	44	27	48	4	

(2) Activities that have long duration estimates. Taking corrective measures that will reduce a 20-day activity by 20 percent—that is, by 4 days—has a larger impact than totally eliminating a 1-day activity. Usually, longer-duration activities present the opportunity for larger reductions.

Look again at Table 13-1: There may be more opportunity to reduce the 55-day duration estimate for "Mail Questionnaire & Get Responses" by 5 days (9 percent) than to reduce the shorter duration estimates of other activities on the critical path.

There are various approaches to reducing the duration estimates of activities. One obvious way is to apply more resources to speed up an activity. This could be done by assigning more people to work on the activity or asking the people working on the activity to work more hours per day or more days per week. Additional appropriate resources might be transferred from concurrent activities that have positive slack. Sometimes, however, adding people to an activity may in fact result in the activity's taking longer, because the people already assigned to the activity are diverted from their work in order to help the new people get up to speed. Another approach is to assign a person with greater expertise or more experience to perform or help with the activity, so as to get it done in a shorter time than was possible with the less experienced people originally assigned to it.

Reducing the scope or requirements for an activity is another way to reduce its duration estimate. For example, it might be acceptable to put only one coat of paint on a room rather than two coats, as originally planned. In an extreme case, it may be decided to totally eliminate some activities, deleting them and their durations from the schedule.

Increasing productivity through improved methods or technology is yet another approach to reducing activities' durations. For example, instead of having people keyboard data from a customer survey into a computer database, optical scanning equipment might be used.

Once specific corrective actions to reduce the negative slack have been decided on, the duration estimates for the appropriate activities must be revised in the network plan. Then a revised schedule needs to be calculated to evaluate whether the planned corrective actions reduce the negative slack as anticipated.

In most cases, eliminating negative slack by reducing durations of activities will involve a trade-off in the form of an increase in costs or a reduction in scope. For a more thorough discussion of this topic, see the appendix on time-cost trade-off at the end of this chapter. If the project is way behind schedule (has substantial negative slack), a substantial increase in costs and/or reduction in work scope or quality may be required to get it back on schedule. This could jeopardize elements of the overall project objective: scope, budget, schedule, and/or quality. In some cases, the customer and contractor or project team may have to acknowledge that one or more of these elements cannot be achieved. Thus, for example, the customer may have to extend the required completion time for the entire project, or there may be a dispute over who should absorb any increased cost to accelerate the schedule—the contractor or the customer.

Some contracts include a bonus provision, whereby the customer will pay the contractor a bonus if the project is completed ahead of schedule. Conversely, some contracts include a penalty provision, whereby the customer can reduce the final payment to the contractor if the project is not completed on time. Some of these penalties can be substantial. In either of these situations, effective schedule control is crucial.

The key to effective schedule control is to aggressively address any paths with negative or deteriorating slack values as soon as they are identified, rather than hoping that things will improve as the project goes on. Addressing schedule problems early will minimize the negative impact on cost and scope. If a project gets too far behind, getting back on schedule becomes more difficult, and it doesn't come free. It requires spending more money or reducing the scope or quality.

On projects that don't have negative slack, it's important not to let the slack deteriorate by accepting delays and slippages. If a project is ahead of schedule, a concentrated effort should be made to keep it ahead of schedule.

Schedule Control for Information Systems Development

Controlling the schedule for the development of an information system is a challenge. Numerous unexpected circumstances arise that can push an IS development project beyond its originally scheduled due date. However, just as with any other type of project, the key to effective project control is to measure actual progress and compare it to planned progress on a timely and regular basis and to take necessary corrective action immediately.

Like other forms of schedule control, schedule control for IS development projects is carried out according to the steps discussed earlier in this chapter. A project control process such as the one illustrated in Figure 12.1 should be used for comparing actual performance with the schedule. Once the customer and the project team agree on changes, these changes should be recorded and the schedule should be revised.

Among the changes that commonly become necessary during IS development projects are the following:
- Changes to input screens—such as added fields, different icons, different colors, different menu structures, or completely new input screens.
- Changes to reports—such as added fields, different subtotals and totals, different sorts, different selection criteria, different order of fields, or completely new reports.
- Changes to on-line queries—such as different ad hoc capabilities, access to different fields or databases, different query structures, or additional queries.
- Changes to database structures—such as additional fields, different data field names, different data storage sizes, different relationships among the data, or completely new databases.

- Changes to software processing routines—such as different algorithms, different interfaces with other subroutines, different internal logic, or new procedures.
- Changes to processing speeds—such as higher throughput rates or response times.
- Changes to storage capacities—such as an increase in the maximum number of data records.
- Changes to business processes—such as changes in work or data flow, addition of new clients that must have access, or completely new processes that must be supported.
- Changes to software resulting from hardware upgrades or, conversely, hardware upgrades resulting from the availability of more powerful software.

Questions

1. How to calculate an updated project schedule once data have been collected on the actual finish time of completed activities and the effects of any project changes?
2. Schedule control involves four steps, what are they?
3. What paths must be applied a concentrated effort to accelerate project progress?
4. When analyzing a path of activities that have negative slack, which kinds of activities should be focused on?
5. What is the obvious way to reducing the duration estimates of activities?
6. What are the other ways to reducing the duration estimates of activities?
7. What is the key to effective schedule control?
8. On projects that don't have negative slack, what's important to do?
9. What can push an information system project beyond its originally scheduled?
10. What are the changes that commonly become necessary during information system development project?

Vocabulary, Phrases and Expressions

network-based planning：基于网络的计划
Gantt chart：甘特图
software packages：软件包
completed activities：已完成活动
database：数据库
supplier：供应商
preliminary review：初步评审
schedule control：进度控制
corrective action：纠正措施
negative slack：负时差

positive slack：正时差
top priority：最高优先级
productivity：生产率
a bonus provision：奖励条款
a penalty provision：惩罚条款
information system：信息系统

参 考 译 文

第13单元　进度控制(2)

更新项目进度

基于网络的计划和进度安排允许对项目进度计划进行动态变更。由于网络式计划(图解)和进度计划(表)是相互独立的，对它们进行人工更新比甘特图更容易一些。然而，可以使用各式各样的软件包来自动更新进度计划、网络图、预算以及网络——甘特图转换。

一旦收集到已完成活动的实际结束时间和项目变更所带来影响的有关数据，就可以计算出最新的项目进度。这些计算以第10单元提出的方法为依据：
- 未完成活动的最早开始和结束时间可以沿网络图正向推算得出，但它们是以已完成活动的实际完成时间和未完成活动的工期估计为基础的。
- 未完成活动的最迟开始和结束时间可以沿网络图反向推算得出。

进度控制方法

进度控制包括以下4个步骤：
(1) 分析进度，找出哪些地方需要采取纠正措施。
(2) 确定应采取哪种具体的纠正措施。
(3) 修改计划，将纠正措施列入计划。
(4) 重新计算进度，估计计划采取的纠正措施的效果。

如果计划采取的纠正措施仍无法获得满意的进度安排，则必须重复以上步骤。

在整个项目实施过程中，每次重新计算进度计划——无论是在实际数据或项目变更被列入进度计划之后，还是纠正措施被列入计划之后——都有必要分析这一新的进度计划，以决定是否需要进行进一步的关注。进度分析应该包括识别关键路径和任何有负时差的活动路径，以及那些与先前的进度计划相比已偏离预定进度的路径(时差变坏的路径)。

加快项目进度的重点应放在有负时差的路径上，时差的数值决定了努力的优先级。例如，负时差最大的路径优先级最高。

我们必须找出能够消除负时差的纠正措施，这些纠正措施必须减少有负时差路径上的活动的工期估计。切记，活动路径时差是由路径上的全部活动共享的，因此，路径上任何活动预计工期的变更都会引起该路径上时差的相应变更。

当分析有负时差的活动路径时，应将精力集中在以下两种活动上：
(1) 近期内的活动(即正在进行或随后即将开始的活动)。减少活动工期的一种明智做法是，对即将到来期间内的活动采取积极的纠正措施，而不是打算对将来期间内的活动采取纠正措施。如果把减少活动工期的纠正措施推迟到遥远的将来，会发现负时差甚至比发现时更糟糕。随着项目的进展，可以用来采取纠正措施的时间总是越来越少。

研究表 13-1 可以发现，减少关键路径上近期活动"评审建议并确定最终调查表"或"打印问卷调查表"的工期，比将纠正措施推迟到最后一个活动"准备报告"要好得多。

表 13-1 更新后的市场调研项目速度

	活动	负责人	工期估计	最早		最迟		总时差	实际完成时间
				开始	结束	开始	结束		
1	识别目标消费者	Susan							2
2	设计初始问卷调查表	Susan							11
3	试验性测试问卷调查表	Susan							30
4	评审建议并确定最终调查表	Susan	15	30	45	25	40	−5	
5	准备邮寄标签	Steve	2	45	47	48	50	3	
				开始	结束	开始	结束		
6	打印问卷调查表	Steve	10	45	55	40	50	−5	
7	开发数据分析软件	Andy	12	45	57	88	100	43	
8	设计元件测试数据	Susan	2	45	47	98	100	53	
9	邮寄问卷调查表并获得反馈	Steve	55	55	110	50	105	−5	
10	测试软件	Andy	5	57	62	100	105	43	
11	输入反馈数据	Jim	7	110	117	105	112	−5	
12	分析结果	Jim	8	117	125	112	120	−5	
13	准备报告	Jim	10	125	135	120	130	−5	
14	为标签订购新数据库	Steve	21	23	44	27	48	4	

(2) 工期估计长的活动。减少一项具有 20 天工期的活动 20%的时间，即 4 天的纠正措施，会比完全除去一项只有 1 天工期的活动的纠正措施有更大的影响。总的来说，工期较长的活动缩减的可能较大。

再看一下表 13-1，"邮寄问卷调查表并获得反馈"估计需要 55 天时间，从中减少 5 天 (9%)，将比从关键路径上其他具有较短工期估计的活动中省出时间的机会多。

有多种方法可以缩短活动的工期估计。一种显而易见的方法是投入更多的资源以加快活动进程。分派更多的人手来完成一项活动，或者要求活动的工作人员增加每天的工作时间或每周的工作天数，均可以加快活动进程。增加的相应资源可以从当前有正时差的活动中转移过来。然而，有时候在一项活动中增加人员，实际上却会延长活动的工期，这是因为原有工作人员为帮助新人熟悉工作而分散了精力。另一种方法是指派一位经验更丰富的人去完成或帮助完成这项活动，这样，与最初派出的无经验的人相比，能用更短的时间完成任务。

缩小活动范围或降低活动要求是缩短活动工期的另一种方法。例如，房间内可以只涂一层油漆，而不像最初计划的那样涂两层油漆。在特殊情况下，也可以将一些活动和它们的工期从进度中除去。

通过改进方法或技术来提高生产率是缩短活动工期的另一种方法。例如，可以通过光学扫描设备将从客户调查中得到的数据输入计算机数据库，而不是用键盘人工输入。

一旦减少负时差的具体纠正措施被确定下来，就必须修正网络计划中相应活动的工期估计，然后计算出一个修改过的进度，以评价计划采取的纠正措施能否像预期的那样减少负时差。

在绝大多数情况下，通过缩短活动的工期来消除负时差时，需在成本增加或范围缩小之间进行权衡(为了更全面地讨论这个问题，可参照本章附录"时间-成本平衡法")。如果项目落后于进度(有很大的负时差)，为了使项目按进度进行，往往需要大幅提高项目成本和/或缩小工作范围、降低质量标准，这可能危及整个项目目标的各个要素：范围、预算、进度和/或质量。在某些情况下，客户和承包商或项目团队可能不得不承认这些要素中的一个或多个不可能实现。这样，客户就不得不延长整个项目的要求完工时间，否则，因加快进度而增加的成本由谁负担，是客户还是承包商？这就会引起争议。

一些合同含有奖励条款，即如果项目提前完成，客户就给予承包商奖励。相反的，一些合同含有惩罚条款，即如果项目未按进度完成，客户将减少给承包商的最终付款，而且一些惩罚可能还相当严厉。有效的进度控制在上述两种情况下均至关重要。

有效进度控制的关键是尽可能早地、果断地将主要精力放在有负时差或时差变坏的路径上，而不应寄希望于随着项目的进展情况会自动改善。尽早处理进度问题会减少对成本和范围的负面影响。如果项目远远落后于进度，赶上原进度会更加困难，而且这需要代价，要投入更多的财力，或者缩小项目范围，或者降低质量标准。

对于没有负时差的项目，重要的是不要使它出现耽搁或延误而最终造成时差的减少。如果项目的实际进度快于计划进度，要尽力保持这种状况。

信息系统开发项目的进度控制

控制信息系统开发项目的进度是一项难度很大的工作。大量无法预测的情况会使信息系统开发项目远远超出它预定的进度日期。然而，就像任何其他类型的项目一样，有效项目进度控制的关键是监控实际进程，及时、定期地将它与计划进度进行比较，并立即采取必要的纠正措施。

类似于其他类型的进度控制，信息系统开发项目的进度控制应按照本章前面论述的步骤进行。如图12.1所示，项目控制过程应该是将实际进程与计划进度进行比较的过程。一旦客户与项目团队就变更达成一致，就应记录下这些变更，并修改进度计划。

信息系统开发项目中会出现如下一些难以避免的变更：
- 界面的变更——如增加的字段、不同的图标、不同的颜色、不同的菜单结构、按钮以及全新的输入屏幕。
- 报告的变更——如增加的字段、不同的小计和合计、不同的分类、不同的选择标准、不同的字段顺序或全新的报告。

- 在线查询的变更——如各种非预先安排的查询能力,对不同字段或数据库的访问,不同的查询结构或额外的查询。
- 数据库结构的变更——如增加的字段、不同的数据字段名、不同的数据存储空间、数据间不同的关系或全新的数据库。
- 软件处理路径的变更——如不同的算法、与其他子路径的不同衔接、不同的内部逻辑或全新的程序。
- 处理速度的变更——如更高的输出速率和更短的反应时间。
- 存储能力的变更——如数据记录最大容量的提高。
- 业务处理的变更——如工作或数据流的变更、新增客户的进入或全新程序的支持。
- 硬件更新引起的软件变更,或相反的,功能更强大的软件的出现引起的硬件更新。

Unit 14 Innovation and Technological & Economic Feasibility

Innovation and Technological Feasibility

The planning for a construction project begins with the generation of concepts for a facility which will meet market demands and owner needs. Innovative concepts in design are highly valued not for their own sake but for their contributions to reducing costs and to the improvement of aesthetics, comfort or convenience as embodied in a well-designed facility. However, the constructor as well as the design professionals must have an appreciation and full understanding of the technological complexities often associated with innovative designs in order to provide a safe and sound facility. Since these concepts are often preliminary or tentative, screening studies are carried out to determine the overall technological viability and economic attractiveness without pursuing these concepts in great detail. Because of the ambiguity of the objectives and the uncertainty of external events, screening studies call for uninhibited innovation in creating new concepts and judicious judgment in selecting the appropriate ones for further consideration.

One of the most important aspects of design innovation is the necessity of communication in the design/construction partnership. In the case of bridge design, it can be illustrated by the following quotation from Lin and Gerwick concerning bridge construction:

(1) The great pioneering steel bridges of the United States were built by an open or covert alliance between designers and constructors. The turnkey approach of designer-constructor has developed and built our chemical plants, refineries, steel plants, and nuclear power plants. It is time to ask, seriously, whether we may not have adopted a restrictive approach by divorcing engineering and construction in the field of bridge construction.

(2) If a contractor-engineer, by some stroke of genius, were to present to design engineers today a wonderful new scheme for long span prestressed concrete bridges that made them far cheaper, he would have to make these ideas available to all other constructors, even limiting or watering them down so as to "get a group of truly competitive bidders". The engineer would have to make sure that he found other contractors to bid against the ingenious innovator.

(3) If an engineer should, by a similar stroke of genius, hit on such a unique and brilliant scheme, he would have to worry, wondering if the low bidder would be one who had any concept of what he was trying to accomplish or was in any way qualified for high class technical work.

Innovative design concepts must be tested for technological feasibility. Three levels of technology are of special concern: technological requirements for operation or production, design resources and construction technology. The first refers to the new technologies that may be introduced in a facility which is used for a certain type of production such as chemical processing or nuclear power generation. The second refers to the design capabilities that are available to the designers, such as new computational methods or new materials. The third refers to new technologies which can be adopted to construct the facility, such as new equipment or new construction methods.

A new facility may involve complex new technology for operation in hostile environments such as severe climate or restricted accessibility. Large projects with unprecedented demands for resources such as labor supply, material and infrastructure may also call for careful technological feasibility studies. Major elements in a feasibility study on production technology should include, but are not limited to, the following:

- Project type as characterized by the technology required, such as synthetic fuels, petrochemicals, nuclear power plants, etc.
- Project size in dollars, design engineer's hours, construction labor hours, etc.
- Design, including sources of any special technology which require licensing agreements.
- Project location which may pose problems in environmental protection, labor productivity and special risks.

An example of innovative design for operation and production is the use of entropy concepts for the design of integrated chemical processes. Simple calculations can be used to indicate the minimum energy requirements and the least number of heat exchange units to achieve desired objectives. The result is a new incentive and criterion for designers to achieve more effective designs. Numerous applications of the new methodology has shown its efficacy in reducing both energy costs and construction expenditures.

The choice of construction technology and method involves both strategic and tactical decisions. For example, the extent to which prefabricated facility components will be used represents a strategic construction decision. In turn, prefabrication of components might be accomplished off-site in existing manufacturing facilities or a temporary, on-site fabrication plant might be used. Another example of a strategic decision is whether to install mechanical equipment in place early in the construction process or at an intermediate stage. Strategic decisions of this sort should be integrated with the process of facility design in many cases. At the tactical level, detailed decisions about how to accomplish particular tasks are required, and such decisions can often be made in the field.

Construction planning should be a major concern in the development of facility designs, in the preparation of cost estimates, and in forming bids by contractors. Unfortunately, planning for the construction of a facility is often treated as an after thought by design professionals. This contrasts with manufacturing practices in which the assembly of devices is a major concern in design. Design to insure ease of assembly or construction should be a major concern of engineers and architects. As the Business Roundtable noted, "All too often chances to cut schedule time and costs are lost because construction operates as a production process separated by a chasm from financial planning, scheduling, and engineering or architectural design. Too many engineers,

Unit 14 Innovation and Technological & Economic Feasibility

separated from field experience, are not up to date about how to build what they design, or how to design so structures and equipment can be erected most efficiently."

Example 14.1 Innovative use of structural frames for buildings.

The structural design of skyscrapers offers an example of innovation in overcoming the barrier of high costs for tall buildings by making use of new design capabilities. A revolutionary concept in skyscraper design was introduced in the 1960's by Fazlur Khan who argued that, for a building of a given height, there is an appropriate structural system which would produce the most efficient use of the material.

Before 1965, most skyscrapers were steel rigid frames. However, Fazlur Khan believed that it was uneconomical to construct all office buildings of rigid frames, and proposed an array of appropriate structural systems for steel buildings of specified heights. By choosing an appropriate structural system, an engineer can use structural materials more efficiently. For example, the 60-story Chase Manhattan Building in New York used about 60 pounds per square foot of steel in its rigid frame structure, while the 100-story John Hancock Center in Chicago used only 30 pounds per square foot for a trusted tube system. At the time the Chase Manhattan Building was constructed, no bracing was used to stiffen the core of a rigid frame building because design engineers did not have the computing tools to do the complex mathematical analysis associated with core bracing.

Innovation and Economic Feasibility

Innovation is often regarded as the engine which can introduce construction economies and advance labor productivity. This is obviously true for certain types of innovations in industrial production technologies, design capabilities, and construction equipment and methods. However, there are also limitations due to the economic infeasibility of such innovations, particularly in the segments of construction industry which are more fragmented and permit ease of entry, as in the construction of residential housing.

Market demand and firm size play an important role in this regard. If a builder is to construct a larger number of similar units of buildings, the cost per unit may be reduced.

Nowhere is the effect of market demand and total cost more evident than in residential housing. The housing segment in the last few decades accepted many innovative technical improvements in building materials which were promoted by material suppliers. Since material suppliers provide products to a large number of homebuilders and others, they are in a better position to exploit production economies of scale and to support new product development. However, homebuilders themselves have not been as successful in making the most fundamental form of innovation which encompasses changes in the technological process of homebuilding by shifting the mixture of labor and material inputs, such as substituting large scale off-site prefabrication for on-site assembly.

There are several major barriers to innovation in the technological process of homebuilding, including demand instability, industrial fragmentation, and building codes. Since market demand for new homes follows demographic trends and other socio-economic conditions, the variation in home building has been anything but regular. The profitability of the homebuilding industry has closely matched aggregate output levels. Since entry and exist from the industry are relatively easy, it is not uncommon during periods of slack demand to find builders leaving the market or suspending their operations until better times. The inconsistent levels of retained earnings over a period of years, even among the more established builders, are likely to discourage support for research and development efforts which are required to nurture innovation. Furthermore, because the homebuilding industry is fragmented with a vast majority of homebuilders active only in local regions, the typical homebuilder finds it excessively expensive to experiment with new designs. The potential costs of a failure or even a moderately successful innovation would outweigh the expected benefits of all but the most successful innovations. Variation in local building codes has also caused inefficiencies although repeated attempts have been made to standardize building codes.

In addition to the scale economies visible within a sector of the construction market, there are also possibilities for scale economies in individual facility. For example, the relationship between the size of a building (expressed in square feet) and the input labor (expressed in laborhours per square foot) varies for different types and sizes of buildings.

Example 14.2   Use of new materials.

In recent years, an almost entirely new set of materials is emerging for construction, largely from the aerospace and electronics industries. These materials were developed from new knowledge about the structure and properties of materials as well as new techniques for altering existing materials. Additives to traditional materials such as concrete and steel are particularly prominent. For example, it has been known for some time that polymers would increase concrete strength, water resistance and ability to insulate when they are added to the cement. However, their use has been limited by their costs since they have had to replace as much as 10 percent of the cement to be effective. However, Swedish researchers have helped reduce costs by using polymer microspheres 8 millionths of an inch across, which occupy less than 1 percent of the cement. Concretes made with these microspheres meet even the strict standards for offshore structures in the North Sea. Research on micro-additives will probably produce useful concretes for repairing road and bridges as well.

Example 14.3   Green Buildings.

The Leadership in Energy and Environmental Design (LEED) Green Building Rating System is intended to promote voluntary improvements in design and construction practices. In the rating system, buildings receive points for a variety of aspects, including reduced energy use, greater use of daylight rather than artificial lights, recycling construction waste, rainfall runoff reduction, availability of public transit access, etc. If a building accumulates a sufficient number of points, it may be certified by the Green Building Alliance as a "green building". While some of these aspects may increase construction costs, many reduce operating costs or make buildings more attractive. Green building approaches are spreading to industrial plants and other types of construction.

Questions

1. What's one of the most important aspects of design innovation in the design/construction partnership?
2. Innovation design concepts must be tested for technological feasibility. Three levels of technology are of special concern. What are they?
3. What should technological feasibility studies include?
4. Is it true that innovation is often regarded as the engine which can introduce construction economies and advance labor productivity?
5. Who promote the housing segment to accept many innovation technical improvements in building material in the last few decades?
6. Why do material suppliers support new product development?
7. What are major barriers to innovation in the technological process of homebuilding?
8. Is the variation in home building regular? Why?
9. Why is it common during periods of slack demand to find builders leaving the market or suspending their operations until better times?
10. How to identity the "green building"?

Vocabulary, Phrases and Expressions

innovation：创新
technological feasibility：技术可行性
technology required：技术要求
project size：项目规模
project location：项目所在地
innovative design：创新性设计
prefabrication：配件预先制造
strategic decisions：战略决策
tactical decisions：战术决策
field experience：现场经验
economic feasibility：经济可行性
labor productivity：劳动生产率
residential housing：住宅建筑
material suppliers：材料供应商
economy of scale：因经营规模扩大而得到的经济节约；规模经济
homebuilder：住宅开发商
expected benefits：期望收益
laborhour：工时
green building：绿色建筑

参 考 译 文

第 14 单元 创新和技术与经济的可行性

创新和技术可行性

一个建设工程项目的规划设计开始于一个能满足市场和业主需求的设施方案的产生。设计中的创新理念弥足珍贵,不仅仅是为了设计本身,而是由于创新性的理念能降低成本,且能改善设施的美观程度、舒适性或便利性。然而,施工方以及设计人员必须尊重且完全理解与创新性设计相关联的技术复杂性,以保证设施的安全与牢固。由于这些方案经常是初步的或意向性的设计,需要进行方案审查研究,以便在陷入过多的细节问题之前,确定方案的技术可行性和经济性。鉴于研究对象的模糊及外界条件的不确定性,方案审查研究要求在构思新方案时不受任何禁锢地创新,而在下一阶段选择方式时则要有明智的判断。

设计创新的一个最重要的方面在于设计/施工方之间必要的沟通。在桥梁设计案例中,下列摘自林和戈尔维克的有关桥梁设计的评论显示了这种沟通的必要性:

(1) 美国伟大的先锋钢铁桥梁,是由设计方和施工方之间开放式的或变相的合作而建成的。化工厂、提炼厂、钢铁厂和核电站都是以设计一施工的交钥匙方式建成的。现在应该严肃地自问,我们是否在桥梁建设领域中采用了将工程设计和施工分离开的工作方式。

(2) 假定一个天才的承包商要提交给设计工程师一个新的、造价低廉的大跨度预应力混凝土桥梁施工方案,他将不得不对所有其他承包商解释其想法,甚至限制或减少其中的新颖之处,以便"得到一组竞争性投标者"。工程师将不得不寻找其他的承包商,以提出针对创新者的标书。

(3) 如果一个同样天才的工程师构思了一个独特的方案,他就不得不担心低价中标者是否有同样的思路来完成其方案,或是否有资格承担如此高技术的工作。

创新的设计方案必须经过技术可行性的检验。有3个层次的技术需要得到关注:操作或生产的技术要求、设计资源以及施工技术。第一个指的是在生产设施中引进特定的新技术,如化工生产程序或核能发电;第二个指的是设计方所拥有的设计能力,如新的计算方法或新型材料;第三个指的是可用来施工的新技术,如新的设备或新的施工方法。

在不利环境中,如恶劣气候或者通行困难的条件下,一个新的设施可能涉及操作复杂的新技术。对某些资源如劳动力供应、材料和基础设施有着不同寻常要求的大型项目,也可能要求细致的技术可行性研究。研究应包括如下主要因素(但并不仅限于此):

- 按技术要求如油料、石油化工、核电站等分类的项目类型。
- 按总投资、工程设计人员的工作时间、建造工时等确定项目的大小。
- 设计,包括任何特定的、需要授权许可的技术资源等。
- 选择可能造成诸如环境保护、生产效率和其他特殊风险的项目地点。

一个经营和生产过程的创新性设计的例子是在化学加工过程设计中熵的应用。通过很简单的计算即可显示要达到期望目标所需的最低能量和最少数量的热交换单元。这种结果对设计人员实现设计目标起到了新的激励作用,并成为新的标准。新方法在多个工程设计中的应用有效地降低了能量成本和工程建设开支。

施工技术和方法的选择同时涉及了技术和最佳施工方案的决定。例如，在何种程度上使用预制构件是一个方针性的决定。相对应地，构件的预制可以在工厂中完成，也可以在现场进行。另外一个方针性决定的例子是在施工阶段的早期或中间阶段安装机械设备。此类方针性的决定在很多情况下应该与设施的设计过程综合考虑。在策略性的层次要求做出如何完成一项特定任务的具体决定，此类决定往往可以在现场做出。

在设施的设计过程、造价估算过程和承包商投标过程中，施工计划应该是一个主要内容。然而很可惜，一个设施的施工计划往往被设计人员认为应该是后期考虑的问题。与此相反的是，在制造业中，设备的组装是设计中一个备受关注的问题。便于组装和施工的设计应该是工程师和建筑师关注的一个重点。如商业圆桌会议所评论的："由于施工被作为一个与财务计划、进度计划及工程和建筑设计相分离的生产过程，很多缩短工期和降低成本的机会就被浪费掉了。脱离了工地现场经验，太多的工程师不知道如何建造他们所设计的东西，或者如何设计实际的结构和设备。

例 14.1 大楼结构框架的创新性的使用。

利用一种新的设计方法为克服高层建筑造价高的问题提供一个创新的实例。在 20 世纪 60 年代，法兹勒·汉介绍了其革命性的摩天大楼的设计概念，他认为对于任何一个给定高度的建筑物都有一个特定的结构模式能最有效地利用建筑材料。

在 1965 年以前，绝大多数的摩天大楼为刚性框架结构。然而，法兹勒·汉相信用刚性框架建造所有的办公大楼是不经济的，提出了特定高度钢结构大楼的适用结构体系方案。通过选择一个适用结构体系，一个工程师可以更有效地使用结构材料。例如，纽约 60 层的曼哈顿银行大楼的刚性框架结构，其用钢量为每平方英尺 60 磅，而芝加哥 100 层的约翰·汉考克中心的桁架筒体系的用钢量仅为每平方英尺 30 磅。在建造曼哈顿大楼时，由于工程设计人员没有使用计算工具进行复杂的核心支撑数学分析计算，所以大楼的刚性框架的核心没有利用支撑进行加固。

创新与经济可行性

创新经常被认为是提高施工的经济性和劳动生产率的动力。对于在工业生产技术、设计能力、施工设备和方法等领域中某些类型的创新而言，这显然是正确的。然而，由于创新在经济上不可行，也往往受到多种条件的限制，特别是在建筑工业的某些进入门槛较低、特别散乱的领域，如住宅建筑领域，尤其如此。

在这方面市场需求和公司的规模扮演了重要的角色。如果建造大量同类型的建筑，单个建筑的成本将会降低。

没有其他领域能够像住宅建筑一样明显地受到市场需求和总造价的影响。在过去的几十年中，受到材料供应商的推动，住宅建设领域接受了很多建筑材料方面的创新性技术。因为，材料供应商为相当数量的住宅开发商和其他公司提供产品，他们更容易享受到规模产品经济所带来的效益，并支持新产品的开发。然而，住宅开发本身还没有成功地形成一种最基本的创新模式，这种模式可以通过转移劳动力和改变材料的供应方式，如用大规模的工厂预制代替现场组装，从而使住宅建造的技术过程适应实际情况的变化。

住宅建造的技术过程创新是有障碍的，如需求的不稳定、分散，以及不成规模的工业和建设规范等。由于新住宅的市场需求受到人口增长规律和其他社会经济条件的影响，住宅建设的变化从来不会有规律可循。住宅开发商的盈利情况与其综合产出量密切相关。由于进入和退出这个市场相当容易，所以经常可以看到在市场需求不足时，开发商便会离开市场或暂停他们的经营活动，直到经营形势好转。对一般的开发商，甚至是历史悠久的开发商而言，在一定时期内变幻不定的营业收入水平也很可能对其进行研究和开发的努力起到消极的作用，而这正是培育创新技术的条件。此外，由于住宅建设工业是由绝大多数活动在不同区域的、分散的开发商构成的，普通的开发商发现用新技术进行试验的代价极其昂贵。失败的潜在成本或即使一个一般成功的创新成本都会超出期望的收益，除非创新得到了极大的成功。即使有反复不断的尝试以使建设规范实现标准化，但各地建设规范的不同仍然造成了效率低下。

除了在一个建筑市场分支领域具有显而易见的规模经济效益之外，在单一设施之中同样有规模经济效益的可能性。例如，建筑规模(以平方英尺表示)和劳动力供应(以每平方英尺的工时表示)之间的关系随着建筑类型的规模的变化而变化。

例14.2 新材料的使用。

近年来，建筑业涌现出了几乎是整套的新建筑材料，这些新材料主要来自航天和电子工业。人们需要了解这些新材料的结构和特性，并采用新的技术将其开发成建筑材料。传统材料如混凝土和钢材的添加剂就是其中一个典型的例子。例如，人们已经了解在水泥中加入聚合材料可以增强混凝土的强度、防水性能和绝缘性能。然而，由于必须替换多达10%的水泥以达到使用效果，这些材料的使用受到了成本的限制。不过，瑞典研究人员通过使用粒径为 $1/(8\times10^4)$ 英寸的聚合材料降低了成本，这些材料仅需替代1%的水泥。用这种粒径聚合材料做成的混凝土能满足北海海洋建筑标准的苛刻要求。微粒添加剂的研究可能也会有助于生产用于修补道路和桥梁的混凝土。

例14.3 绿色建筑。

能源和环境设计引导组织(LEED)的绿色建筑评定系统旨在促进设计和施工实践的改进。在评定系统中，对大楼的各个方面进行评分，如能耗的降低、更多地利用日光而非人工照明、建筑废物的循环利用、降雨排水的回收、公共交通的可用性等。如果一座建筑累计了足够的分数，就会被绿色建筑联盟认证为"绿色建筑"。这些要求会增加工程造价，但更多的是会降低运营成本或使大楼更具魅力。绿色建筑的思想正在向工业建筑和其他类型的工程建筑传播。

Unit 15   Claims, Disputes and Arbitration

Contractor's Claims

If the Contractor considers himself to be entitled to any extension of the Time for Completion and/or any additional payment, under any Clause of these Conditions or otherwise in connection with the Contract, the Contractor shall give notice to the Employer, describing the event or circumstance giving rise to the claim. The notice shall be given as soon as practicable, and not later than 28 days after the Contractor became aware, or should have become aware, of the event or circumstance.

If the Contractor fails to give notice of a claim within such period of 28 days, the Time for Completion shall not be extended, the Contractor shall not be entitled to additional payment, and the Employer shall be discharged from all liability in connection with the claim. Otherwise, the following provisions of this Sub-Clause shall apply.

The Contractor shall also submit any other notices which are required by the Contract, and supporting particulars for the claim, all as relevant to such event or circumstance.

The Contractor shall keep such contemporary records as may be necessary to substantiate any claim, either on the Site or at another location acceptable to the Employer. Without admitting liability, the Employer may, after receiving any notice under this Sub-Clause, monitor the record-keeping and/or instruct the Contractor to keep further contemporary records. The Contractor shall permit the Employer to inspect all these records, and shall (if instructed) submit copies to the Employer.

Within 42 days after the Contractor became aware (or should have become aware) of the event or circumstance giving rise to the claim, or within such other period as may be proposed by the Contractor and approved by the Employer, the Contractor shall send to the Employer a fully detailed claim which includes full supporting particulars of the basis of the claim and of the extension of time and/or additional payment claimed. If the event or circumstance giving rise to the claim has a continuing effect:

- this fully detailed claim shall be considered as interim.
- the Contractor shall send further interim claims at monthly intervals, giving the accumulated delay and/or amount claimed, and such further particulars as the Employer may reasonably require.
- the Contractor shall send a final claim within 28 days after the end of the effects resulting from the event or circumstance, or within such other period as may be proposed by the Contractor and approved by the Employer.

Within 42 days after receiving a claim or any further particulars supporting a previous claim, or within such other period as may be proposed by the Employer and approved by the Contractor, the Employer shall respond with approval, or with disapproval and detailed comments. He may also request any necessary further particulars, but shall nevertheless give his response on the principles of the claim within such time.

Each interim payment shall include such amounts for any claim as have been reasonably substantiated as due under the relevant provision of the Contract. Unless and until the particulars supplied are sufficient to substantiate the whole of the claim, the Contractor shall only be entitled to payment for such part of the claim as he has been able to substantiate.

The Employer shall proceed in accordance with Sub-Clause 3.5 [Determinations] to agree or determine the extension (if any) of the Time for Completion (before or after its expiry) in accordance with Sub-Clause 8.4[Extension of Time for Completion], and/or the additional payment (if any) to which the Contractor is entitled under the Contract.

The requirements of this Sub-Clause are in addition to those of any other Sub-Clause which may apply to a claim. If the Contractor fails to comply with this or another Sub-Clause in relation to any claim, any extension of time and/or additional payment shall take account of the extent (if any) to which the failure has prevented or prejudiced proper investigation of the claim, unless the claim is excluded under the second paragraph of this Sub-Clause.

Appointment of the Dispute Adjudication Board

Disputes shall be adjudicated by a DAB in accordance with Sub-Clause 20.1 [Obtaining Dispute Adjudication Board's Decision]. The Parties shall jointly appoint a DAB by the date 28 days after a Party gives notice to the other Party of its intention to refer a dispute to a dispute to a DAB in accordance with Sub-Clause 20.4.

The DAB shall comprise, as stated in the Particular conditions, either one or three suitably qualified persons ("the members"). If the number is not so stated and the Parties do not agree otherwise, the DAB shall comprise three persons.

If the DAB is to comprise three persons, each Party shall nominate one member for the approval of the other Party. The Parties shall consult both these members and shall agree upon the third member, who shall be appointed to act as chairman.

However, if a list of potential members is included in the Contract, the members shall be selected from those on the list, other than anyone who is unable or unwilling to accept appointment to the DAB.

The agreement between the Parties and either the sole member ("adjudicator") or each of the three members shall incorporate by reference the General Conditions of Dispute Adjudication Agreement contained in the Appendix to these General Conditions, with such amendments as are agreed between them.

The terms of the remuneration of either the sole member or each of the three members shall be mutually agreed upon by the Parties when agreeing the terms of appointment. Each Party shall be responsible for paying one-half of this remuneration.

If at any time the Parties so agree, they may appoint a suitably qualified person or persons to replace any one or more members of the DAB. Unless the Parties agree otherwise, the appointment will come into effect if a member declines to act or is unable to act as a result of death, disability, resignation or termination of appointment. The replacement shall be appointed in the same manner as the replaced person was required to have been nominated or agreed upon, as described in this Sub-Clause.

The appointment of any member may be terminated by mutual agreement of both Parties, but not by the Employer or the Contractor acting alone. Unless otherwise agreed by both Parties, the appointment of the DAB (including each member) shall expire when the DAB has given its decision on the dispute referred to it under Sub-Clause 20.4, unless other disputes have been referred to the DAB by that time under Sub-Clause 20.4, in which event the relevant date shall be when the DAB has also given decisions on those disputes.

Failure to Agreement Dispute Adjudication Board

If any of the following conditions apply, namely:
- the Parties fail to agree upon the appointment of the sole member of the DAB by the date stated in the first paragraph of Sub-Clause 20.2.
- either Party fails to nominate a member (for approval by the other Party) of a DAB of three persons by such date.
- the Parties fail to agree upon the appointment of the third member (to act as chairman) of the DAB by such date.
- the Parties fail to agree upon the appointment of a replacement person within 42 days after the date on which the sole member or one of the three members declines to act or is unable to act as a result of death, disability, resignation or termination of appointment.

Then the appointing entity or official named in the Particular Conditions shall, upon the request of either or both of the Parties and after due consultation with both Parties appoint this member of the DAB. This appointment shall be final and conclusive. Each Party shall be responsible for paying one-half of the remuneration of the appointing entity or official.

Obtaining Dispute Adjudication Board's Decision

If a dispute (of any kind whatsoever) arises between the Parties in connection with, or arising out of, the Contract or the execution of the Works, including any dispute as to any certificate, determination, instruction, opinion or valuation of the Employer, then after a DAB has been appointed pursuant to Sub-Clause 20.2 [Appointment of the DAB] and 20.3[Failure to Agree DAB], either Party may refer the dispute in writing to the DAB for its decision, with a copy to the other Party. Such reference shall state that it is given under this Sub-Clause.

For a DAB of three persons, the DAB shall be deemed to have received such reference on the date when it is received by the chairman of the DAB.

Both Parties shall promptly make available to the DAB all information, access to the Site, and appropriate facilities, as the DAB may require for the purposes of making a decision on such dispute. The DAB shall be deemed to be not acting as arbitrator(s).

Within 84 days after receiving such reference, or the advance payment referred to in Clause 6 of the Appendix-General Conditions of the Dispute Adjudication Agreement, whichever date is later, or within such other period as may be proposed by the DAB and approved by both Parties, the DAB shall give its decision, which shall be reasoned and shall state that it is given under this Sub-Clause. However, if neither of the Parties has paid in full the invoices submitted by each Member pursuant to Clause 6 of the Appendix, the DAB shall not be obliged to give its decision until such invoices have been paid in full. The decision shall be binding on both Parties, who shall promptly give effect to it unless and until it shall be revised in an amicable settlement or an arbitral award as described below. Unless the Contract has already been abandoned, repudiated or terminated, the Contractor shall continue to proceed with the Works in accordance with the Contract.

If either Party is dissatisfied with the DAB's decision, then either Party may, within 28 days after receiving the decision, give notice to the other Party of its dissatisfaction. If the DAB fails to give its decision within the period of 84 days (or as otherwise approved) after receiving such reference or such payment, then either Party may, within 28 days after this period has expired, give notice to the other Party of its dissatisfaction.

In either event, this notice of dissatisfaction shall state that it is given under this Sub-Clause, and shall set out the matter in dispute and the reason(s) for dissatisfaction. Except as stated in Sub-Clause 20.7[Failure to Comply with Dispute Adjudication Board's Decision] and Sub-Clause 20.8[Expiry of Dispute Adjudication Board's Appointment], neither Party shall be entitled to commence arbitration of a dispute unless a notice of dissatisfaction has been given in accordance with this Sub-Clause.

If the DAB has given its decision as to a matter in dispute to both Parties, and no notice of dissatisfaction has been given by either Party within 28 days after it received the DAB's decision, then the decision shall become final and binding upon both Parties.

Amicable Settlement

Where notice of dissatisfaction has been given under Sub-Clause 20.4 above, both Parties shall attempt to settle the dispute amicably before the commencement of arbitration. However, unless both Parties agree otherwise, arbitration may be commenced on or after the fifty-sixth day after the on which notice of dissatisfaction was given, even if no attempt at amicable settlement has been made.

Arbitration

Unless settled amicably, any dispute in respect of which the DAB's decision (if any) has not become final and binding shall be finally settled by international arbitration. Unless otherwise agreed by both Parties:

- the dispute shall be finally settled under the Rules of Arbitration of the International

Unit 15 Claims, Disputes and Arbitration

Chamber of Commerce.
- the dispute shall be settled by three arbitrators appointed in accordance with these Rules.
- The arbitration shall be conducted in the language for communications defined in Sub-Clause 1.4[Law and Language].
- The arbitrator(s) shall have full power to open up, review and revise any certificate, determination, instruction, opinion or valuation of (or on behalf of) the Employer, and any decision of the DAB, relevant to the dispute.
- Neither Party shall be limited in the proceedings before the arbitrator(s) to the evidence or arguments previously put before the DAB to obtain its decision, or to the reasons for dissatisfaction given in its notice of dissatisfaction. Any decision of the DAB shall be admissible in evidence in the arbitration.
- Arbitration may be commenced prior to or after completion of the Works. The obligations of the Parties and the DAB shall not altered by reason of any arbitration being conducted during the progress of the Works.

Failure to Comply with Dispute Adjudication Board's Decision

In the event that:
- neither Party has given notice of dissatisfaction within the period stated in Sub-Clause 20.4[Obtaining Dispute Adjudication Board's Decision].
- the DAB's related decision (if any) has become final and binding.
- a Party fails to comply with this decision.

Then the other Party may, without prejudice to any other rights it may have, refer the failure itself to arbitration under Sub-Clause 20.6 [Arbitration]. Sub-Clause 20.4[Obtaining Dispute Adjudication Board's Decision] and Sub-Clause 20.5[Amicable Settlement] shall not apply to this reference.

Expiry of Dispute Adjudication Board's Appointment

If a dispute arises between the Parties in connection with, or arising out of, the Contract or the execution of the Works and there is no DAB in place, whether by reason of the expiry of the DAB's appointment or otherwise:

Sub-Clause 20.4 [Obtaining Dispute Adjudication Board's Decision] and Sub-Clause 20.5[Amicable Settlement] shall not apply, and the dispute may be referred directly to arbitration under Sub-Clause 20.6[Arbitration].

Questions

1. Shall the employer be discharged from all liability in connection with the claim if the contractor fails to give notice of a claim within a period of 28 days?
2. Where shall contractor keep contemporary records as may be necessary to substantiate

any claim?
3. When shall the contractor send to the employer a fully detailed claim?
4. What shall a fully detailed claim include?
5. When shall the employer respond the claim with approval, or with disapproval and detailed comments?
6. What amounts for any claim shall be included in each interim payment?
7. Who shall be appointed to constitute the dispute adjudication board?
8. If either party is dissatisfied with the DAB's decision, what may either party do?
9. In what circumstance, the DAB's decision shall become final and binding upon both parties?
10. How shall the dispute be settled by international arbitration?

Vocabulary, Phrases and Expressions

additional payment：追加付款
claim：索赔
discharge from：释放；使免除
contemporary record：同期记录
a final claim：最终的索赔报告
interim payment：期中付款
time for completion：竣工时间
disputes：争端
dispute adjudication agreement：争端裁决协议
dispute adjudication board：争端裁决委员会
invoice：发票；发货单
an amicable settlement：友好解决
arbitral award：仲裁裁决；公断书
dissatisfaction：不满；不平
international arbitration：国际仲裁
Rules of Arbitration of the International Chamber of Commerce：国际商会仲裁规则

参考译文

第15单元 索赔、争端和仲裁

承包商的索赔

如果承包商认为，根据本条件任何条款或与合同有关的其他文件，他有权得到竣工时间的任何延长期和(或)任何追加付款，承包商应向雇主发出通知，说明引起索赔的事件或情况。该通知应尽快在承包商觉察或应已觉察该事件或情况后 28 天内发出。

如果承包商未能在上述 28 天期限内发出索赔通知，则竣工时间不得延长，承包商应无权获得追加付款，而雇主应免除有关该索赔的全部责任。如果承包商及时发出索赔通知，应适用本款以下规定。

承包商还应提交所有有关该事件或情况的、合同要求的任何其他通知，以及支持索赔的详细资料。

承包商应在现场或雇主认可的另外地点保持用以证明任何索赔可能需要的此类同期记录。雇主收到根据本款发出的任何通知后，在未承认责任前，可检查记录保持情况，并且可以指示承包商保持进一步的同期记录。承包商应允许雇主检查所有这些记录，并向雇主(若有指示要求)提供复印件。

在承包商觉察(或应已觉察)引起索赔的事件或情况后 42 天内，或在承包商可能建议并经雇主认可的其他期限内，承包商应向雇主递交一份充分详细的索赔报告，包括索赔的依据、要求延长的时间和(或)追加付款的全部详细资料。如果引起索赔的事件或情况具有连续影响，则：

- 上述充分详细的索赔报告应被视为中间的。
- 承包商应按月向雇主递交进一步的中间索赔报告，说明累计索赔的延误时间和(或)金额，以及雇主可能合理要求的更详细的资料。
- 承包商应在引起索赔的事件或情况产生的影响结束后 28 天内，或在承包商可能建议并经雇主认可的其他期限内，递交一份最终索赔报告。

雇主在收到索赔报告或对过去索赔的任何进一步证明资料后 42 天内，或在雇主可能建议并经承包商认可的其他期限内做出回应，表示批准或不批准并附具体意见。他还可以要求任何必需的进一步的资料，但他仍要在上述时间内对索赔的原则做出回应。

每次期中付款应包括已根据合同有关规定证明有依据的、对任何索赔的应付款额。除非并直到提供的详细资料足以证明索赔的全部要求是有依据的以前，承包商只有权得到索赔中他已能证明是有依据的部分。

雇主应按照第 3.5 款［确定］的要求，就以下事项进行商定或确定：根据第 8.4 款［竣工时间的延长］的规定，应给予的竣工时间(其期满前或后)的延长期(如果有)；和(或)根据合同，承包商有权得到的追加付款(如果有)。

本款各项要求是对适用于索赔的任何其他条款的追加要求。如果承包商未能达到本款或有关任何索赔的其他条款的要求，除非该索赔根据本款第二段的规定被拒绝，对给予任何延长期和(或)追加付款，应考虑承包商此项未达到要求对索赔的彻底调查造成阻碍或影响(如果有)的程度。

争端裁决委员会的任命

争端应按照第 20.1 款[取得争端委员会的决定]的规定，由争端裁决委员会(简称 DAB)裁决。双方应在一方向另一方发出通知，提出按第 20.4 款将争端提交 DAB 的意向后 28 天内，联合任命一个 DAB。

DAB 应按专用条件中的规定，由具有适当资格的 1 名或 3 名人员("成员")组成。如果对委员会人数没有规定，且双方没有另外协议，DAB 应由 3 人组成。

如果 DAB 由3人组成，各方均应推荐一人，报他方认可，双方应同这些成员协商，并商定第三名成员，此人应任命为主席。

但如果合同中包括有备选成员名单，除有不能或不愿接受 DAB 的任命外，成员应从名单上的人员选择。

双方与该唯一成员(裁决人)或该 3 人成员的每个人间的协议书应参考本通用条件附录的争端裁决协议书的一般条件，结合他们间商定的此类修订意见拟订。

该唯一成员或 3 人成员中的每个人的报酬条件，应由双方在协商任命条件时共同商定。每方应负担上述报酬的一半。

如果经双方同意，他们可以在任何时候任命一位或几位有适当资格的人员，替代 DAB 的任何一位或几位成员。除非双方另有协议，在某一成员拒绝履行职责，或因其死亡、无行为能力、辞职或任命期满而不能履行职责时，上述替代任命即告生效。替代任命应按照本条款所述对被替代人在提名或商定时所需的同样方式进行。

对任何成员的任命，可以经过双方相互协议终止，但雇主或承包商都不能单独采取行动。除非双方另有协议，对 DAB(包括每位成员)的任命应在 DAB 已就根据第 20.4 款提交给它的争端做出决定时期满，除非这时又有其他争端根据第 20.4 款提交给 DAB，在此情况下，相应的期满日期应是 DAB 也对这些争端做出决定时。

对争端裁决委员会未能取得一致时

如果下列任一情况适用，即：
- 到第 20.2 款第一段规定的日期，双方未能就 DAB 唯一成员的任命达成一致意见。
- 到该日期，任一方未能提名 DAB 三人成员中的一人(供一方认可)。
- 到该日期，双方未能就 DAB 第 3 位成员(将担任主席)的任命达成一致意见。
- 在唯一成员或 3 人成员中的一人拒绝履行职责，或因其死亡、无行为能力、辞职、或任命期满而不能履行职责后 42 天内，双方未能就任命一名替代人员达成一致意见。

这时，在专用条件中指定的任命实体或职员，应在任一方或双方请求下，并经过双方进行应有的协商后，任命 DAB 该成员。此项任命应是最终的、决定性的。每方应负责支付给该指定实体或官员报酬的一半。

取得争端裁决委员会的决定

如果双方间发生了有关或起因于合同或工程实施的争端(不论任何种类)，包括对雇主的任何证明、决定、指示、意见或估价的任何争端，在已依照第 20.2 款[争端裁决委员会的任命]和第 20.3 款[对争端裁决委员会未能取得一致]的规定任命 DAB 后，任一方可以将该争端事项以书面形式提交给 DAB，并将副本发送给另一方，委托 DAB 做出裁定。此项委托应说明是根据本款规定做出的。

对于 3 人 DAB，该 DAB 应被认为在其主席收到委托的日期已收到该项委托。

双方应立即向 DAB 提供，DAB 为对该争端做出决定可能需要的所有资料、现场进入权及相应设施。DAB 应被认为不是在进行仲裁人的工作。

DAB 应在收到此项委托或附录——争端裁决协议书一般条件第 6 条中提到的预付款额两者中较晚的日期后 84 天内，或在可能由 DAB 建议并经双方认可的此类其他期限内，提出它的决定,决定应是有理由的,并说明是根据本款规定提出的。但是,如果任一方未能对每位成员按照附录第6条的规定提交的发票全部付清,在直到该发票全部被付清前,DAB应有权不提交它的决定。决定应对双方具有约束力,双方都应立即遵照执行,除非并直到如下文所述,决定在友好解决或仲裁裁决中应做修改。除非合同已被放弃、拒绝或终止,承包商应继续按照合同完成工程。

如果任一方对DAB的决定不满意,可以在收到该决定通知后28天内,将其不满向另一方发出通知。如果DAB未能在收到此项委托或此项付款后84天(或经认可的其他)期限内提出其决定,则任一方可以在该期限期满后28天内向另一方发出不满的通知。

在上述任一情况下,表示不满的通知应说明是根据本款规定发出的,并应说明争端的事项和不满的理由。除第20.7款[未能遵守争端裁决委员会的决定]和第20.8款[争端裁决委员会任命期满]所述情况外,除非已按本款规定发出表示不满的通知,任一方都无权着手争端的仲裁。

如果DAB已就争端事项向双方提交了它的决定,而任一方在收到DAB决定后28天内均未发出表示不满的通知,则该决定应是最终的,对双方均有约束力。

友好解决

如果已按照上述第20.4款发出了表示不满的通知,双方应在着手仲裁前,努力以友好方式来解决争端。但是,除非双方另有协议,仲裁可以在表示不满的通知发出后第56天或其后着手进行,即使未曾做过友好解决的努力。

仲裁

对于经DAB做出的决定(如果有)未能成为最终的和有约束力的任何争端,除非已获得友好解决,应通过国际仲裁对其做出最终裁决。除非双方另有协议:
- 争端应根据国际商会仲裁规则最终解决。
- 争端应由按照上述规则任命的3位仲裁人负责解决。

仲裁应以第1.4款[法律和语言]规定的交流语言进行。

仲裁人应有权公开、审查和修改与该争端有关的雇主(或其代表)发出的任何证书、确定、指示、意见或估价,以及DAB的任何决定。

任一方在仲裁人的诉讼中,应不受以前为获得DAB的决定而向其提供的证据或论据,或在其表示不满的通知中提出的不满意理由的限制。DAB的任何决定都应该可以作为仲裁中的证据。

仲裁在工程竣工前或竣工后都可以着手进行。双方与DAB的义务不得因为在工程进行过程中正在进行任何仲裁而改变。

未能遵守争端裁决委员会的决定

在以下情况下:
- 任一方在第20.4款[取得争端裁决委员会的决定]中规定的期限内均未发出表示不满的通知。
- DAB的有关决定(如果有)已成为最终的、有约束力的。
- 有一方未遵守上述决定。

这时，另一方可以在不损害其可能拥有的其他权利的情况下，根据第 20.6 款[仲裁]的规定，将上述未遵守决定的事项提交进行仲裁。在此情况下，第 20.4 款[取得争端裁决委员会的决定]和第 20.5 款[友好解决]的规定应不适用。

争端裁决委员会任命期满

如果双方间因与合同或工程实施相关或由其引起的问题产生争端，或者因 DAB 任命期满或其他原因，没有 DAB 进行工作，则：第 20.4 款[取得争端裁决委员会的决定]和第 20.5 款[友好解决]的规定应不适用；此项争端可以根据第 20.6 款[仲裁]的规定，直接提交进行仲裁。

Unit 16　Sample Forms of Securities

Form of Bid Security (Bank Guarantee)

WHEREAS,_____ [Name of Bidder] (hereinafter called "the Bidder") has submitted ____his bid dated_____ [Date] for the construction of _____ [Name of contract] (hereinafter called "the Bid").

KNOW ALL MEN by these presents that We _____ [Name of Bank] of [Name of Country] having our registered office at (hereinafter called " the Bank ") are ____bound unto_____ [Name of Employer](hereinafter called"the Employer")in the sum of _____ for which payment well and truly to be made to the said Employer the Bank binds himself, his successors and assigns by these presents.

SEALED with the Common Seal of the said Bank this _____ day of _____.

The conditions of this obligation are:

(1) If the Bidder withdraws his Bid during the period of bid validity specified in the Form of Bid.

(2) If the Bidder having been notified of the acceptance of his Bid by the Employer during the period of bid validity.

① fails or refuses to execute the Form of Agreement in accordance with the Instructions to Bidders if required.

② fails or refuses to furnish the Performance Security, in accordance with the Instruction to Bidders.

We undertake to pay to the Employer up to the above amount upon receipt of his first written demand, without the Employer having to substantiate his demand, provided that in his demand the Employer will note that the amount claimed by him is due to him owing to the occurrence of one or both of the two conditions, specifying the occurred condition or conditions.

This Guarantee will remain in force up to and including the date_____days after the deadline for submission of bids as such deadline is stated in the Instructions to Bidders or as it may be extended by the Employer, notice of which extension(s) to the Bank is hereby waived. Any demand in respect of this Guarantee should reach the Bank not later than the above date.

DATE_____ SIGNATURE OF THE BANK_____
WITNESS_____ SEAL_____
(Signature, Name, and Address)

Form of Bid Security(BOND)

BOND NO._____ DATE BOND EXECUTED_____

By this Bond We _____ [Name of Bidder] (hereinafter called "the Principal")as Principal and_____ [Name of Surety]of the country of _____ [Name of

Country of Surety], authorized to transact business in the country of_____ [Name of Country of Employer] (hereinafter called "the Surety")are held and firmly bound unto [Name of Employer] (hereinafter called "the Employer")as Obligee, in the sum of_____for the payment of which sum, well and truly to be made, we, the said Principal and Surety bind ourselves, our successors and assigns, jointly and severally, firmly by these presents.

SEALED with our seals and dated this_____day of_____.

WHEREAS, the Principal has submitted a written Bid to the Employer dated the day of____ _____, for the construction of _____ (hereinafter called the "Bid").

NOW, THEREFORE the conditions of this obligation are:

(1) If the Principal withdraws his Bid during the period of bid validity specified in the Form of Bid.

(2) If the Principal having been notified of the acceptance of his Bid by the Employer during the period of bid validity:

① fails or refuses to execute the Form of Agreement in accordance with the Instructions to Bidders, if required.

② fails or refuses to furnish the Performance Security in accordance with the Instructions to Bidders.

Then this obligation shall remain in full force and effect, otherwise it shall be null and void.

PROVIDED HOWEVER, that the Surety shall not be:

① liable for a greater sum than the specified penalty of this bond.

② liable for a greater sum than the difference between the amount of the said Principal's Bid and the amount of the Bid that is accepted by the Employer.

The Surety executing this instrument hereby agrees that its obligation will remain in force up to and including the date_____ days after the deadline for submission of Bids as such deadline is stated in the Instructions to Bidders or as it may be extended by the Employer, notice of which extension(s) to the Surety is hereby waived.

PRINCIPAL_____SURETY_____

SIGNATURE (S)_____SIGNATURE (S)_____

NAME (S) AND TITLE (S)_____NAME (S)_____

SEAL_____

Performance Bank Guarantee (Conditional)

THIS AGREEMENT is made on the_____day of_____between_____ [name of bank] of_____ [address of bank] (hereinafter called "the Guarantor") of the one part and_____ [name of Employer] of_____ [address of Employer] (hereinafter called "the Employer") of the other part.

WHEREAS

(1) This Agreement is supplemental to a contract (hereinafter called the Contract) made between_____ [name of contractor]of_____ [address of Contractor] (hereinafter called

the Contractor) of the one part and the Employer of the other part whereby the Contractor agreed and undertook to execute the Works of_____ [name of Contract and brief description of the Works] for the sum of_____ [amount in Contract currency] being the Contract Price.

(2) The Guarantor has agreed to guarantee the due performance of the Contract in the manner hereinafter appearing.

NOW THEREFORE the Guarantor hereby agrees with the Employer as follows:

① If the Contractor (unless relieved from the performance by any clause of the Contract or by statute or by the decision of a tribunal of competent jurisdiction) shall in any respect fail to execute the Contract or commit any breach of his obligations thereunder then the Guarantor will indemnify and pay the Employer the sum of_____ [amount of Guarantee] _____ [in words], such sum being payable in the types and proportions of currencies in which the Contract Price is payable, provided that the Employer or his authorized representative has notified the Guarantor to that effect and has made a claim against the Guarantor not later than the date of issue of the Defects Liability Certificate.

② The Guarantor shall not be discharged or released from his guarantee by an arrangement between the Contractor and the Employer, with or without the consent of the Guarantor, or by any alteration in the obligations undertaken by the Contractor, or by any forbearance on the part of the Contractor, whether as to the payment, time, performance of otherwise, and any notice to the Guarantor of any such arrangement, alteration or forbearance is hereby expressly waived.

Given under our hand on the date first mentioned above.

SIGNED BY_____.   SIGNED BY_____.
For and behalf of the guarantor   For and behalf of the guarantor
in the presence of_____.   in the presence of_____.

Performance Bank Guarantee (Unconditional)

To: [name and address of Employer]

WHEREAS _____ [name and address of Contractor] (hereinafter called "the Contractor") has undertaken, in pursuance of Contract No. _____ dated _____ to execute [name of Contract and brief description of Works] (hereinafter called "the Contract.");

AND WHEREAS it has been stipulated by you in the said Contract that the Contractor shall furnish you with a Bank Guarantee by a recognized bank for the sum specified therein as security for compliance with his obligations in accordance with the Contract;

AND WHEREAS we have agreed to give the Contractor such a Bank Guarantee;

NOW THEREFORE we hereby affirm that we are the Guarantor and responsible to you, on behalf of the Contractor, up to a total of _____ [amount of Guarantee], _____ [amount in words], such sum being payable in the types and proportions of currencies in which the Contract Price is payable, and we undertake to pay you, upon your first written demand and without cavil or argument, any sum or sums within the limits of _____ [amount of Guarantee] as aforesaid without your needing to prove or to show grounds or reasons for your demand for the sum specified therein.

We hereby waive the necessity of your demanding the said debt from the Contractor before presenting us with the demand.

We further agree that no change or addition to or other modification of the terms of the Contract or of the Works to be performed thereunder or of any of the Contract documents that may be made between you and the Contractor shall in any way release us from any liability under this guarantee, and we hereby waive notice of any such change, addition, or modification.

This guarantee shall be valid until the issue of defect liability certificate.

SIGNATURE AND SEAL OF THE GUARANTOR_____

Name of Bank:_____

Address:_____

Date:_____

Performance Bond

By this Bond_____ [name and address of Contractor] as Principal (hereinafter called " the Contractor ") and_____ [name, legal title and address of surety, bonding company or insurance company] as Surety (hereinafter called "the Surety"), are held and firmly bound unto _____ [name and address of Employer] as Obligee (hereinafter called "the Employer") in the amount of_____[amount of Bond]_____[in words], for the payment of which sum well and truly to be made in the types and proportions of currencies in which the Contract Price is payable, the Contractor and the Surety bind themselves, their heirs , executors , administrators, successors and assigns, jointly and severally, firmly by these presents.

WHEREAS the Contractor has entered into a written Agreement with the Employer dated the _____day of_____ for_____ [name of Contract] in accordance with the documents, plans, specifications and amendments thereto, which to the extent herein provided for, are by reference made part hereof and are hereinafter referred to as the Contract.

NOW, THEREFORE the Condition of this Obligation is such that, if the Contractor shall promptly and faithfully perform the said Contract (including any amendments thereto) then this obligation shall be null and void; otherwise it shall remain in full force and effect. Whenever the Contractor shall be, and declared by the Employer to be, in default under the Contract, the Employer having performed the Employer's obligations thereunder, the Surety may promptly remedy the default, or shall promptly:

(1) complete the Contract in accordance with its terms and conditions.

(2) obtain a bid or bids from qualified Bidders for submission to the Employer for completing the Contract in accordance with its terms and conditions, and upon determination by the Employer and the Surety of the lowest responsive Bidder, arrange for a Contract between such Bidder and Employer and make available as work progresses (even though there should be a default or a succession of defaults under the Contract or Contracts of completion arranged under this paragraph) sufficient funds to pay the cost of completion less the Balance of the Contract

Price; but not exceeding, including other costs and damages for which the Surety may be liable hereunder, the amount set forth in the first paragraph hereof. The term "Balance of the Contract Price", as used in this paragraph, shall mean the total amount payable by Employer to Contractor under the Contract, less the amount properly paid by Employer to Contractor.

(3) pay the Employer the amount required by Employer to complete the Contract in accordance with its terms and conditions up to a total not exceeding the amount of this Bond.

The Surety shall not be liable for a greater sum than the specified penalty of this Bond.

Any suit under this Bond must be instituted before the expiration of one year from the date of the issuing of the Defects Liability Certificate.

No right of action shall accrue on this Bond to or for the use of any person or corporation other than the Employer named herein or the heirs, executors, administrators, successors and assigns of the Employer.

In testimony whereof, the Contractor has hereunto set his hand and affixed his seal, and the Surety has caused these presents to be sealed with his corporate seal duly attested by the signature of his legal representative, this_____day of_____.

SIGNED ON_____   SIGNED ON_____
On behalf of_____   On behalf of_____
BY_____   BY_____
In the capacity of_____   In the capacity of_____
In the presence of_____   In the presence of_____

Bank Guarantee for Advance Payment

To:_____[name of Employer]_____[address of Employer]_____[name of Contract]

Gentlemen:

In accordance with the provisions of the Conditions of Contract, ("Advance Payment") of the above-mentioned Contract,_____[name and Address of Contractor] (hereinafter called "the Contractor") shall deposit with _____ [name of Employer] a bank guarantee to guarantee his proper and faithful performance under the said Clause of the Contract in_____
_____ [amount of Guarantee]_____[in words].

We, the_____[bank or financial institution], as instructed by the Contractor, agree unconditionally and irrevocably to guarantee as primary obligator and not as Surety merely, the payment to _____ [name of Employer] on his first demand without whatsoever right of objection on our part and without his first claim to the Contractor, in the amount not exceeding ____[amount of Guarantee]_____ [in words].

We further agree that no change or addition to or other modification of the terms of the Contractor or of Works to be performed or of any of the Contract documents which may be made between _____[name of Employer] and the Contractor, shall in any way release us from any liability under this guarantee, and we hereby waive notice of any such change, addition or modification.

This guarantee shall remain valid and in full effect from the date of the advance payment under the Contract until_____[name of Employer] receives full repayments of the same amount from the Contractor.

        Yours truly,
        SIGNATURE AND SEAL:_____
        Name of Bank/Financial Institution:_____
        Address:_____
        Date:_____

Questions

1. If the bidder withdraws his bid during the period of bid validity specified in the form of bid, what should the bank do in accordance with the bank guarantee for bid?
2. If the successful bidder fail or refuse to furnish the performance security, what should the bank do in accordance with the bank guarantee for bid?
3. What are the conditions of the bank's obligations in accordance with the bank guarantee for bid?
4. What are the conditions of the surety's obligations in accordance with the bid security?
5. If the principal withdraws his bid during the period validity specified in the form of bid, what should the surety do in accordance with the bid security?
6. Shall the surety be liable for a greater sum than the specified penalty of the bond in accordance with the bid security?
7. Shall the surety be liable for a greater sum than the difference between the amount of the principle's bid and the amount of the bid that is accepted by the employer in accordance with the bid security?
8. What are the bank's obligations in accordance with the conditional performance bank guarantee?
9. What are the obligations of the surety in accordance with the performance bond?
10. What are the conditions of the surety's obligations in accordance with the performance bond?

Vocabulary, Phrases and Expressions

bidder：投标者
registered office：注册办事处；总公司
successor：继承人

assignee：受让人
by these presents：[律]根据本文件
the period of bid validity：投标有效期
written demand：书面要求
guarantee：保证；保证书；担保；抵押品
remain in force：在有效期中，仍然有效
witness：证人；作证
principal：委托人；当事人
surety：保证人；担保人
obligee：债权人；权益人
amount of guarantee：担保金额
legal title：权利证书；法定权利
bonding company：担保公司
insurance company：保险公司
heir：继承者；承袭者
executor：执行者；被指定遗嘱执行者
administrator：管理人员
successor：接任者
obligation：义务；债务
balance of the contract price：合同价格余额
penalty：处罚；罚款
legal representative：法定代表
financial institution：金融机构

参 考 译 文

第16单元　各类保证范例格式

投标保证格式(银行保函)

鉴于_____[投标者名称](以下称"投标者")已于_____[日期]为实施_____[合同名称]递交了其投标书(以下称"投标书")。

兹以本文件证明我们，_____[国家名称]在_____[地点]设有注册办事处的_____[银行名称](以下称"银行")以一笔金额为_____的款项向_____[雇主名称](以下称"雇主")担保；银行将依照本保函，约束自身、其继承人和受让人，完全准确地向雇主支付上述款额。

银行于_____盖章承认。

履行这一义务的条件如下：

(1) 如果投标者在投标书格式中规定的投标有效期内撤回其投标书。
(2) 在投标有效期内已接到雇主中标函的投标者，如果：
① 在被要求时，未能或拒绝按投标者须知签署协议书；
② 未能或拒绝按投标者须知递交履约保证。

一旦接到雇主的第一次书面要求且其中注明：由于发生了上述一种或两种情况，其要求的赔偿额是应付的，并对情况做出了说明，我们即向雇主支付上述担保款额，而无需雇主为其要求出具任何证据。

本保函有效期为递交投标书截止日期后_____天(含_____天)，该截止日期在投标邀请书中加以说明，可由雇主加以延长，上述延期无需通知银行。有关本保函的任何要求应在不迟于上述日期前通知银行。

日期_____ 银行签字_____

证人_____ 签章_____

(签名，姓名，地址)

投标保证格式(担保)

担保书第_____号 担保生效日期_____

根据此担保，我们_____ [投标人名称](以下称"委托人")作为委托人同获准在_____ [雇主国家的名称]从事业务的_____ [担保人国家的名称]的_____ [担保人名称](以下称"担保人")，坚定且真诚地负责向权益人_____[雇主名称](以下称"雇主")担保，担保总额为_____。我们委托人和担保人共同地且各自地严格遵守本文件的规定，约束自己及各自的继承人和受让人完全准确地支付上述款额。

双方已于_____签章为据。

鉴于委托人已于_____日向雇主递交了_____的工程的书面投标书(以下称"投标书")。

为此，履行本义务的条件如下：
(1) 如果委托人在投标书说明的投标有效期内撤回其投标书。
(2) 在投标有效期内已接到雇主中标函的委托人，如果：
① 在被要求时，未能或拒绝按投标者须知签署协议；
② 未能或拒绝按投标者须知递交履约保证。
则本担保义务保持完全有效。否则，本担保义务将终止并无效。

但担保人将不负责支付：
① 超过本担保书所列的赔偿金额的款额；
② 超过上述委托人的投标书的金额与雇主所接受的投标书金额之差额的款额。

签署本文件的担保人同意本文件的有效期为递交投标书截止日期后____天(含___天)，该截止日期在投标邀请书中加以说明，可由雇主加以延长，上述延期无需通知担保人。

委托人_____   担保人_____

签 名_____   签 名_____

姓名及地址_____   姓 名_____

　　　　　　　　　　　　　　盖　章

银行履约保函(有条件的)

本保证书以地址为_____[银行地址]的_____[银行名称](以下称"保证人")为一方,以地址为_____[雇主地址]的_____[雇主名称](以下称"雇主")为另一方,于_____订立。

鉴于:

(1) 本保证书为以地址为_____[承包商地址]的_____[承包商名称](以下称"承包商")为一方,以雇主为另一方而订立的合同价格为_____[按合同价格要求的货币的数额]的合同(以下称"合同")的补充,根据该合同承包商已同意承担并实施_____[工程及合同名称]工程。

(2) 保证人同意保证以下文所述方式正确履行合同。

在此,保证人向雇主承诺:

① 如果承包商在任何方面未能履行合同或合同规定的义务(除非合同条款、法规或有主管权限的法庭决定免除其义务),保证人将偿付雇主总额为_____[担保金额]_____[文字数目]的款额,但条件是雇主或其授权的代表须为此通知保证人且在不迟于签发缺陷责任证书之日前提出要求。

② 承包商与雇主之间经过或未经保证人同意的协议,或承包商承担的义务的任何变更,或承包商方面的任何宽限,无论是否涉及付款、时间或履约,均不解除保证人所承担的保证义务。此类协议、变更或宽限无需通知保证人。

兹于本保函开具日期双方签字为据。

由_____   由_____
代表保证人   代表雇主
在_____(证明人)的证明下   在_____(证明人)的证明下
签名_____   签名_____

银行履约保函(无条件的)

致:_____[雇主名称]
_____[雇主地址]

鉴于:_____[承包商名称及地址](以下称"承包商")根据_____[日期]签字的编号为_____的合同,已承担实施_____[工程及合同名称](以下称"合同");

鉴于:你方在上述合同中规定,承包商应向你方递交一封由你方认可的银行开具的银行保函,以其中规定的金额作为承包商履行其合同中规定的义务的保证。

鉴于:我们已同意为该承包商提供此项银行保函。

在此,我们确认:作为保证人,我们代表承包商向你方负责,将以支付合同价格的货币种类和比例向你方支付担保总额为_____[保证金数额]_____[文字数目]的款额。一旦接到你们的第一次书面要求,我们即无条件无争议地向你方支付上述担保金额_____[保证金数额]内的一笔或数笔款额。支付上述款额时,不需要你方为索取上述款额出示证明或提出理由。

我们认为,在你方向我们提出要求之前,你方无需向承包商提出索取上述债款的要求。

我们进一步同意,合同条款、依据合同条款拟实施的工程或你方与承包商可能签订的任何合同文件等方面的任何更改、增加或修正,均不解除本保函中我们的任何责任,并且我们在此不要求你方向我们发送有关上述更改、增加或修正的通知。

本保函有效期截止到签发缺陷责任证书之日。

保证人签字和盖章 _____
银行名称 _____
地　　址 _____
日　　期 _____

履约担保

根据此履约担保，_____[承包商名称及地址]作为委托人(以下称"承包商")同_____(担保人、担保公司或保险公司名称、法定资格及地址)作为担保人(以下称"担保人")，坚定而真诚地为作为权益人的_____[雇主名称及地址](以下称"雇主")担保，担保金额为_____[担保金额]_____[文字数目]。承包商和担保人共同地且各自地严格根据本文件规定，约束自己及各自的继承人、遗嘱执行人、遗产管理人、继任人和受让人，完全准确地以支付合同价格的货币种类和按比例支付上述款额。

鉴于承包商与雇主根据合同文件、计划、规范及其修正内容为_____[合同名称]于_____签署了协议书。按此处列明的内容，上述文件以参照形式构成该协议书的组成部分，以下统称为"合同"。

为此，特立约如下：如果承包商能迅速忠实地履行上述合同(包括对其任何修正的内容)，则本担保义务将终止并无效，否则本担保义务将保持完全有效。无论何时，如果承包商违背合同且雇主声明承包商违约，而雇主已履行了其在合同中规定的义务，则担保人应迅速地为违约进行补偿，或应立即：

(1) 根据合同条款和条件完成合同。

(2) 为按照合同条款和条件完成本合同，从合格的投标人处选取一份或数份投标书，提交雇主；在雇主和担保人共同确定标价最低且符合要求的投标人之后，安排该投标人与雇主签署合同。还应根据工程进度安排充足的资金，用于支付扣除合同价格余额之外的竣工费用(即使在如此安排的一项或多项合同的执行中还会出现违约或多次违约)，但包括担保人可能应支付的其他费用和损失，总金额不得超过上述第一段所列的担保金额。本段中的"合同价格余额"是指，按合同雇主应付给承包商的全部金额减去雇主已合理付给承包商的金额后余下的款额数量。

(3) 按雇主的要求支付给雇主款额，以用于根据合同条款和条件完成合同，但总额不得超过本担保书所担保的金额。

担保人不负责支付大于本担保书所规定的赔偿金额的款额。

根据本担保书的诉讼必须在从签发缺陷责任证书日期算起的一年期满之前提出。

除本担保书指定的雇主或雇主的继承人、遗嘱执行人、遗产管理人、继承人和受让人外，任何个人或组织均无权对本担保提出诉讼，也不得行使这种权力。

承包商已签字盖章，担保人已由其法定代表签字并加盖公章，特此为证。签署日期_____。

于_____[日期]　　　　　　　　于_____[日期]
由_____　　　　　　　　　　由_____
以_____的资格　　　　　　　以_____的资格

代表_____   代表_____
在_____ 证明下   在_____ 证明下
签字   签字

银行预付款保函

致：_____ [雇主名称]_____ [雇主地址]_____ [合同名称]

先生们：根据上述合同中合同条件第 60.1 款（"预付款"）的规定，_____ [承包商名称及地址]（以下称"承包商"）应向_____ [雇主名称]提交一份银行保函，以保证其正确忠实地履行上述合同条款所规定的义务，保证金额为_____ [保证金额]_____ [文字数目]。

我们_____ [银行或金融机构]，按照承包商的指示，无条件地且不可撤回地同意作为主要债务人而不仅仅是担保人，向雇主保证，在雇主第一次提出要求时，我们即毫无异议地向雇主付款，但金额不得超出_____ [保证金额]_____ [文字数目]，且你方无需先向承包商提出上述要求。

我们还同意，合同条款、据此合同拟实施的工程或_____ [雇主名称]与承包商可能签订的任何合同文件等方面的更改、增加或修正，均不解除本保函中我们的任何责任。并且，我们在此不要求你方向我们发送有关上述更改、增加或修正的通知。

本保函的有效期为：自合同规定的预付款支付之日起到_____ [雇主名称]从承包商收回全部偿还的预付款为止。

你的忠实的，_____
签名盖章_____
银行或金融机构名称_____
地址_____
日期_____

参 考 文 献

[1] Chris Hendrickson. *Project Management for Construction* [M]. Second Edition prepared for world wide web publication, 2008.

[2] [美]克里斯·T·翰觉克森. 建设项目管理[M]. 徐勇戈，曹吉鸣，等译. 北京：高等教育出版社，2005.

[3] FIDIC. *Guide to the Use of FIDIC－Conditions of Contract for Works of Civil Engineering Construction* [M]. Fourth Edition. Lausanne, 1989.

[4] 周可荣. 国际工程管理专业英语阅读选编[M]. 北京：中国建筑工业出版社，2005.

[5] Jack Gido, James P. Clements. *Successful Project Management* [M]. South-Western College Publishing, 1999.

[6] [美]吉多，克莱门斯. 成功的项目管理[M]. 张金成，译. 北京：机械工业出版社，2004.

[7] FIDIC. *FIDIC Conditions of Contract For EPC/Turnkey Projects -The Silver Book* [M]. Lausanne, 1989.

[8] 张水波. FIDIC 设计——建造与交钥匙工程合同条件应用指南[M]. 北京：中国建筑工业出版社，1999.

[9] Project Management Institute. *A Guide to the Project Management Body of Knowledge* [M]. Newtown Square, Pennsylvania, 2000.

[10] Barrie, Donald S., Boyd C. Paulson. *Professional Construction Management* [M]. McGraw-Hill, 1984.

[11] Ahuja, H. N., W. J. Campbell. *Estimating: From Concept to Completion* [M]. Prentice Hall, 1987.

[12] Clark, J. E. *Structural Concrete Cost Estimating* [M]. McGraw-Hill, 1983.

[13] Moder, J.C. Phillips, E. Davis. *Project Management with CPM, PERT and Precedence Diagramming* [M]. Van Nostrand Reinhold Company, 1983.

[14] Baker, K. *An Introduction to Sequencing and Scheduling* [M]. John Wiley, 1974.

[15] Willis, E. M. *Scheduling Construction Projects* [M]. John Wiley, 1986.

21世纪全国应用型本科土木建筑系列实用规划教材(已出版)

序号	书名	定价	标准书号	出版日期
1	建筑设备	35.00	978-7-301-10475-0	2008.11(第4次印刷)
2	土木工程测量	35.00	978-7-301-10472-9	2008.1(第3次印刷)
3	工程项目管理	32.00	978-7-301-10438-5	2008.7(第3次印刷)
4	工程造价管理	24.00	978-7-301-10277-0	2008.11(第3次印刷)
5	建设工程监理概论	26.00	978-7-301-10436-1	2008.5(第3次印刷)
6	工程量清单的编制与投标报价	25.00	978-7-301-10433-0	2007.2(重印)
7	材料力学	27.00	978-7-301-10485-9	2007.2(重印)
8	土木工程材料	35.00	978-7-301-10437-8	2008.11(第3次印刷)
9	工程经济学	34.00	978-7-301-10504-7	2007.2(重印)
10	有限单元法	17.00	978-7-301-10435-4	2007.2(重印)
11	工程招标投标管理	20.00	978-7-301-10266-4	2008.11(第3次印刷)
12	土木工程计算机绘图	28.00	978-7-301-10763-8	2008.7(第3次印刷)
13	工程地质	20.00	978-7-301-10517-7	2009.1(第3次印刷)
14	结构力学简明教程	20.00	978-7-301-10520-7	2007.6(重印)
15	建筑工程施工组织与管理	20.00	978-7-301-10432-3	2008.11(第3次印刷)
16	流体力学	20.00	978-7-301-10477-4	2007.6(重印)
17	理论力学	26.00	978-7-301-10474-3	2007.6(重印)
18	土力学	18.00	978-7-301-10448-4	2007.6(重印)
19	混凝土结构设计原理	28.00	978-7-301-10449-9	2007.6(重印)
20	建设法规	20.00	978-7-301-10201-1	2008.11(第3次印刷)
21	结构抗震设计	25.00	978-7-301-10476-7	2007.6(重印)
22	弹性力学	22.00	978-7-301-10473-6	2007.6(重印)
23	工程力学	30.00	978-7-301-10902-1	2007.6(重印)
24	工程事故分析与工程安全	22.00	978-7-301-10447-7	2007.6(重印)
25	砌体结构	20.00	978-7-301-10302-9	2007.6(重印)
26	工程合同管理	23.00	978-7-301-10743-0	2007.6(重印)
27	高层建筑施工	32.00	978-7-301-10434-7	2007.12(重印)
28	高层建筑结构设计	23.00	978-7-301-10753-9	2007.12(重印)
29	力学与结构	42.00	978-7-301-10519-1	2009.2(重印)
30	荷载与结构设计方法	20.00	978-7-301-10754-6	2008.7(重印)
31	混凝土结构设计	28.00	7-301-10518-5	2006.12

序号	书名	定价	标准书号	出版日期
32	土木工程施工	42.00	978-7-301-11344-8	2008.3(重印)
33	房屋建筑学	36.00	978-7-301-11496-4	2008.2(重印)
34	工程结构检测	20.00	978-7-301-11547-3	2007.2
35	钢结构设计原理	32.00	7-301-10755-2	2007.2
36	基础工程	32.00	7-301-11300-5	2007.2
37	土木工程课程设计指南	25.00	978-7-301-12019-4	2007.7
38	桥梁工程	52.00	978-7-301-12333-1	2008.1
39	土木工程概预算与投标报价	28.00	978-7-301-12334-8	2007.12
40	室内装饰工程预算	30.00	978-7-301-13579-2	2008.6
41	建设项目评估	35.00	978-7-301-13880-9	2008.8
42	房屋建筑学(上：民用建筑)	32.00	978-7-301-14882-2	2009.2
45	工程管理专业英语	24.00	978-7-301-14957-7	2009.3

电子书(PDF 版)、电子课件和相关教学资源下载地址：http://www.pup6.com/ebook.htm，欢迎下载。

欢迎免费索取样书，请填写并通过 E-mail 提交教师调查表，下载地址：http://www.pup6.com/down/教师信息调查表 excel 版.xls，欢迎订购。

联系方式：010-62750667，wudi1979@163.com，linzhangbo@126.com，欢迎来电来信。